HIKING TRAILS 1
Southern Vancouver Island
Greater Victoria and Vicinity

Revised and expanded by Gail F. Harcombe

FOURTEENTH EDITION, 2017

VANCOUVER ISLAND TRAILS
INFORMATION SOCIETY (VITIS)

Fourteenth edition copyright © 2017 Vancouver Island Trails Information Society

Original copyright © 1972 Outdoor Club of Victoria Trails Information Society First edition Hiking Trails, Victoria and Southern Vancouver Island December 1972. Reprinted: January, February and November 1973 and February 1974. Revised: 1975, 1977, 1979, 1981, 1987, 1990, 1993, Vancouver Island Trails Information Society (name change) 1997 Revised: 1997, 2007, 2017

Maps
Annie Weeks and Patrice Snopkowski, Beacon Hill Communications Group

Illustrations
Judy Trousdell

Cover photo: Rolly Patton
Photo of Betty Burroughs: Jo-Anne Richards, Works Photography

Photos
Credits are shown with the photos

Book design
Frances Hunter, Beacon Hill Communications Group

Printed and Bound in Canada:
Friesens of Altona, MB.
Distribution: Orca Book Publishers,
Victoria, BC.

Library and Archives Canada Cataloguing in Publication

Hiking trails 1 : southern Vancouver Island greater Victoria and vicinity. — Fourteenth edition / revised and expanded by Gail F. Harcombe.

(Hiking trails of Vancouver Island ; 1) Includes bibliographical references and index. ISBN 978-0-9877797-1-7 (softcover)

1. Hiking--British Columbia—Victoria Region—Guidebooks. 2. Trails—British Columbia—Victoria Region—Guidebooks. 3. Victoria Region (B.C.)—Guidebooks. I. Harcombe, G. F. (Gail Felicity), 1952–, editor II. Vancouver Island Trails Information Society, issuing body III. Title: Southern Vancouver Island greater Victoria and vicinity. IV. Series: Hiking trails of Vancouver Island; 1

GV199.44.C22V53
2017   917.11'28045   C2016-907848-5

MIX
Paper from responsible sources
FSC
www.fsc.org   FSC® C016245

Vancouver Island Trails Information Society (VITIS)

website: www.hikingtrailsbooks.com   *telephone*: Victoria area 250-474-5043
e-mail: trails@hikingtrailsbooks.com   *toll free*: 1-866-598-0003

This book is dedicated to the memory of
BETTY BURROUGHS, *who for more than 50 years*
shared, motivated, and enhanced hiking experiences
through the Outdoor Club of Victoria and Vancouver Island
Trails Information Society, and helped with the
production of these books in so many ways.

Contents

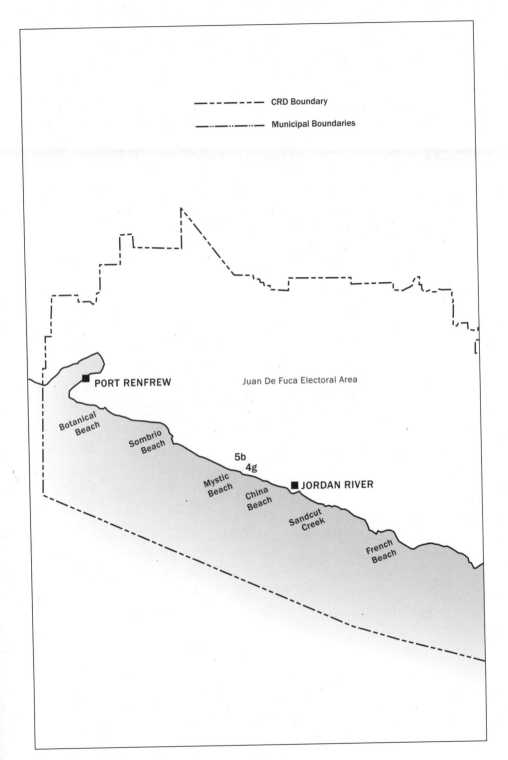

CRD Boundary
Municipal Boundaries

PORT RENFREW

Juan De Fuca Electoral Area

Botanical Beach

Sombrio Beach

5b
4g

Mystic Beach

China Beach

JORDAN RIVER

Sandcut Creek

French Beach

General Map and Key to Hiking Areas

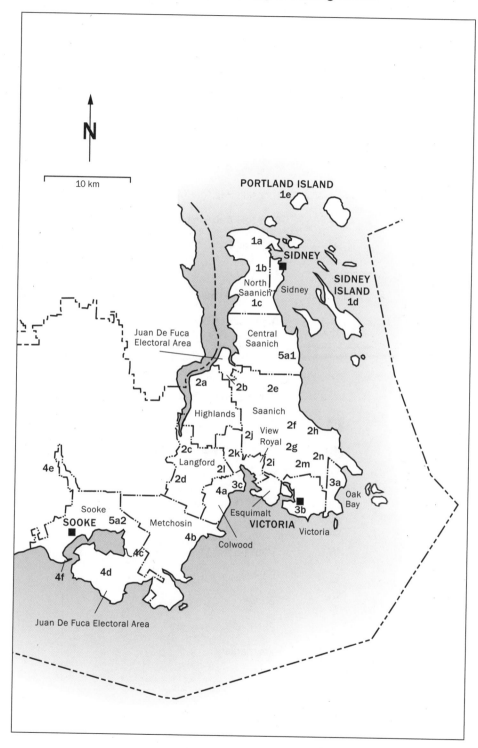

N

10 km

PORTLAND ISLAND
1e

1a

SIDNEY
1b
North
Saanich
Sidney

SIDNEY
ISLAND
1d

1c

Central
Saanich
5a1

Juan De Fuca
Electoral Area

2a   2b   2e

Highlands   Saanich

View   2f   2h
Royal
2j   2g

2c   2k   2i   2n

Langford   2l   2m

4e   2d   3c   3a

4a   Oak
Esquimalt   3b   Bay

Sooke   VICTORIA
SOOKE   5a2   Metchosin   Victoria
4b
Colwood
4c

4f   4d

Juan De Fuca Electoral Area

LEGEND

‑ ‑ ‑ ‑ ‑ ‑ ‑	Trail
‑ ‑ ‑ ‑ ‑ ‑ ‑	Trail described in text
••••••••••••••	Rugged trail
················	Rugged trail described in text
—··—··—··	Galloping Goose Regional Trail
■‑··■‑··■‑··	Lochside Regional Trail
——————	E&N Rail Trail completed
============	E&N Rail Trail future development
—⑰—	Highway
——————	Other paved road
‑ ‑ ‑ ‑ ‑ ‑	Gravel or dirt road
—┼—┼—┼—	E&N Railway
▬▬▬	Parks/green spaces
—·—·—·—	Park boundary; park described in text
P	Parking
Ⓟ	Limited parking
Ⓥ	Viewpoint of interest
⋀	Camping
Ⓣ	Toilets
W	Drinking water
⌐	Shelter
)(	Bridge
⚓	Anchorage
55 29	km markers

Editor's Note

Hiking is great for so many reasons. It is a good escape from life's often busy pace, a way to get exercise with the benefit of fresh air and amazing surroundings, affordable, and a way to share a new experience/adventure with friends and family. It can also be a way to increase your knowledge and appreciation of the beautiful outdoors. We hope you find this revised and expanded edition of *Hiking Trails 1* useful as you explore the amazingly diverse and spectacular area that is southern Vancouver Island.

What is new

Overall look!

We decided that since this book is one in a series, the *Hiking Trails of Vancouver Island*, it should follow the same format as the other books in the series: Book 2 South-Central Vancouver Island and the Gulf Islands; and Book 3 Northern Vancouver Island. The new format includes more colour and the text is a bit less compact, making it easier to read. You will notice, too, that the cover design is now the same as the other books.

New and updated hikes!

Hiking Trails 1, 14th edition, features more than 140 walks and hikes. The previous edition of the *Hiking Trails 1* was compiled and published in 2007, and needless to say, there have been changes to parks, roads, and trails in the intervening years. We've updated descriptions of the hikes that have been retained for this edition, and have added a number of short walks and longer hikes, most within a short drive from downtown Victoria. Some, especially those around lakes and nature sanctuaries, are fairly level and easy.

The maps!

All the maps are new in this edition. All but one hike has its own map, and all maps are in the same format and in colour. Every effort was made to include clear access information and use the colours to differentiate between hikes that are described in the text and those that are in the area but not described. Please note that some areas have many many trails, and it is difficult to include all, especially those that exist but are not "official" routes. Consequently, you may find yourself faced with more trails on the ground than we have on our maps. Every effort has been made to ensure the accuracy of the maps in *Hiking Trails 1* (at the time of printing). However, the maps in this book are not a substitute for NTS maps or other detailed guides/maps. See Information Sources, p.226, for a list of sources for maps.

What is (almost) the same

As much as possible, the tremendous work done by previous editors has been retained. Alterations to text were primarily kept to updates, so for those familiar with previous editions, you will find much of the content unchanged. As before, all hikes are described using the same format, although in a slightly different order than in the 13th edition. When access or some aspect of the trails had changed, those sections have been updated. The hikes are suitable for a variety of abilities and interests, from some that are especially good for families to those much more strenuous for the experienced hiker. The hikes described in this edition are within the Capital Regional District (CRD), and, as before, are grouped within areas, and those areas are ordered from north to south and then to the west (see map p.6). A number of the beautiful (and fun) illustrations by Judy Trousdell are again included.

Should you find any glaring errors or discrepancies, please send your updates to the Vancouver Island Trails Information Society (VITIS) at trails@hikingtrailsbooks.com Updates are periodically posted on the VITIS website www.hikingtrailsbooks.com

How to Use this Book

Hiking Trails 1 features 32 hiking areas, grouped into four sections by geographic location, and with a fifth section that includes regional trail descriptions. There are over 140 described hikes, and many chapters also include short descriptions of nearby hiking spots and/or area highlights.

Maps

The book's map legend is on page 8, following the General Map that shows locations for featured hikes. All but one chapter has an accompanying map—for Whiffin Spit, it was not considered necessary to include a map since the hike is very easy—chances of getting lost are slim.

Difficulty/Distance

Easy: The trail is generally level with little or no elevation gain or hills. The trail's surface may be paved, boardwalk, gravel, chip or dirt. A number of these are wheelchair-accessible (see Accessible Areas p.215)

Moderate: These trails may be muddy and uneven, with roots and branches, elevation changes, creek crossings and some steep hills. Unmarked junctions may be confusing. Typically climbs are moderate in length and steepness.

Strenuous: On these trails expect frequent elevation changes and long, steep hills. You may encounter slick logs, blowdowns and tricky creek crossings. Trails may be longer distances and be steep, narrow, rough and uneven. These routes are prone to slippery, muddy conditions and are often less maintained and sometimes overgrown. These trails traverse difficult, more remote terrain and may not be suitable for children or inexperienced hikers.

Distances: Wherever possible one-way (or loop) hiking distances are noted. Occasionally average hiking times are listed. These are subjective ratings and hiking times will depend on an individual's pace, one's degree of fitness, the trail's condition, the weather and the time of year. Use these as general guides only.

Highlights

Provides a brief summary of what the hike offers, scenic highlights, what you will discover in the area and when is the best time to go.

Cautions

Important information on hazards, potential problem spots, localized conditions and other things to watch out for and know prior to your hike are detailed here.

Access

Concise directions are found under this heading.

Hike Descriptions

The featured hikes are described in detail, and trails are shown in red on the accompanying maps.

Worth Noting/Of Interest

Here you may find interesting facts on plants, animals, birds and landforms, as well as area background information, historical notes, local regulations and restrictions, and hints that will help to ensure your hike is a safe and enjoyable one.

Nearby

This section briefly describes some additional parks, trails and/or points of interest close to the featured area.

Hints and Cautions

Hiking Trails 1 contains basic information for finding area trailheads and descriptions for some, but not all, of the possible hikes in Greater Victoria and the immediate vicinity. Many of the trails are under municipal, regional, provincial, or federal park administration, and these will generally have warning signs for any safety concerns the agency may have. Please pay attention to the information in those signs.

Each hike described in this book contains precautionary notes and reminders of things to watch for.

This book does not include details on equipment and food; that is part of your pre-trip planning. This planning is essential, particularly if you are considering hiking in the more remote areas or any of the more strenuous hikes. It is recommended that only experienced hikers attempt the remote trails.

Hiking

Key points:

- Be aware that conditions on trails can change quickly, particularly those on beaches, or near headlands and channels. Rogue waves may happen without warning and hikers have been swept off rocks. Keep children and pets under close supervision. Hiking in the off-season or after periods of extended precipitation can be challenging, even on easy to moderately difficult trails, so be prepared for adverse conditions.

- Protect the environment by staying on the trails. Do not disturb plants or wildflowers, or damage trees and any of the natural surroundings.

- Pack out what you pack in. Leave nothing and take nothing.

- Respect private property. Ask for permission to enter. Close gates that were closed. Leave open those that were open.

Weather: Check the weather forecast before setting out, but remember that weather can change unexpectedly. A fine, warm sunny day can turn wild, wet and windy with little warning. Cold, damp fogs may be experienced even in the summer, and they can be accompanied by strong, cold westerly winds in the Juan de Fuca Strait. Hilltops are more exposed to wind, and temperatures can be several degrees cooler. *Waterproofing Tip*—Articles placed in an orange plastic garbage bag inside your backpack will remain dry in the wettest weather and the bag can be used as a distress signal in an emergency.

Trip Planning: Tell your family or a close friend where you are going, with whom, and when you expect to return. Leave a note on your notice board, in your appointment calendar or desk diary, or even a short phone message.

Do not hike alone: Take one or more companions and take extra food and water (and a whistle), even on day hikes. Start your hike early in the day, to enjoy the cool of the morning, and plan to finish early. This will give you a safe margin of time to deal with any unforeseen experiences. If you are new to the community, we suggest you join a hiking club or group. Many community recreation centres and the YM/YWCA include hiking programs in their recreation schedules. Hiking with a group allows you to hike trails that require a vehicle to be parked at both ends of the trail, such as the coast trail in East Sooke Regional Park or the Metchosin Shoreline Pearson College to Devonian route.

Avoiding falls: Going uphill is generally easier and safer than coming down. On hikes that include hill climbs, take your time. Descend slowly and cautiously. Beware of loose stones, moss-covered rocks, protruding tree roots, wet logs and especially arbutus leaves.

Avoiding getting lost: Stay on the main trail. If you are uncertain as to which is the proper route, take your time in deciding which one to follow. Carry a compass—a compass can help for orienting maps to the terrain and often for simply deciding on direction of travel.

While most of the hikes in this book do not require navigation by map and compass, this skill is a necessity if you are to hike in some of the larger backcountry areas beyond Victoria, such as East Sooke or Gowlland Todd parks. A map and compass are essential if you should choose to go cross-country between trails, something that is not generally recommended, and certainly not without these tools. It is amazing how quickly one can become turned around and lost. GPS units and cell phones are also useful, but remember that these may not work in steep, mountainous terrain or heavily forested areas.

When hiking in an unfamiliar area, remember that unlogged ridges are generally easier to negotiate than valleys, and logging roads and bodies of water moving downstream usually lead out. Deer trails can also be good routes along valley floors and up ridges.

Maps are available from many park organizations and municipalities and may provide more detailed information than is found in the maps in this book. It is recommended that these be acquired if any of the more difficult areas are visited. Because topographical maps show the shape of the land, they are the most suitable type of map for most outdoor activities. They show the topography or shape of the land in addition to other features such as roads, rivers, lakes, etc.

If you feel lost, stop hiking. Stay calm. Often this is all it takes to get your bearings. Gauge the amount of daylight remaining and prepare to spend the night outdoors if necessary. Come daylight, move to open ground where air or ground searchers can spot you. Signal your position by blowing your whistle and tie your orange emergency bag in a place where it can be seen from the air.

Garbage in, garbage out: Take nothing but photographs and memories and leave nothing but footprints.

Fires: Fires are not permitted in most parks and are generally not necessary on a day hike. Fires are usually banned in the summer because of the very dry conditions. Be aware of and follow seasonal fire regulations and closures. Humans cause 60–80% of forest fires—never smoke while hiking. If you must smoke, do so at rest stops and ensure that any cigarettes and matches are completely extinguished. If you see a fire, report it at once. 1-800-663-5555 or *5555 from your cell phone.

Gear: Wear sturdy but comfortable hiking boots or walking shoes. Carry good raingear and spare warm clothing. A small daypack for food and water, matches, maps, and other essentials is advised, but weight should be kept to a minimum. Leave a change of dry clothing in the trunk of your car for your return.

Water: Carry your own supply of drinking water as a precaution against water-borne parasites (more likely on the more remote hikes).

Hypothermia: A combination of wet and wind can lead to hypothermia, a lowering of the body's core temperature that brings on uncontrolled shivering, forgetfulness, malaise and reluctance to keep moving. Stay warm, add a layer of clothing if the temperature drops and you feel cool. Stay dry—put your rain gear on at the earliest opportunity. Recognize the early symptoms and find shelter from wind or rain—break for a snack or warm drink.

Hyperthermia (Heat exhaustion and heat stroke): Hyperthermia is overheating of the body core brought on in warm weather by vigorous exercise and several contributory factors. On your hikes, drink plenty of water, wear a hat, dress lightly (shed excess layers of clothing), and rest frequently in shady spots.

Camping: Camp in designated areas when possible.

Parking: Park only in designated areas. If parking on the roadside, be sure to check for restrictions. Automobile break-ins are an unfortunate possibility. Leave valuable items at home or keep them with you. If you leave anything in your car, lock it in the trunk. Leave nothing on your vehicle dashboard or on the seats where it can be seen.

Dogs: Dogs are welcome in most regional parks and trails, but must be under control. Nearly all parks require dogs to be leashed. Specific information on these requirements will be posted. Remember that unleashed dogs can chase wildlife and damage fragile ecosystems. Always clean up after your pet. (See also Dog-friendly Hikes, p.222).

Flora and Fauna

Flora: Greater Victoria and the area surrounding it offers a diversity of flora for you to enjoy. Many of the trails described in this book take you to places where there are towering conifers, and some take you where you can see Garry oak, arbutus and big-leaf maple. Many species of flowering plants and shrubs (both native and horticultural varieties) are to be found. While the spring and summer are the most flamboyant, with showy displays of wildflowers, the fall and winter provide ample opportunity to observe other plants such as fungi, mosses and lichens. This area also has many evergreen trees and shrubs, giving the landscape its green hue year-round. Check the "Best time to go" comments in the hike descriptions to get the best experience. Remember—leave wildflowers where you find them—it is illegal to pick flowers in any of the parks or ecological reserves. Poison oak is rare, but you may encounter stinging nettles or devil's club. Because there are some poisonous plants in the Greater Victoria vicinity, eat berries and mushrooms only if you are certain they are edible.

East Sooke Park is a prime example of the excellent viewing opportunities in the area. In the spring and summer, flower enthusiasts may find a variety of species. Look for Indian paintbrush, fringe cup, orange honeysuckle, patches of stonecrop, monkey flower, hardtack, white clover, harvest brodiaea, white campion, blue camas, death camas, western buttercup, red columbine, small-flower alumroot, Queen Anne's lace, seaside woolly sunflower, hedge nettle, cluster white rose, fairy orchids, red elderberry, sea blush, Columbia tiger lily, nodding onion, white triteleia and mullein and many more. (See also Nature Walks, p.218).

Fauna: Hiking in this area means that you have an opportunity to see wildlife in natural habitats. Marine life such as seals and whales are always a treat, and there are many species of birds that call this area home (at least for portions of the year). Nothing to fear from snakes—there are no poisonous snakes on Vancouver Island. Deer are likely the most commonly observed wild animal, but on some trails, you will be hiking in bear and Cougar territory. Bear sightings are rare, and Cougar sightings are especially rare. Attacks are extremely rare. Bear and Cougar will sense you before you sense them. They will generally avoid you, but you can take some basic precautions, such as leaving your pet at home, making noise while hiking, watching for signs such as droppings and tracks, particularly around berry patches and streams with spawning salmon. Never approach cubs or kittens.

Birdwatching

When hiking Vancouver Island trails, one cannot help noticing the diversity of birds that inhabit our rocky and sandy shoreline, tidal mud flats, deciduous forests, dense old growth cedar and Douglas-fir stands, and inland rocky hilltops and Garry oak meadows. The diversity of habitat attracts an ever-changing mix of avifauna, making southern Vancouver Island an excellent place for birdwatching (see Nature Walks, p.218, for a list of some of the area's top birding spots).

September to December are the prime months to birdwatch as summer migrants may linger, vagrants and juveniles wander west, Asian species migrate south, and pelagic species move into Juan de Fuca

The Turkey Vulture is mostly brownish-black, with silvery-grey flight feathers beneath that contrast with the darker leading edge of the wing. With its bald red head, it can appear as if its head is missing! Slightly smaller than the Bald Eagle, it soars with an unsteady, rocking motion, wings upturned in a distinctive U-shape or dihedral.

A mature Bald Eagle has a dark body, white head and white tail (the bird is not actually bald...the name comes from an old meaning of the species name meaning white-headed). With a wingspan of 1.8-2.3 m, it soars and glides with flat outstretched wings.

The Osprey has a white head with a dark eye-stripe, a clear white belly and wings that are light on the undersides, but dark on the topside. It flies and soars with wings held in the shape of a flattish letter "M". Although the wingspan is similar to the Turkey Vulture, the much lighter colouring, slimmer body, and narrower wings help one tell them apart.

On your trip to Portland and Sidney Islands, watch for cormorants, an easily identified and common diving sea bird. They may fly low over the water, usually in single file, and will often be seen standing on rocks, a log or a navigation buoy holding their wings out to dry after a deep dive. These dark goose-sized birds with long necks and bills absorb water into their wing feathers, and they are able to dive to 46 or more metres. Another unusual feature is that their webbed feet have four toes, which enables them to cling to vertical cliffs where they nest. The extra toe also allows them to feed on sand lance and shoaling Pacific herring.

The Great Blue Heron is another common resident of our coast. It is Canada's largest ("tallest") bird, standing over one metre high with a wingspan of just under two metres, but their weight rarely exceeds 2.5 kg. Herons are a gregarious species nesting in colonies, normally high in the treetops, often a long way from the water. They eat a wide variety of prey and forage day or night. They can usually be seen standing perfectly still on rocks or docks, in shallow or deep water (often up to their 'tummies') waiting for their prey to come within striking distance of their long bills. This ungainly-looking bird takes its prey with great speed and is equally at home in fields as it is in or near water.

Strait and Georgia Strait. Goldstream Provincial Park is a great place to view Bald Eagle during the salmon spawning, and Beechey Head, in East Sooke Park, is a prime spot to witness the annual fall Turkey Vulture migration—"Hawk Watch". The migration usually starts in mid-September and runs through the end of October, peaking around the end of September.

Late spring can also offers great birdwatching opportunities. Some more recognizable rare species that have turned up in our region include Snowy Owl, Tropical Kingbird, and Cattle Egret. Other rare species that seem to make an annual visit include Lazuli Bunting, Rock Sandpiper, Eurasian Wigeon, Brown Pelican, Short-eared Owl, and Green Heron.

Year-round species of interest include Brandt's and Pelagic cormorants, Marbled Murrelet, Harlequin Duck, Mute Swan, Glaucous-winged Gull, Great Blue Heron, Black Oystercatcher, Bald Eagle (look for these when on coastal hikes and on your trip over to Portland or Sidney Island). Red-tailed Hawk, Anna's Hummingbird, Sky Lark, California Quail, Bushtit, Bewick's Wren, and many others can be found further inland.

For information on birding locations around Greater Victoria and other areas, visit www.birding.bc.ca or contact VNHS or Rocky Point Bird Observatory (www.rpbo.org). The Victoria Natural History Society (VNHS) (www.vicnhs.bc.ca), the Capital Regional District's Parks Division (www.crd.bc.ca/parks), and Swan Lake Christmas Hill Nature Sanctuary (www.swanlake.bc.ca) regularly schedule bird walks —check the websites for information about where and when.

1

Saanich Peninsula Including Near Islands

1a. Horth Hill Regional Park/Lands End Area MAP 1a

Horth Hill Regional Park

DIFFICULTY/DISTANCE Easy to moderate/30 minutes, out and back hike

HIGHLIGHTS Named after a pioneering family who settled the area in 1860, this (36 ha) CRD regional park in North Saanich features a series of hiking trails that traverse three distinct forest zones. Horth Hill Regional Park, created in 1966, has hiking and equestrian trails that meander through park forests. Several trails climb up to a viewpoint near the Horth Hill summit (140 m). Trails are well posted and there is an information board. Elevation gain from the parking lot to the summit is approximately 90 m, with some trails a steeper climb than others. The park is open sunrise to sunset.

Best time to go Enjoy panoramic views of Satellite Channel, the Saanich Peninsula, and Gulf Islands from viewpoints at any time of year; in spring, enjoy the profusion of wildflowers and in the fall, mushrooms are waiting to be discovered.

ACCESS Follow Highway #17 (Pat Bay Hwy) north of Victoria and Sidney, almost to Swartz Bay. Take the Wain Road exit, follow the Wain Road overpass to cross the highway, then turn right on Tatlow Road. Travel about 500 m to the signed, gated parking lot on the right. Allow approximately 35 minutes driving time from Victoria. The park is open from sunrise to sunset.

Map 1a Horth Hill Regional Park/Lands End Area

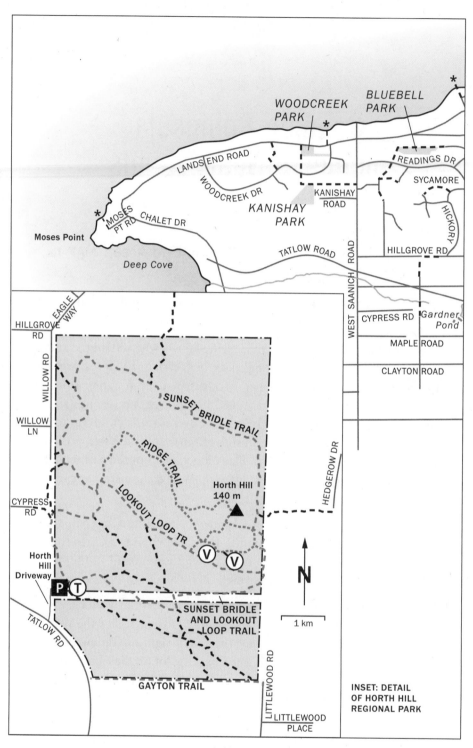

Map 1a Horth Hill Regional Park/Lands End Area

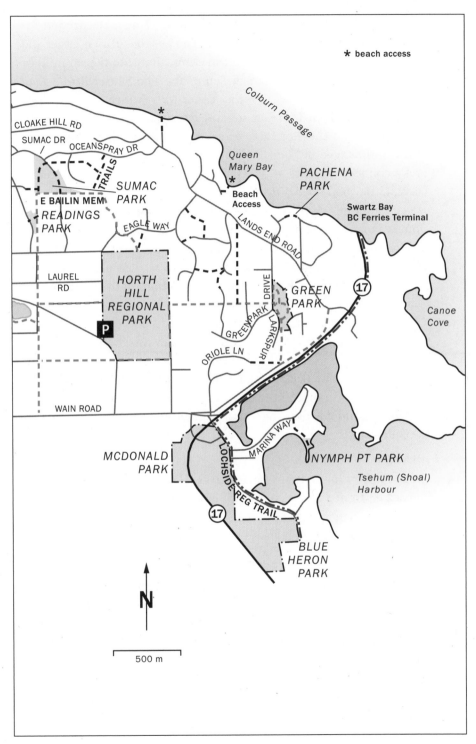

★ beach access

HIKE DESCRIPTIONS From the main parking lot, the northern trail through the forest soon divides. The *Ridge Trail* is steeper and has loose gravel requiring proper footwear. The *Lookout Trail* is easier and is often used as a bridle path. You can climb almost to the summit for spectacular vistas of the Saanich Peninsula. The *Sunset Bridle Trail* loops around base of the hill for an easier walk, which you will share with horse and rider. There are unnamed trails in the southern section of the park, and there are also unnamed trails running through the centre of the Lookout Loop Trail, allowing for shorter hikes if desired. Trails connect the park to local streets at several points: Hedgerow Drive, Littlewood Road, Cypress Rad, Willow Lane, and Eagle Way.

As you climb Horth Hill, look for exposed weathered outcrops of Comox Formation sandstone. Horth Hill is a cuesta or hogback hill with its smooth slope to the north and its sharp drop-off to the south. There are other hogback hills on the Saanich Peninsula that also display evidence of glacier grooves. The deep fjord of the Saanich Inlet is testimony to the force of glacial action.

Three forest communities are represented here. First, the heavily shaded western redcedar, then the Douglas-fir/swordfern community at middle elevations, and lastly, near the summit, are the dry, open slopes of the Garry oak landscape. Look for the ladyslipper orchid in the spring and mushrooms in the fall. At the viewpoint below the summit, a panorama unfolds over the Saanich Peninsula, Satellite Channel and the Gulf Islands.

NEARBY

Green Park One of many small parks in the area, Green Park may be reached from a trail that extends east from Horth Hill. Green Park is ideal for picnics, with two man-made ponds and an open meadow, which is seasonally wet. Horses are allowed in the park.

Lands End Area

The Municipality of North Saanich has created a series of hiking and bridle trails connecting numerous small natural parklands and ecological reserves. Highlights include waterfront parks, Horth Hill trails, a ravine at the head of Peregrine Place, small wooded parks, and a number of beach accesses that provide walking enjoyment. Several of these parks, and at various spots along the route, offer good birdwatching depending on time of year (e.g., Nymph Point Park). A moderate to strenuous loop route starting at the end of Swartz Bay

Road offers a variety of terrain, a combination of paved roadways and unpaved trails, including the gentler perimeter trails of Horth Hill Regional Park. It can be completed in about 3.5 hours.

Detailed trail maps and lists of parks are available at the North Saanich municipal office or online at www.northsaanich.ca or from CRD (www.crd.bc.ca).

WORTH NOTING

- Dogs are allowed off leash in North Saanich community parks, provided they are accompanied and under control, with the exception of Dominion Brook Park and the portion of Cy Hampson Park east of Lochside Drive, where dogs are allowed but must be on a leash at all times.
- Please remember to dispose of your dog's waste with the rest of your garbage.

Map 1b Airport Trail

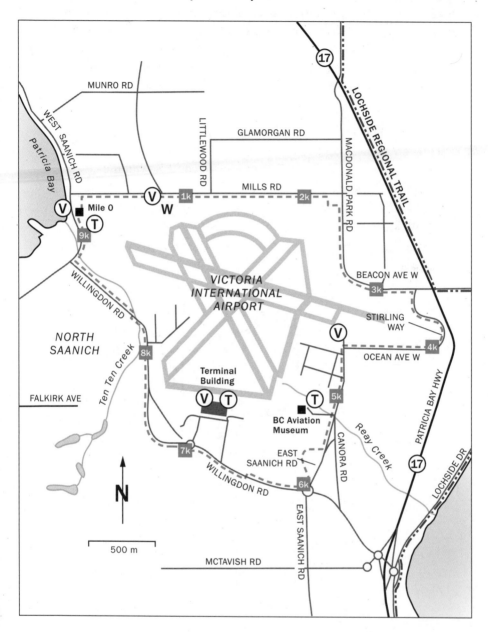

1b. "The Flight Path" Trail (Airport Trail) MAP 1b

DIFFICULTY/DISTANCE Easy/9.3 km loop

HIGHLIGHTS Although it may seem an odd choice to include this trail in a book about hiking trails, particularly since it is completely paved, the Victoria International Airport's Multi-Use Path (MUP), "The Flight Path," provides a safe off-road route through the natural beauty of the Saanich Peninsula—one with variety and some spectacular views—and connects to regional trails and a number of other hikes in the area.

Best time to go Any time—each season brings changes in the landscape and views.

CAUTIONS This is a popular trail, depending on the weather, so be aware of those around you and listen for cyclists' bells to ensure a safe hike. NOTE: the paved path can be slippery when wet or icy.

ACCESS From Victoria, travel north on Highway #17 (about 17 km), and take Exit 26 toward Victoria/Anacortes/San Juan Islands. At the first roundabout take the 3rd exit onto McTavish Road. At the second roundabout, take the 1st exit onto Canora Road. Continue straight (road forks—take the left fork) onto Willingdon Road. At the roundabout, take the 2nd exit to stay on Willingdon Road. Turn right onto Kitty Hawk Road.

From Sidney or Swartz Bay (ferries), travel south on Highway #17, and take Exit 26 toward McTavish Road/Victoria International Airport/Mill Bay. At the roundabout, take the 1st exit onto Canora Rd. Follow the directions above from Canora Road to the airport.

Parking is available at the airport and in limited areas along some of the adjacent roads—be sure to check the signs! The trail is open sunrise to sunset and can be reached from many access points along the route.

HIKE DESCRIPTION Created especially for walking and cycling, this 9.3 km trail circles the Victoria International Airport and winds through gently rolling, mostly open terrain. Accommodating users of all ages, this is a route for walking, jogging, and cycling (dog walking, and even scooters or in-line skates are also often seen). It takes about 1 hour if cycling at a fairly steady pace. Benches and picnic tables are situated at spots along the trail, as are "hydration stations" (for you and your dog). Signage along the route provides information on geographical points of interest and local history, as well as designating kilometre distances (as part of the "Heartsmart" initiative that promotes good health through exercise like distance walking).

There are many access points along the route, the most popular of them being West Saanich Road and Ocean Avenue. Along the flat portion on Mills Road, one can look south toward the Mt. Newton valley and see John Dean Park, one of the oldest provincial parks in B.C. The highest point along the trail, Hospital Hill, overlooks the airport, and on a clear day, you may be lucky enough to have views of the Malahat and Cowichan Valley hills and westerly mountains. The portion of the route along West Saanich offers views of Patricia Bay, and Dickson Woods. The stand of trees near the airport terminal is a great spot to rest and watch birds. From the eastern portion of the trail, Mt. Baker can sometimes be seen in all its snow-capped glory.

WORTH NOTING

- Watch for Bald Eagle, Common Raven, and Osprey putting on a flight display while you watch for planes and helicopters. Patricia Bay is often full of birds such as cormorants, Surf Scoter, Bufflehead, and the odd sandpiper.
- Dogs are permitted but must be on leash at all times. Please remember to dispose of your dog's waste with the rest of your garbage.

NEARBY From Beacon Avenue, in the town of Sidney, the Lochside Trail and Galloping Goose Trail systems are easily accessible, linking south to Victoria (29 km) and north to Swartz Bay (5 km).

Bald Eagle (*Haliaeetus leucocephalus*). KIM CAPSON

1c. John Dean Provincial Park   MAP 1c

DIFFICULTY/DISTANCE   Easy to moderate/up to 6 km, one-way

HIGHLIGHTS   John Dean Provincial Park, on Mount Newton (known to the First Nations W̱SÁNEĆ tribe as ȽÁU,WELṈEW̱, meaning "place of refuge"), harbours one of the Saanich Peninsula's last stands of old-growth Douglas-fir and Garry oak. Numerous hiking trails (approximately 6 km of trails, ranging from easy walks to more difficult hikes) crisscross Mount Newton's south and east slopes through these beautiful ecosystems. The area has been described as "the most beautiful example of dry east coast Douglas-fir old-growth in the entire Victoria area." This pristine 174-hectare natural park overlooks the pastoral Saanich Peninsula, and from a number of viewpoints, hikers can see the Gulf Islands and Cascade Mountains. There are easy paths through the forest or more strenuous routes that climb to scenic viewpoints. The park's Garry oak hilltops explode with spring wildflowers. No wonder the park is a favourite destination for family day hikes.

Best time to go   Spring for wildflowers; spring to fall for hikes and views.

CAUTIONS

- Bring your own drinking water—potable water is not available in the park.
- Park trails and side paths can be confusing as they are not all marked. Review the trail map carefully and look for trail signposts at key junctions. At Pickles Bluff there are no barricades, so stay away from the bluff's sheer edge.
- Some park trails are steep, narrow and rough. Protruding roots, loose gravel and trailside bushes may impede progress. Other routes are easier and follow old roads or more level terrain. Mossy rock faces are slick in wet weather. Wear proper footwear.
- The park road is closed to vehicles from November through March.

ACCESS   From Victoria, travel approx. 19 km north on Highway #17 (Pat Bay), and turn left onto Mt. Newton Cross Road. Turn right on East Saanich Road, then left onto Dean Park Road and follow the park road to the parking area. From Victoria, allow about 35 minutes driving time.

From Sidney or Swartz Bay (ferries), travel south on Highway #17, and take Exit 26 to McTavish Road/Victoria International Airport/Mill Bay. At the first roundabout, take the 2nd exit to McTavish Road. At the second roundabout, take the 1st exit and stay on McTavish Road.

Turn left onto East Saanich Road. Continue to Dean Park Road, turn right and follow the park road to the parking area.

There are trail accesses from Alec Road via the Merrill Harrop Trail (bridle path), and from Thomson Place via the Gail Wickens Trail (bridle path). The park is open from 8 am to sunset.

Check the park map at the information shelter near the parking area and plot your own hiking route. A popular loop, one that will take you to the West Viewpoint and Pickles Bluff, follows the West Viewpoint, Woodward, Thomson Cabin or ȽÁU,WELṈEW trails. The latter is one of the park's steepest trails. You can shorten your hike around the halfway point by taking the Illahie Trail, near Emerald Pool, back to the parking area. If your hiking route includes the more rugged Surveyor's Trail (which accesses Cy's Viewpoint), be aware there are steep switchbacks to negotiate near Canyon Creek.

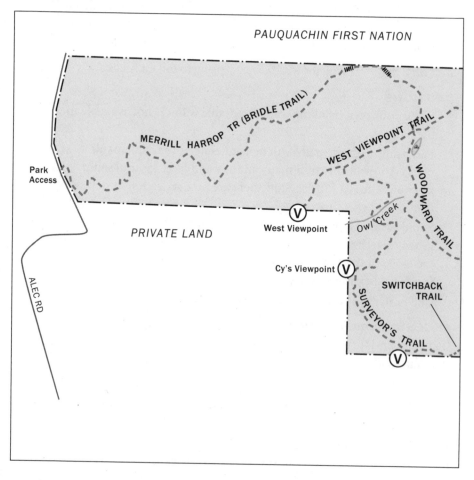

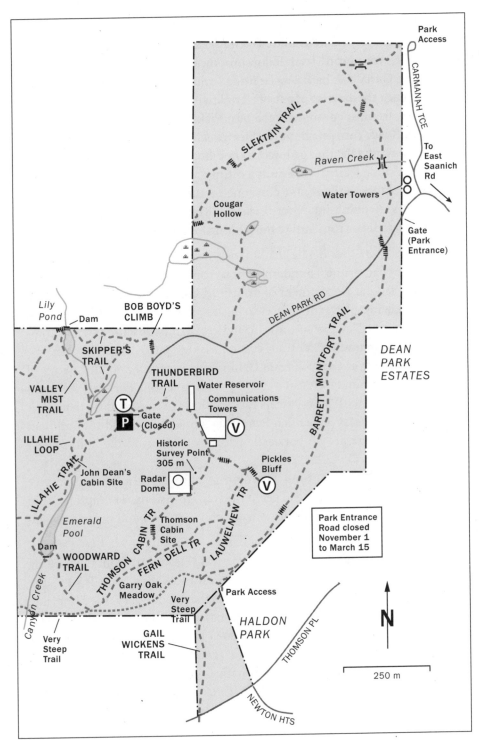

HIKE DESCRIPTIONS   A number of the hikes described below, together with others shown on the map, can be combined for a moderate to strenuous hike: From Alec Road, take the Merrill Harrop Trail to Woodward Trail; follow Woodward Trail past the Emerald Pool where Garry oak meadows begin to replace the forest; Woodward Trail becomes the Barrett Montfort Trail, with views across to Sidney and James Islands; continue north past Pickles Bluff and cross John Dean Park Road; turn left onto the Slektrain Trail and follow the trail back to the road; take the road west to Bob Boyd's Climb Trail, then descend down stone stairs to the gully bottom; at the trail junction turn west onto Skipper's Trail and continue to the junction with Woodward, West Viewpoint and Merrill Harrop Trails. Retrace your steps along the Merrill Harrop Trail to the parking lot on Alec Road.

Pickles Bluff   Moderate/0.5 km, one-way: From the parking area hike up the road or the Thunderbird Trail (on the left, parallel to the road) to the federal Department of Transport communication towers. From the viewing platform in a clearing are views over the Gulf Islands. The Mount Newton summit (333 m) is slightly obscured by the communication towers. Continue east for Pickles Bluff.

Keep left at the Thomson Cabin Trail junction and, after a set of steps, left again at the ȽÁU,WELNEW Trail junction. The final approach (with more steps) is very steep. Pickles Bluff is a rock outcrop that offers a view southeast of Saanich Peninsula, James Island and the San Juan Islands. There are no barricades, so stay away from the bluff's sheer edge.

If you turn right onto Thompson Cabin Trail (follow the service road for a short distance to get to the trail) to visit the Thompson Cabin site, you will pass an historic survey point (305 m) and radar dome on the way.

Valley Mist Trail   Easy/0.5 km, one-way: Head west from the parking area on a wide path and turn north on the Valley Mist Trail to the beautiful lily pond near the park's northern boundary. In the spring, look for Northern Pacific Treefrog, newts, and pond lilies. The West Viewpoint Trail begins near the dam at the pond's north end. You can loop around the pond (on Skipper's Trail or on Skipper's Trail to start and stay left at the intersection with Bob Boyd's Climb—steep with steps—and onto the road) and return to the parking area in about 20–30 minutes.

West Viewpoint   Moderate/1 km, one-way: Take the Valley Mist Trail to the lily pond and turn west, up the steps, on the West Viewpoint Trail. It is a sharp incline at first then it becomes a more gradual climb and the trail narrows. Watch for roots and loose rocks. Keep straight ahead at the junction where the Woodward and Merrill Harrop trails meet the West Viewpoint Trail. At the end of the trail is a lookout over Finlayson Arm and Brentwood Bay. Allow about an hour (one-way) from the parking area.

Merrill Harrop Trail   Moderate/1.5 km one-way: From Alec Road, the Merrill Harrop Trail, named for a local horseman and a former jockey who trained many a horse and rider in the Saanich Peninsula, climbs through a mixed evergreen/arbutus forest. After a number of wooden and stone steps, it connects at the east end with the Woodward and West Viewpoint trails.

John Dean to Centennial Park   Moderate, strenuous at start/approx. 4 km one-way: Follow the Gail Wickens Horse Trail (very steep at the top) through Haldon Park to the intersection of Thompson Road to Mt. Newton Cross Road. Turn east along the Cross Road then south on Malcolm Road, through farmland and woodlands, to Hovey Road and Tomlinson Road accesses to Centennial Park (see description of the park in section **NEARBY**).

WORTH NOTING

- In 1921, John Dean donated 32 ha of his property to the province as parkland...the first donated provincial park in B.C. Over the years, additional donated lands have increased the park to 174 ha.
- Spring wildflowers in the woods and meadows include shooting stars, blue camas, trilliums, red paintbrush, sea blush and calypso orchids.
- Do not pick any wildflowers.
- Mount Newton's forests are a mix of Douglas-fir, western redcedar, grand fir, arbutus and Garry oak.
- Look for Pileated Woodpecker (Canada's largest) on dead snags. Scan the skies for eagles, Turkey Vulture, hawks and ravens.
- Please stay on marked trails at all times. The Friends of John Dean Park Association is responsible for signage and trail maintenance with the goal of counteracting soil erosion, vegetation destruction and soil compaction.

- Dogs must be on leash at all times. You are responsible for their behaviour and disposal of their waste.
- Horses are permitted only on the Merrill Harrop Trail.

NEARBY

Dominion Brook Park (4.5 ha)   Access as for John Dean Park to East Saanich Road. Travel south on East Saanich Road to pass the Panorama Leisure Centre and watch for the park entrance, on the left. Dominion Brook Park has three ponds, a small stream (Dominion Brook), a ravine and sunken garden. There are rare and exotic plant species. Dominion Brook Park features many heritage trees and shrubs. The park originated as a federal horticultural demonstration garden back in 1913. The Friends of Dominion Brook Park, a non-profit society, maintains the park and is working toward its restoration. Park facilities include toilets and a picnic area. Dogs must be leashed.

Coles Bay Regional Park (3.6 ha)   Access from Victoria via Highway #17 (Pat Bay) and then West Saanich Road (#17A) to Ardmore Drive. Turn left and left again on Inverness Road (signed) to the gated entrance. From Victoria, allow 30 minutes travel time. The park is open from sunrise to sunset. Toilets and picnic facilities near the parking area are wheelchair accessible but the beach and trails are not. From the parking area, follow the beach or the nature trails through a mixed forest of Douglas-fir, bigleaf maple and large western redcedar down to Coles Bay, on Saanich Inlet. The hike takes approximately 10 minutes, one-way. The rock, pebble and mud beach is best visited at low tide.

Centennial Park (18.42 ha)   This community park, situated between Wallace Drive and Graham Creek, has a number of walking trails and natural areas, and also boasts sports fields, children's playgrounds, picnic shelter, lacrosse box, and lawn bowling green. There is excellent parking and park facilities. Wheelchair access is limited to the main areas of the park. Some trails are shared with cyclists and equestrians. From the park, you can follow a route south along Wallace, then along a right-of-way beside a ditch, then west onto Kersey Road. Follow Kersey to West Saanich and continue on a grassy trail past greenhouses to Greig Avenue and the delightful Gore Park—beautiful with wildflowers in the spring.

1d. Sidney Spit   MAP 1d

DIFFICULTY/DISTANCE   Easy/varies: 2 km loop and 1.5-2.5 km one-way trails

HIGHLIGHTS   Sidney Spit, the northern tip of Sidney Island, lies about 5 km southeast of the town of Sidney. Formerly a provincial marine park, Sidney Spit is now part of the Gulf Islands National Park Reserve (GINPR). Located in the southern Georgia Strait, the park reserve includes properties on 16 islands, over 30 reefs and islets, their adjoining waters and intertidal zones (see Parks Canada website for information www.pc.gc.ca). The 400 ha park on Sidney Island features trails that access two long, sandy beach spits, salt marshes, a tranquil lagoon, tidal flats and scenic viewpoints. The park is renowned for its birdwatching (particularly migratory shorebirds), wildlife viewing and striking seascapes. In spring, look for Purple Martin near the docks and resident Orca in the waters off the island. In summer, Orca are often sighted and bioluminescence "lights" the waters. In the fall, birdwatchers will see Brandt's Cormorant.

Best time to go   May to September.

CAUTIONS
- **Visitors camping on the island must be registered at a designated campsite before the last ferry leaves for the day.**
- Potable water is available but it has high sodium content. It is best to bring your own fresh water.
- Annual public safety closures November 1 to end of February to facilitate traditional hunting by Coast Salish First Nations.

ACCESS
Sidney Spit is accessed by water only. A seasonal (May 15–September 30) foot-passenger ferry operates from Sidney—the trip takes about 25 minutes. Sheltered anchorage for boats and kayaks is available on the west side of the spit, and mooring and docking is also available. Check with Parks Canada for ferry schedules, current fees, accessibility and regulations (see p.226).

Map 1d   Sidney Spit

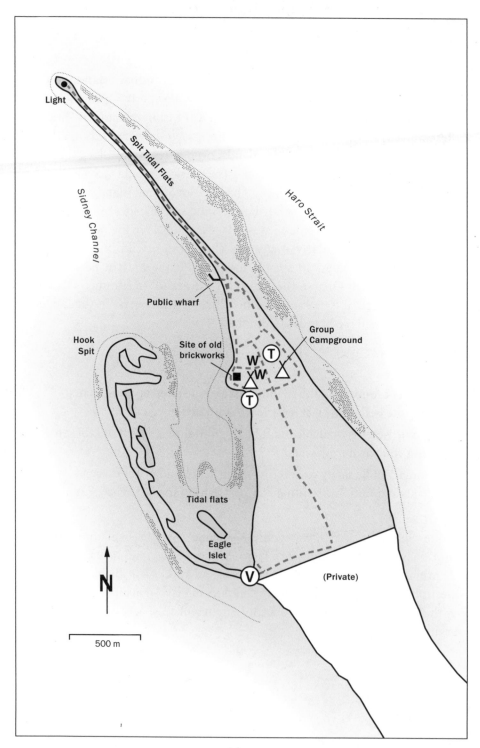

Light

Spit Tidal Flats

Sidney Channel

Haro Strait

Public wharf

Hook Spit

Site of old brickworks

Group Campground

W   T
W
T

Tidal flats

Eagle Islet

(Private)

N

500 m

HIKE DESCRIPTIONS

East Beach and the Bluff   Easy/2.2 km loop: From the public wharf, the trail climbs east to the bluff. Here there are great views over Miners Channel to Mandarte and the Halibut islands. In clear weather, Mount Baker will dominate the backdrop. The trail parallels the bluff along Sidney Island's east side and then swings inland through uplands of arbutus and Douglas-fir, meadows and open fields. Continue past the camping areas and follow the signposts back to the public wharf, near the day-use area.

Sidney Spit   Easy/2 km, one-way: From the public wharf you can hike for 2 km, all the way to the marine navigation light at the tip of Sidney Spit. Time your hike for low tides, which expose the tidal flats and assist your beachcombing efforts. The spectacular white sand peninsula is littered with gnarled driftwood and beach grasses and offers little protection from the sun. Gear up accordingly.

Lagoon and Hook Spit   Easy/2.5 km, one-way: From the public wharf, swing right, past West Beach and the camping area and then follow the inland trail south to the park boundary and a junction. The trail to the left goes east to the bluff that overlooks Miners Channel. Turn right and hike west. As the trail approaches tidewater, there is a short, steep hill. The head of the lagoon is a park highlight and birdwatcher's paradise. At lower tides, the exposed mudflats harbour tiny Dungeness and Red Rock Crabs feeding in a dense carpet of eelgrass. The inner lagoon, salt marshes, tidal flats and spit are sensitive ecosystems. Parks Canada reminds visitors that access in these areas is restricted to a narrow corridor along Hook Spit's outer fringe. The land south of the lagoon is privately owned.

WORTH NOTING

- Situated on the edge of the Pacific Flyway, Sidney Island is a superb habitat for migrating shorebirds. The lagoon is a year-round bird-watching destination. Sidney Island has the southern Gulf Islands' largest Great Blue Heron colony, estimated at well over 100 pairs. Brant (geese) are numerous in March and April.
- On your trip over to Sidney Island, watch for marine mammals, cormorants, Rhinoceros Auklet and Heermann's Gull.
- Fallow deer are a common sight in the island's meadows and open grassy fields.

- The park has no garbage facilities. If you bring it in, pack it out.
- Camping (tenting) is permitted (27 sites) by reservation (see p.226). Fees apply. Carry a portable stove if you camp.
- Dogs must be on a leash at all times. Please remember to dispose of your dog's waste with the rest of your garbage.
- Check out the geocaching program in the park.
- Sidney Island Brick and Tile Company operated on the island from 1906 to 1915, and brick remnants are still visible along the shoreline and in the forest. The bricks for Victoria's Empress Hotel were produced at the site of the old brick works.

NEARBY

D'Arcy Island

This 83 hectare island, also part of the GINPR, is just south of Sidney Island and was once a leper colony at the turn of the 1900s. Short trails through a forest of arbutus and Douglas-fir lead to tiny coves and cobble beaches. Camping is permitted on the island (seven sites, pit toilets), but there is **no potable water** and **no campfires**. Please camp only in designated sites to avoid damaging sensitive habitats or cultural features.

1e. Portland Island   MAP 1e

DIFFICULTY/DISTANCE   Moderate/up to 6.5 km loop

HIGHLIGHTS   Portland Island, also referred to as "Princess Margaret Island", is part of Parks Canada's Gulf Islands National Park Reserve. Originally named in 1858 after the flagship HMS Portland, the 575 ha island was given to Princess Margaret in 1958 to commemorate her visit to the province, and the name changed at that time. She returned it to B.C. in 1967. Located off the south tip of Saltspring Island, at the tip of the Saanich Peninsula, the island features a network of trails, including an up-and-down coastal route, that lead to spectacular seascapes, pocket beaches and excellent opportunities for wildlife viewing. The island was used by First Nations people, and a number of shell middens are visible along the beaches.

Best time to go   May to September.

CAUTIONS

- There is no potable water on Portland Island.
- Camping is permitted (fees apply) on a first-come, first-served basis from May 15 to September 30.

ACCESS
Portland Island is marine access only—accessible by boat, kayak, or pre-booked water taxi service from Sidney, landing at Princess Bay. There is no scheduled ferry service. For more information and current park fees, contact Parks Canada (see p.226).

HIKE DESCRIPTION   Portland Island is largely undeveloped, but there are well-established, signed trails that crisscross and circle the island. The inland trails wind through forests of arbutus and Garry oak. The shoreline loop trail is accessible from any of the three camping areas.

The most popular hike is the *Princess Margaret Perimeter Trail*, a moderate 6.5 km (3-hour loop) that follows the rugged coast trail and snakes around the island. If your time is limited, explore only part of the shoreline. Between Princess Bay and Arbutus Point, there are plenty of seascapes, tiny bays and pocket coves, shell beaches, wave-etched sandstone rocks and bluffs. The Royal Cove Trail (30 minutes to Royal Cove or Arbutus Point), *Kanaka Bluffs Trail* near Arbutus Point (15 minutes), and the *Pellow Islets Trail* (15 minutes) are highlights.

Map 1e   Portland Island

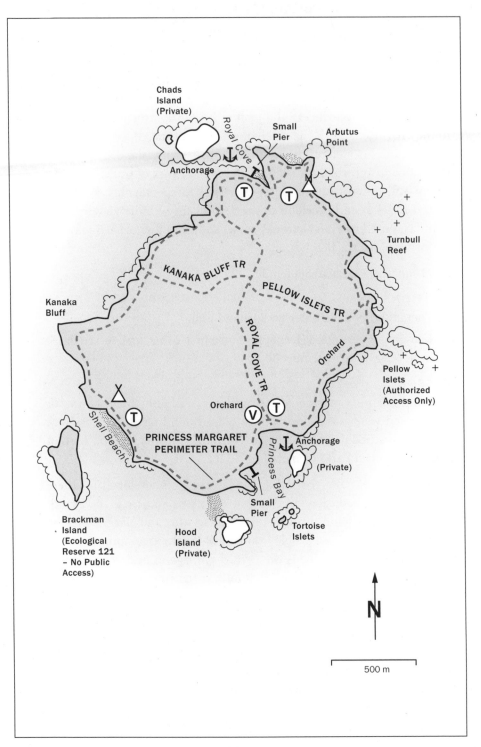

Chads Island (Private)

Royal Cove

Small Pier

Arbutus Point

Anchorage

Turnbull Reef

KANAKA BLUFF TR

PELLOW ISLETS TR

Kanaka Bluff

ROYAL COVE TR

Orchard

Pellow Islets (Authorized Access Only)

Shell Beach

Orchard

PRINCESS MARGARET PERIMETER TRAIL

Princess Bay

Anchorage

(Private)

Brackman Island (Ecological Reserve 121 – No Public Access)

Small Pier

Hood Island (Private)

Tortoise Islets

N

500 m

Portland Island has an abundance of wildlife. Watch for Red-tailed Hawk, Bald Eagle and Turkey Vulture soaring overhead. Scan shoreline shallows for foraging Black Oystercatcher or Great Blue Heron. The waters near offshore islands are where to look for Harbour Seal. If you are lucky you may see these animals hauled-out on tide-exposed rocks. The island is home to Black-tail Deer, River Otter, Mink, and many Raccoon.

WORTH NOTING

- Camping is permitted in three designated areas:
  - Princess Bay (open field, space for 12 tents, composting toilet).
  - Shell Beach (six designated sites, pit toilet).
  - Arbutus Point (six designated sites, composting toilet).
- No campfires are permitted.
- Pack out all your garbage.
- Dogs must be on a leash at all times. Please remember to dispose of your dog's waste with the rest of your garbage.
- Princess Bay and Royal Cove provide good seasonal anchorage. In summer, the Royal Victoria Yacht Club provides information through the park's Marine Hosts at a float in Princess Bay. Best swimming is at Princess Bay's shell beach.
- The park's shell middens (refuse piles) date back 3000 years and attest to early native use of the island. These protected archaeological sites should not be disturbed. On the island's southeast side are the remnants of two old orchards.
- The smaller islands around Portland Island (Hood Island, the Tortoise Islets and Chad Island) are privately owned. Do not trespass. Pellow Islets are authorized access only. There is no public access on Brackman Island, an ecological reserve.

OF INTEREST

In 1991, the freighter MV G.B. Church was sunk off Portland Island's northeast shore to become B.C.'s first artificial reef.

Gowlland Tod forest. JESSICA HARCOMBE FLEMING

2

Saanich, Highlands and Adjacent Municipalities

2a. Gowlland Tod Provincial Park   MAP 2a

DIFFICULTY/DISTANCE   Easy to strenuous/1.5 km to 5 km or longer, one-way

HIGHLIGHTS   Gowlland Tod Provincial Park (1280 ha), created in 1995, encompasses picturesque shorelines and forests at Tod Inlet and the rugged 430 m high Gowlland Range, a series of hills and outcrops that loom above Saanich Inlet's Finlayson Arm, creating the view along the Malahat Drive. This fascinating region, in the Highlands District, has more than 25 km of trails to explore, many of which follow old logging and mining roads to striking viewpoints. And when in the area, don't miss a hike to the top of Lone Tree Hill Regional Park, just east of Gowlland Tod (see p.48).

Vibrant wildflowers cover the rocky outcrops through the spring and early summer. The park's forests of Douglas-fir, bigleaf maple, alder, western redcedar and arbutus provide an undisturbed, natural habitat for Cougar, Black Bear, Black-tailed Deer, River Otter, Mink, Red Squirrel and other wild animals. Over 100 bird species have been noted.

Best time to go   Spring and summer for wildflowers, but the park is a perfect destination for short day hikes or more extended jaunts any time of year.

CAUTIONS
- Gowlland Tod Park is a wilderness region and the territory of Cougar and Black Bear. Be alert. Keep children close by. Keep all pets leashed. BC Parks recommends you leave your animals at home.

Map 2a Gowlland Tod Provincial Park

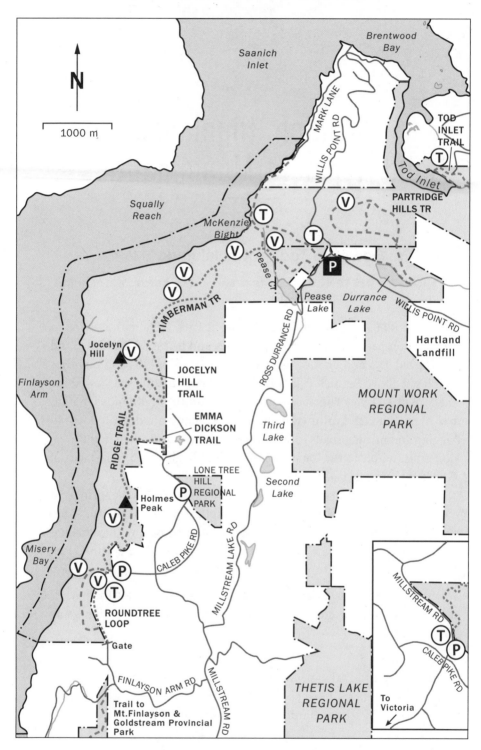

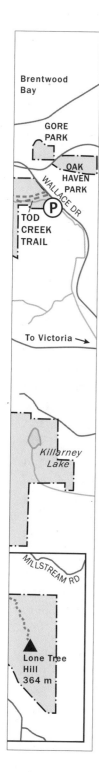

- Be prepared for wet, foggy weather. Wear adequate clothing and footwear. Bring rain gear and emergency supplies. If you are visiting in the wet months, you will encounter mud, slick trails and places where the old roads and trails are flooded into surrounding swampland.
- Stay on marked trails to protect the park's rare and fragile ecosystems, particularly around the rocky, open slopes and grassy meadows. Numerous unmarked trails, confusing old roads and bridle paths crisscross the area. Respect adjacent private property and do not trespass.
- Potable water is not available in the park.
- There is no boat launch in the park. The nearest launch is located at Brentwood Bay.
- Please ride horses and bikes at a walking speed and only on designated trails.

ACCESS   BC Parks has established three park entry points. Hours are sunrise to sunset.

*Wallace Drive (**Tod Inlet** Access)*   From Victoria take Highway #17 (Pat Bay), then West Saanich Road to Wallace Drive and turn left. The trailhead is on the left (west) side of Wallace Drive, opposite Quarry Lake (fenced). Roadside parking is limited. The main trail to Tod Inlet is not wheelchair accessible.

*Ross-Durrance Road (**Timberman Trail** Access)*   From Victoria take Highway #17 (Pat Bay), then West Saanich Road to Wallace Drive and turn left. At Willis Point Road, turn left again and continue beyond Durrance Lake to Ross-Durrance Road. Turn left one more time to the parking lot, also on the left. (Mount Work Regional Park hikers share this lot.)

*Caleb Pike Road (**Ridge Trail/Mount Finlayson Trail** Access)*   Follow Highway #1 (Trans-Canada) west from Victoria and take Exit 14 (Langford/Millstream Road). Keep north onto Millstream Road to Caleb Pike Road. Turn left (west) and continue a short distance to the parking lot.

HIKE DESCRIPTIONS

Tod Inlet Moderate/1.5 km, one-way: The trail is not wheelchair accessible. There is a choice of routes. From the roadside parking on Wallace Drive, continue past the information kiosk on a wide trail (an old road with a gentle grade) that heads directly to the inlet or turn left and follow the twisting, up-and-down path along Tod Creek. The latter route is worth a visit in the spring, when white fawn lilies and trilliums carpet the forest floor. The rare phantom orchid is much more elusive. The trails end on the idyllic shores of Tod Inlet.

Timberman Trail to Jocelyn Hill Strenuous/5 km, one-way: From the McKenzie Bight access look for the marked Timberman Trail on Ross-Durrance Road's west side. Soon after you cross Pease Creek is the junction (on the right) with the Cascade Trail, a link to the McKenzie Bight Trail (see p.52). Keep left on the Timberman Trail for Jocelyn Hill and, en route, three spectacular viewpoints. The first reveals the wide expanse of Saanich Inlet. At a major junction, keep left for Jocelyn Hill. The path to the right climbs to the Malahat viewpoint and is well worth the side trip. The third viewpoint overlooks Squally Reach. Expect many steep sections and repetitive up-and-down hiking. The trail curves around Jocelyn Hill's southeast slope before veering north on the final pitch to the summit. From here you can extend your hike south to the Caleb Pike parking lot or even further to Mount Finlayson and Goldstream Park (too long for a day hike).

At the top of Jocelyn Hill (434 m), the breathtaking view takes in the Olympic Mountains, Finlayson Arm, Bamberton, Squally Reach, Saanich Inlet and the Gulf Islands. Watch for Bald Eagles, a variety of hawks (Cooper's, Red-tailed and Sharp-shinned), Peregrine Falcons, ravens and other resident and migrant raptors. You may spot a Golden Eagle or Townsend's Solitaire. More common are Red Crossbills, Cassin's Vireos, Blue Grouse and Merlin. Here and elsewhere in the park's upland forests look for camas, white fawn lilies, larkspur and other spring wildflowers. Jocelyn Hill is known for its April bloom of gold stars.

Ridge Trail to Jocelyn Hill via Holmes Peak Strenuous/to Holmes Peak 1.2 km, one-way; to Jocelyn Hill 4 km, one way: From the Caleb Pike trailhead, descend behind the information kiosk on the Ridge Trail and keep right at the signposted junction. If you hike the trail in late April or early May, look for the delicate ladyslippers and a profusion of shooting stars. Holmes Peak (329 m) offers a fine vista of the Gowlland Range and Finlayson Arm.

Several bridle paths link to the Ridge Trail. Watch for markers to stay on the main trail and ignore any side paths. After a long, arduous climb you will reach upland forest where arbutus, hairy manzanita, and isolated stands of hardy shore pines cling to the exposed rocky outcrops. Follow the markers to the Jocelyn Hill summit. Extend your hike north to the McKenzie Bight access, near Durrance Lake, then stretch your trek even further by adding a hike up Mount Work (see p. 49). CAUTION This is a very long, arduous hike, generally too long for a day trip. Use of a car shuttle for the return trip may help.

Emma Dickson Trail to Jocelyn Hill via Ridge Tail Moderate to strenuous/approx. 2 km one-way: One of the shortest routes to Jocelyn Hill, and one with access to great views, is the Emma Dickson Trail from Stonecrest subdivision, just past the intersection of Emma Dickson Road and Millstream Road. The trail is a bridle path, so you may be sharing the route with horses. From the subdivision, walk through the woods (west)—there is a short steep stretch to a viewpoint but the rest of the trail to the intersection with the Ridge Trail cliff route is relatively easy walking. From here, you can choose the bridal trail or the steeper Ridge Trail (no horses) to the intersection where both meet the Lower Jocelyn Loop and from there, take the loop trail then the Jocelyn Hill Trail. You can retrace your steps on the return, or choose the longer route via the Jocelyn Hill Trail and Timberman Trail back to the intersection with the Lower Jocelyn Loop. You can also continue on the Timberman Trail from the intersection with the Jocelyn Hill Trail, all the way to McKenzie Bight, enjoying the viewpoints as you go.

Rowntree Loop Moderate/1.9 km loop: From the Caleb Pike Road trailhead, travel south on the road (an even, steady grade), or descend behind the information kiosk on the sign-posted Ridge Trail. Be sure to keep left at the fork. The trail drops to several rewarding viewpoints and then climbs again to eventually reach the road, near the park boundary. These are multi-use trails (hiking, cycling and equestrian) so be courteous.

Partridge Trail Moderate to strenuous/approx. 4.5–5 km loop: CAUTION This loop trail is not signed or maintained. Access is from Durrance Lake. From Willis Point Road, turn right onto Durrance

Close. Parking in the parking lot near the lake is very limited but parking on the shoulder of Willis Point Road is permitted. Use extreme caution if parking on the shoulder. The trail goes north from the Durrance Lake loop trail for approx. 600 m. then divides. The trail to the right is slightly longer than the one to the left. Hike approx. 2.5–3 km to the Partridge Hills viewpoint, offering great views of Tod Inlet.

To access the *Mount Finlayson Trail*, continue south on the road and hike between private properties and under power lines to come out on Rowntree Road, near Viart Road. Take Rowntree Road then turn right (west) on Finlayson Arm Road to the marked Mount Finlayson trailhead, on the left (see p.58).

WORTH NOTING

- This park has pit toilets, located at the Tod Inlet, Mackenzie Bight and Caleb Pike trailheads.
- Tod Inlet is home to waterfowl nesting areas and salmon spawning streams. Dogs must be on leash and under control at all times to avoid disturbing sensitive areas. Please remember to dispose of your dog's waste with the rest of your garbage.

NEARBY

Oak Haven Park (10 ha)   Access as for the Tod Inlet trailhead (see map p.42). Continue north on Wallace Drive past the Tod Inlet trailhead to Benvenuto Avenue and turn right (east) to the park. Parking is limited. This municipal park is a mosaic of open, scrub and parkland forest vegetation, featuring large Douglas-fir, arbutus and Garry oak. The rocky open forest habitat supports a rich variety of wildlife, particularly birds, but including animals such as Black-tailed Deer and Red Squirrel, and quite likely (although seldom seen) bats, amphibians and reptiles. Among the rock outcrops look for Indian plum and Nootka rose and other flowering shrubs. Wildflowers include trillium, camas, satin flowers and fawn lilies. The rocky knoll that now comprises the park area, and that used to be informally known as Pitzer's Rock, was the object of some mining activity, mainly worked for copper between about 1896 and 1901 without significant commercial yields. Square pits are clearly visible on the top and southeast slope of this hill.

Gore Park (6.77 ha)   To reach pretty and unspoiled Gore Park, from Benvenuto Avenue keep north on Wallace Drive to Greig Avenue and turn right (east) to the park. This nature park is in a Garry oak ecosystem and has undergone Camas meadow restoration. The spring wildflowers here are a delight, and watch for Coopers Hawk, often seen in the area.

Trails at McKenzie Bight, Mount Work, Durrance Lake and Goldstream Park are also close by (see pp.49, 52, and 55).

OF INTEREST

- The First Nations people called Tod Inlet "the place of the Blue Grouse." Areas in the park have been, and continue to be, important to First Nations peoples for medicinal, ceremonial and spiritual purposes.

- Gowlland Tod protects a significant portion of the natural shoreline of Finlayson Arm, significant in being the only deep-water fjord on Vancouver Island's east coast and one of only four "shallow sill" fjords in the world. Water in the fjord is replenished only once a year, and the resulting rich biodiversity attracts divers. Boaters, too, are attracted to the calm waters of the inlet.

- The Gowlland Range is named for John Thomas Gowlland, RN, a coastal surveyor who served as second master under Captain Richards aboard HMS Plumper (1857–1860) and HMS Hecate (1861–1863). Tod Inlet is named after John Tod, who arrived in B.C. in 1823.

- In February of 2006, University of Victoria scientists and researchers began operating the VENUS project (Victoria Experimental Network Under The Sea) in Tod Inlet. This underwater observatory is designed to retrieve data from the Saanich Inlet seabed, allowing scientists to study and monitor changing conditions on the seabed.

- Wallace Drive, the main approach to the beautiful Tod Inlet trails, follows the old rail bed of the BC Electric Railway, built to serve Tod Inlet and Deep Cove. Tod Inlet was the location of the town site and cement works of the Vancouver Portland Cement Company (1904–1920s) and is adjacent to Butchart Gardens, created by Jenny Butchart from worked-out limestone quarries.

Lone Tree Hill Regional Park

DIFFICULTY/DISTANCE   Moderate to strenuous/1.6 km, one-way

HIGHLIGHTS   The small (32 ha) Lone Tree Hill Regional Park was created in 1982. Named after a solitary, bonsai-like Douglas-fir tree that stood on the summit for over 200 years, it is located in the Highlands District and offers excellent viewpoints, fine examples of dry, rocky outcrop vegetation and birdwatching opportunities.

Best time to go   Particularly nice in the spring and summer.

CAUTIONS
- Avoid the open slopes near the summit.
- Dogs are welcome but fires and camping are not.

ACCESS   **From Victoria**, take Highway #1 (Trans-Canada), leave the highway at Exit 14 and follow the right hand lane onto Millstream Road. Stay on this road, travelling north and at the junction of Millstream Road and Millstream Lake Road, bear left. Millstream Road is signed as a "no through road" at this point. The park is on the right side of the road about 1.5 km beyond Caleb Pike Road. Lone Tree Hill Regional Park is connected to Goldstream Provincial Park by Finlayson Arm Road, a narrow and very winding country road.

HIKE DESCRIPTION   From the parking area, the winding forested trail, at times steep and rocky, climbs steadily for 1.2 km to the summit (364 m). Allow about 1 hour return. At the top there are spectacular views of the Malahat, the Gowlland Range, Victoria and the Olympic Mountains. An arbutus tree now occupies the top of the hill where the Douglas-fir once stood. Stay on the trail to protect the area's delicate ecology.

WORTH NOTING
- The park is a popular birdwatching destination. Soaring Turkey Vulture, Red-tailed Hawk, and Bald Eagle may be seen riding overhead thermals.
- Wildflowers (shooting stars, camas, fairy orchids, sea blush, sedum and fawn lilies) are abundant in the spring, particularly near the summit.

2b. Mount Work   MAP 2b

DIFFICULTY/DISTANCE   Moderate to strenuous/1.7 km to 2.5 km, one way

HIGHLIGHTS   Mount Work Regional Park (697 ha), among the largest in the CRD system, is in the Highlands District, and has 11 km of captivating trails through upland and lowland forests. One trail descends to Saanich Inlet. The steep climb to the summit is somewhat challenging but hikers are treated to a striking view of southern Vancouver Island from the highest point on the Saanich Peninsula. The park has three freshwater lakes—Durrance, Fork, and Pease. Durrance Lake, the most accessible, has an attractive loop trail (and is stocked with catchable Rainbow Trout).

Best time to go   You can hike in the Mount Work area any month of the year, barring times of snow at higher elevations (the summit trails are exposed to the weather).

CAUTIONS
- Mount Work routes are fairly steep in parts and there are several switchbacks. The open rock faces near the summit may be extremely slippery in wet weather.
- Storms and fog may roll in without warning. Gear up for potentially adverse conditions and wear proper footwear.
- Bring your own drinking water and leave enough time to return before dark.
- Please keep to the main trails at all times to protect fragile vegetation.

ACCESS   **To the Main Entrance** (north end trailhead)   From Victoria take Highway #17 (Pat Bay), then West Saanich Road to Wallace Drive and turn left. At Willis Point Road turn left again and continue to Ross-Durrance Road. Turn left one more time to the parking lot, also on the left. (Gowlland Tod Provincial Park hikers park here too.)

For Durrance Lake   Follow directions as above to Willis Point Road. Turn right at Durrance Close, which leads to the parking lot. NOTE that the parking lot is very small and gets very busy in summer. If you do park on the road, make sure your tires are off the pavement, or you may be ticketed.

Map 2b Mount Work

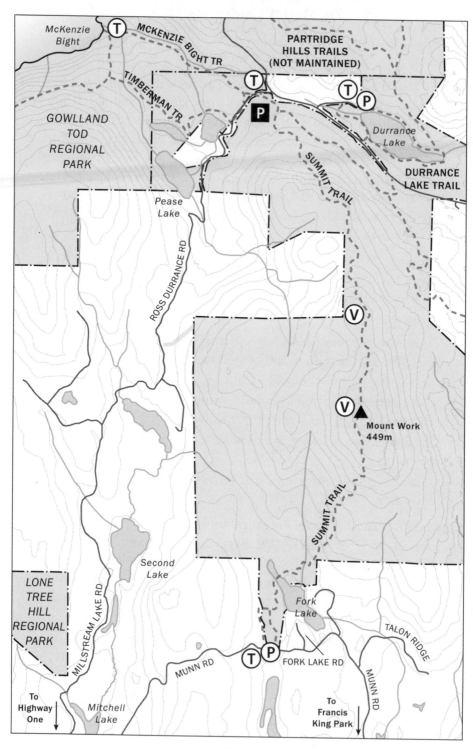

Map 2b Mount Work

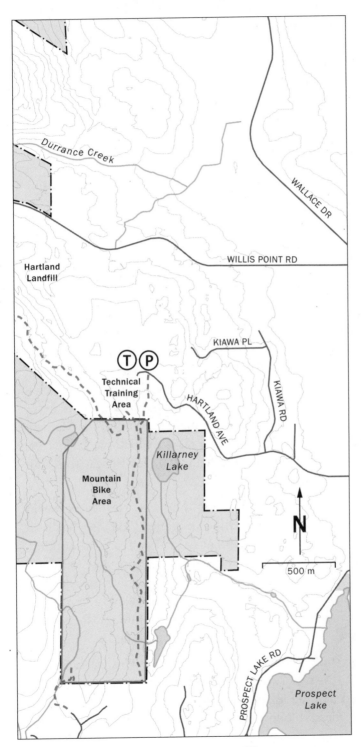

For the Fork Lake (Munn Road) Entrance (south end trailhead) From Victoria, take Highway #1 (Trans-Canada) and take Exit 14 to the Highlands. Keep right at the fork, and turn right at Millstream Lake Road, then slight right at Munn Road to the park entrance and parking area on the right, just past Fork Lake Road.

From Victoria, allow about 40 minutes driving time. The park is open from sunrise to sunset. The north side of Durrance Lake is wheelchair accessible.

HIKE DESCRIPTIONS

Summit Trail Strenuous/from north trailhead, 2.5 km, one way; from south trailhead, 1.8 km, one way: The rugged Summit Trail stretches north to south, from one end of the park to the other. There are steep stretches and series of switchbacks, as well as several "false summits", so pay attention to signage on your way to the top. You have a choice of starting points, but the distance to the top is a little shorter from the Fork Lake trailhead than from the one near Durrance Lake. NOTE: whichever trailhead you choose, and just after you begin hiking, turn right at the first junction for the summit.

The cool, moist, lowland forest consists of mainly maple, western redcedar, alder and Douglas-fir. The drier uplands have Douglas-fir, lodgepole pine and arbutus. There are open areas and beautiful views on the way up that include Central Saanich and the Haro Strait islands. At the top of Mount Work (449 m), the highest point on the Saanich Peninsula, the spectacular summit view takes in Victoria, Lone Tree Hill, Finlayson Arm, the Malahat, Jocelyn Hill, Juan de Fuca Strait and the Olympic Mountains.

Durrance Lake Trail Moderate/1.7 km, one way: Nestled between Mount Work and the Partridge Hills, Durrance Lake (8.4 ha) is a popular hiking, swimming and fishing destination. From the parking lot, the Durrance Lake Trail leads to the lake's east end, close to a dam on Durrance Creek. From here the groomed path narrows considerably and loops back along the lake's south side. The trail follows a serpentine course as it meanders through the damp, boggy lowland forest and eventually emerges on Durrance Close, near the parking lot.

McKenzie Bight Trail Moderate/1.5 km, one way: This pleasant hike traverses a multi-use trail (hiking, biking and equestrians) and starts from the shared parking lot on Ross-Durrance Road. Cross over to the road's west side and follow the sign-posted McKenzie Bight Trail.

It is a steady drop most of the way and the return climb will take you slightly longer than your descent. The trail takes you from Mount Work Regional Park into Gowlland Tod Provincial Park (see p.41). The shady forest floor alongside McKenzie Creek is covered with mosses, lichen and ferns of many types. The ferns are exceptionally thick in the ravine (the grotto), near a fine stand of western redcedar and Douglas-fir. In early April, the Rufous Hummingbird is a common sight.

The trail emerges at McKenzie Bight, close to Squally Reach. There are waterside picnic spots. Take time to examine the diversity of seaweed that flourishes in the estuary near the mud, sand and pebble beach. Harbour seals are sometimes observed offshore. A 21 m wide parkland strip extends northeast from McKenzie Bight along a rough road to the end of Mark Lane. To loop hike back, cross the McKenzie Creek bridge and follow the Cascade and Timberman trails (in Gowlland Tod Provincial Park) to the start. The Cascade Trail (moderate 0.5 km), on McKenzie Creek's west side, passes several clamorous waterfalls and a viewpoint on Pease Creek. For a longer hike, you can continue on the Timberman Trail to several viewpoints: Saanich Inlet Viewpoint, Malahat Viewpoint, and Squally Reach Viewpoint.

Munn Road Loop Trail Easy/630 m: An accessible trail with gradual slopes and smooth gravel surface loops through the forest, treating you to evergreen trees, and a mix of native shrubs, flowers, mosses and ferns. There is an accessible toilet at the trailhead.

WORTH NOTING

- Mount Work is a monadnock, or residual hill, whose hard rock (Wark gneiss) survived the grinding action of scouring glaciers. Evidence of their passing is all around this area. A little to the west lies Finlayson Arm, a glacial fjord. Along the McKenzie Bight Trail look for deposits of layered gravel and clay.
- Wildflowers to look for include fawn lilies, trilliums, shooting stars and Indian paintbrush. Shrubs like Oregon grape and oceanspray are common. Ferns and salmonberries thrive along parts of the Durrance Lake Trail.
- The shrub at Mount Work's summit that resembles an arbutus tree is actually hairy manzanita, a close relative. The clusters of white or pink flowers turn into dark berries in the fall.
- At the Mount Work summit, watch for Turkey Vultures high in the thermals. In the late summer, these large birds congregate here in

small flocks. Their fall migration south begins with a crossing of Juan de Fuca Strait. Other birds of prey to watch for are hawks and Bald Eagles.

- Look for the Pacific Bananaslug underfoot, and Western Red-backed Salamanders near decaying trees.
- Toilets are located at Munn Road access, Durrance Lake and near the parking area on Ross-Durrance Road.
- Keep your dog under control and on the trail at all times. Please stay off surrounding private property.

NEARBY The Mount Work-Hartland mountain bike trails on Mount Work's east slope are also part of the park. The trails here are multiuse, cycling, hiking, and horseback riding. Contact the South Island Mountain Bike Society (SIMBS) for access and permit information at simbs.com.

Just to the east of the Mountain Bike area of the park is the lovely Killarney Lake. There is a short trail around the lake that also connects to trails in the mountain bike area of the park. Best access is from the trail head on Meadowbrook Road, where there is a small amount of parking on the side of the road.

Gowlland Tod Provincial Park abuts Mount Work Park. From the shared Ross-Durrance Road parking lot, a hiking-only trail leads to several viewpoints, Jocelyn Hill and beyond (see p.50). To the north of Durrance Lake are the Partridge Hills. Please note that the trails are not signed or maintained.

Trillium (*Trillium ovatum*).   GAIL F. HARCOMBE

2c. Goldstream/Mount Finlayson

DIFFICULTY/DISTANCE   Easy to strenuous/15 minutes to 1.5 hours or more, one-way

HIGHLIGHTS   Goldstream Provincial Park (388 ha) features almost 16 km of year-round hiking trails through forested uplands and lowlands, each with their own characteristics. The park has 600-year-old Douglas-fir, large western redcedar, arbutus and Garry oak. There are superb opportunities for wildlife viewing and nature appreciation. The fall Chum Salmon run draws thousands of visitors. There is a large picnic area with shelters, and a full-service 173-site campground. Check the BC Parks website for information on fees, reservations and additional trails (see p.226). The Freeman King Visitor Centre near the Goldstream River estuary has seasonal interpretive programs.

Best time to go   A great place to go any time of the year, but the best times are in the spring, late fall, and early to mid-winter: in the spring for wildflowers, including the shade-loving western trillium and the calypso orchid, and birdwatching/wildlife viewing; in the fall for the spectacular salmon run; and in winter for the Eagle Extravaganza (up to 200 eagles have been recorded in one day!).

CAUTIONS
- Use extreme caution if crossing Highway #1.
- Bicycles are allowed on the trail from the parking lot to the Visitor Centre, but are not permitted on hiking trails.
- Hike only on marked trails and obey posted signs to protect both yourself and the park's rare and fragile ecosystems.
- The Mount Finlayson Trail is well known for accidents. It is not recommended for pets or small children. Please take this mountain seriously.
- Avoid the treacherous steep slopes in the Niagara Canyon on the Gold Mine Trail.
- The Goldstream River estuary is closed to the public (including all boaters). Goldstream River and its tributaries have a very limited fishing season and are catch and release only at all times of the year.
- Parts of Goldstream Park are semi-wilderness regions and the territory of Cougar and Black Bear. These backcountry areas are not suitable for dogs or other pets. Be alert. Keep children close by.

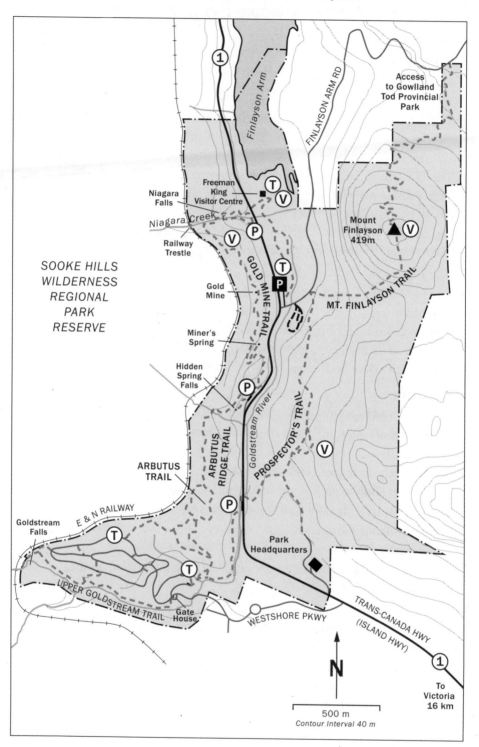

SOOKE HILLS
WILDERNESS
REGIONAL
PARK
RESERVE

Finlayson Arm

FINLAYSON ARM RD

Access
to Gowlland
Tod Provincial
Park

Freeman
King
Visitor Centre

Niagara
Falls

Niagara Creek

Railway
Trestle

Mount
Finlayson
419m

GOLD MINE TRAIL

Gold
Mine

MT. FINLAYSON TRAIL

Miner's
Spring

Hidden
Spring
Falls

Goldstream River

ARBUTUS RIDGE TRAIL

PROSPECTOR'S TRAIL

ARBUTUS
TRAIL

E & N RAILWAY

Goldstream
Falls

UPPER GOLDSTREAM TRAIL

Gate
House

Park
Headquarters

WESTSHORE PKWY

TRANS-CANADA HWY
(ISLAND HWY)

To
Victoria
16 km

N

500 m
Contour Interval 40 m

- Due to the sensitive nature of the salmon spawning cycle, dogs must be kept out of the river.
- Pets/domestic animals must be on a leash and under control at all times and are not allowed in the water, beach areas or park buildings. Please dispose of their excrement.

ACCESS Take Highway #1 (Trans-Canada) about 30 minutes (16 km) west of Victoria to Goldstream Park's southern boundary, where you will see a portal sign. Keep on Highway #1, then turn right into the day-use/picnic area and parking lot, near the junction of the highway and Finlayson Arm Road (at the start of the Malahat drive). There are also three day-use parking lots on the southbound lane of the highway. The more northerly one serves the Niagara Falls viewpoint.

Freeman King Visitor Centre A short trail extends from the day use/picnic area to the Freeman King Visitor Centre. Here you will find historical displays, a gift shop, and a viewing platform close to the Goldstream River estuary and salt marsh. This is an excellent spot to watch for deer, Mink, River Otter, Bald Eagle, migrating hummingbirds (March), and various shorebirds and ducks (late spring/early summer). Please observe the estuary's quiet zone regulations. Several short trails starting from the day-use parking lot are wheelchair accessible.

The Visitor Centre is open daily from 9 am–4:30 pm. School programs occur throughout the week and visitors are welcome to join in. To find out more, phone 250-478-9414. Interpretive programs offered by the Visitor Centre during the spawning Chum Salmon run (usually late October to early December) and the "Eagle Extravaganza" (December to February) are extremely popular. (Likely due to the closure of the estuary, Bald Eagles, once rarely seen here, now abound during the run, and nest during the summer.)

To access the campground (from Victoria), take Highway #1 (Trans-Canada) to Westshore Parkway. Turn left and continue to the roundabout. Take the first exit to Amy Road. Turn left onto Sooke Lake Road, then right onto Golden Gate Road and continue to the campground entrance.

HIKE DESCRIPTIONS As well as the hikes listed below there are several short, interconnecting trails along the river, close to the day-use/picnic area. Many trails have good viewpoints and some join other paths making it easy to create your own loop hike.

Arbutus Trail   Easy/15 minutes, one-way; the Arbutus Ridge, moderate/1.5 hours, one-way: This trail passes through stands of arbutus trees and Garry oak that prefer drier upland areas. The spring season brings a profusion of wildflowers.

Lower Goldstream Trail   Easy/15 minutes, one-way: Winding along the Goldstream River, the trail is a great spot to view the fall Chum Salmon run. Chinook and Coho salmon also enter the river. Watch for River Otter, Mink and American Dipper.

Upper Goldstream Trail   Easy/1/2 hour, one-way: Near the campsite is the trail to hike if you like big trees. Highlights include some of the park's oldest trees and 8 m high Goldstream Falls.

Gold Mine Trail   Moderate/1 hour, one-way: The trail climbs to the top of 47.5 m high Niagara Falls on Niagara Creek. A footbridge spans the Niagara Canyon. Avoid the treacherous steep slopes in this area. The route passes old mine workings and a spring. A short trail accesses the bottom of Niagara Falls. This is not a loop trail, so plan on retracing your steps. There is limited parking near the start of the trail, on the southbound side of the highway. Crossing the highway is extremely dangerous. In summer, it is sometimes possible to use the tunnels (there are two) under the highway.

Prospector's Trail   Moderate/1.5 hours, one-way: Along the trail that links the Group Campsite with the Mount Finlayson Trail, you will see large Douglas-fir, Garry oak and arbutus. Impressive rocks and boulders, some footbridges, and a lookout at an outcrop in an arbutus grove are delights along the way. There is a great viewpoint and old copper mine workings. This is a good hike for a hot day as most of the trail is shaded, but also a good trail in light rain since the trees keep you from getting too wet. You can choose to start with a gentle grade (the first part of the Mount Finlayson trail) and at the fork, take the Prospector's Trail, or take the steep, concrete stairs (lots of stairs!). The trail is fairly narrow and for the most part ascends gradually.

Mount Finlayson Trail   Strenuous/45 minutes to 1 hour, one-way: Beginning in a heavily forested area on the east side of the Goldstream River bridge (close to the day-use/picnic area), the trail accesses one of Victoria's best viewpoints. Be prepared for adverse and changeable weather conditions on the challenging and steady (almost 2 km) climb to the summit (419 m). Wear adequate clothing and footwear.

Overlooking Goldstream Provincial Park. ROLLY PATTON

Beware of exposed, steep drop-offs and bluffs. Some rock scrambling is required. Watch for orange markings with directional arrows placed at the switchbacks to indicate the route. Sections of trail may be extremely slippery when wet. Allow adequate time during daylight hours for your return hike. You should not attempt a summit later than noon, depending on the time of year. Once it is dark, you cannot see the trail and it is far too dangerous to descend.

To descend from the summit, some hikers may prefer to use the "safe" route that snakes down the north flank of Mount Finlayson to Finlayson Arm Road. The trail is 4 km long. At the bottom, follow the trail that links to Gowlland Tod Provincial Park (see map p.42) or circle back to the Goldstream Park parking lot via Finlayson Arm Road. Use caution on this narrow road. There is no sidewalk.

Bear Mountain Resort to Mount Finlayson   Strenuous/1 hour or more one-way: Take the path that runs behind the main building (where the check-in is) to the trail up Mount Finlayson. This hike can be treacherous—the route is very steep, with rough sections of roots and loose rock. About halfway up Mount Finlayson, there is an area where the trail crisscrosses an open rock area. Great views of the Bear Mountain Resort

- The Goldstream area is a traditional First Nations fishing ground and the site of a mid-1800s gold rush. In 1958, the Greater Victoria Water Board donated the land at Goldstream Park to the province. Later additions were acquired in 1994 through the Commonwealth Nature Legacy Program.
- Mt. Finlayson, Finlayson Arm, and Finlayson Road were named after Roderick Finlayson, one of Victoria's founding fathers. Employed by the Hudson Bay Company in Lower Canada, he eventually got a posting to what was then called Fort Victoria.
- The Outdoor Club of Victoria constructed the Arbutus Ridge, Gold Mine, Prospector's and Riverside trails. The club designed and installed the stairs and CRD have adopted that plan for building other trail stairs.

complex from here. Once you reach the summit, you can choose to go down the other side of the mountain (see Mount Finlayson Trail hike description), or descend using the trail that takes you back to the resort.

NEARBY Gowlland Tod Provincial Park trails may be accessed from Finlayson Arm Road (see p.42).

Goldstream Provincial Park. NEIL BURROUGHS

2d. Mount Wells   MAP 2d

DIFFICULTY/DISTANCE   Strenuous/1.3 km, one-way

HIGHLIGHTS   A strenuous climb through Douglas-fir forest and Garry oak ecosystems to the barren rock summit of Mount Wells Regional Park, in Langford, rewards hikers with spectacular views of southern Vancouver Island and the Olympic Mountains. This fragile area explodes with spring wildflowers and there are excellent opportunities for wildlife viewing.

Best time to go   Spring and summer.

CAUTIONS
- Mount Wells Regional Park is a remote wilderness area, and the trail to the summit is steep and challenging. In wet weather, there will be muddy sections and slick rock, so wear proper footwear. Go properly prepared and carry adequate water for the steep ascent.
- Please keep pets on the trail and under control.

ACCESS   **From Victoria,** take Highway #1 (Trans-Canada) north. Turn left onto Westshore Parkway. At the roundabout, take the 1st exit onto Amy Road. Turn left onto Sooke Lake Road, then left again onto Humpback Road. Keep right at the intersection with Irwin Road, and continue to the parking area. From Victoria, allow 30 minutes driving time. The park is open from sunrise to sunset.

There is an alternative "unofficial" access to Mount Wells off Awsworth Road, which isn't quite as steep. Enter Awsworth road off Sooke Road, turn right and park a short way up the hill. There are several trails near here, and another further along Awsworth and at the end of Glenshire Drive.

HIKE DESCRIPTION   Sitting on the edge of the Sooke Hills Wilderness Park Reserve, the largest protected area in the region, the CRD's Mount Wells Regional Park (123 ha) features a steep trail (240 m elevation gain) to the viewpoint at the Mount Wells summit (352 m). From the start on Humpback Road, the park's *Summit Trail* crosses an old water pipeline that once was a flow line out of the now disused Humpback Reservoir. The trail leaves the Douglas-fir forest of the lower regions and ascends through drier, open rocky terrain, where Garry oak, arbutus, hairy manzanita and delicate mosses grow. The route traverses patches of open rock and loose dirt or mud, depending

Map 2d Mount Wells

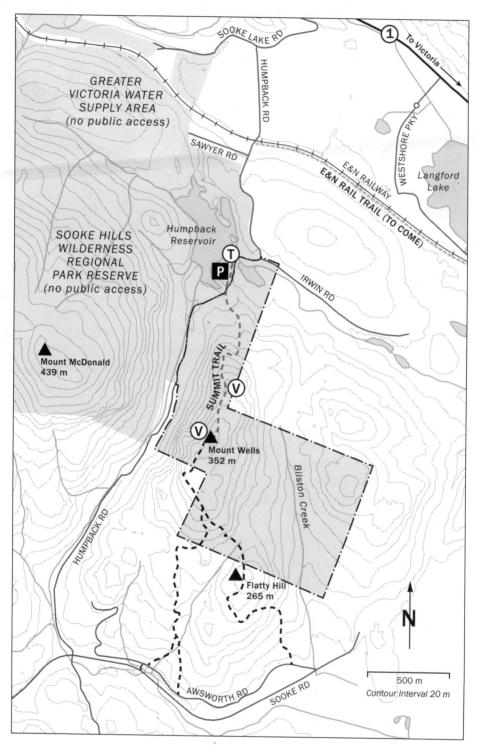

GREATER
VICTORIA WATER
SUPPLY AREA
(no public access)

SOOKE LAKE RD

HUMPBACK RD

SAWYER RD

E&N RAILWAY

E&N RAIL TRAIL (TO COME)

WESTSHORE PKY

To Victoria

1

Langford
Lake

SOOKE HILLS
WILDERNESS
REGIONAL
PARK RESERVE
(no public access)

Humpback
Reservoir

T
P

IRWIN RD

Mount McDonald
439 m

SUMMIT TRAIL

V

V

Mount Wells
352 m

Bilston Creek

HUMPBACK RD

Flatty Hill
265 m

AWSWORTH RD

SOOKE RD

N

500 m
Contour Interval 20 m

on the weather, which can be particularly challenging on the descent. Chain link "railings" have been installed in a few rocky portions, which help on the way up or down. At the top, your reward is a panoramic vista of Victoria, the Juan de Fuca Strait and the Sooke Hills to the west, including Mt. McDonald in the Sooke Hills Park Reserve.

WORTH NOTING

- Mt. Wells has long been used for rock-climbing, and contains steep walls and roof climbs, with grades for every level of climbers.
- In spring, wildflowers are abundant. Look for camas, satin flowers and shooting stars. The endangered prairie lupine grows in only one place in Canada, on Mount Wells. Stay on designated trails to protect the area's fragile vegetation and soil.
- Watch for Turkey Vultures riding overhead thermals. Listen for the drumming calls of Blue Grouse. The park is also habitat for deer, squirrels and Northern Alligator Lizards. The latter are often spotted sunning themselves on rocks.

NEARBY Together, Mount Wells Regional Park and the Sooke Hills Wilderness Regional Park Reserve (4124 ha) provide an undeveloped forest buffer zone for the Victoria area's drinking water supply at Sooke Lake. Both this reserve and Mount Wells Regional Park are part of the Sea to Sea Green Blue Belt, protected forests that separate urban regions from the wilderness areas further west.

What flower or tree is that? Enhance your walk or hike, take time to identify the fauna and flora around you. Carry your plant identification books with you, and take time to notice and identify the different plants along the trail.

Map 2e   Elk/Beaver Lake

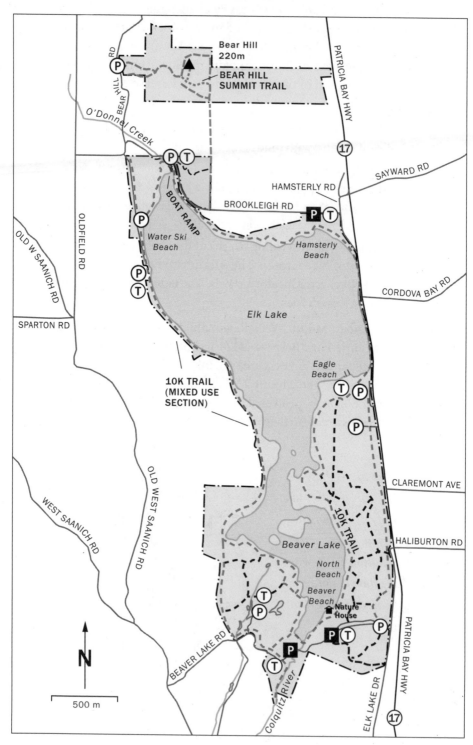

Bear Hill
220m

BEAR HILL
SUMMIT TRAIL

BEAR HILL RD

O'Donnel Creek

PATRICIA BAY HWY

17

SAYWARD RD

HAMSTERLY RD

BROOKLEIGH RD

BOAT RAMP

Water Ski
Beach

Hamsterly
Beach

OLDFIELD RD

OLD W SAANICH RD

CORDOVA BAY RD

SPARTON RD

Elk Lake

Eagle
Beach

10K TRAIL
(MIXED USE
SECTION)

OLD WEST SAANICH RD

WEST SAANICH RD

CLAREMONT AVE

10K TRAIL

HALIBURTON RD

Beaver Lake

North
Beach

Beaver
Beach

Nature
House

BEAVER LAKE RD

Colquitz River

PATRICIA BAY HWY

ELK LAKE DR

17

N

500 m

2e. Elk/Beaver Lake   MAP 2e

DIFFICULTY/DISTANCE   Easy/up to 10 km loop

HIGHLIGHTS   The CRD's Elk/Beaver Lake Regional Park (443 ha) in Saanich sees close to a million visitors a year. It's a multi-use park enjoyed by hikers, equestrians, cyclists, swimmers, paddlers, rowers, fishers, windsurfers, boaters and dog trainers. Elk Lake is the largest lake in the area. A 10 km trail loops around both lakes and there are plenty of shorter paths to explore. The main loop takes about 2–2.5 hours and the shorter loop to the west of Beaver Lake takes about 45 minutes.

Best time to go   Any time of year, depending on use.

CAUTIONS

- Be aware that some of the trails in the park are designated multi-use, and cyclists and equestrians are allowed (on the section of the 10K Trail that runs along the west side of the lakes; equestrians share a portion of the trail between the Jennings Lane parking lot and North Beach area).
- Camping, open fires, and smoking are prohibited in the park.
- Over the years, plants and animals, some of which are detrimental to the ecosystem, have been introduced into the lakes. Never release any fish or other animals into Elk/Beaver Lake.
- Please stay on designated trails and do not disturb animals or plants.
- Keep your dog under control and on the trail at all times.

ACCESS

To Elk Lake   From Victoria, take Highway #17 (Pat Bay) north past Elk Lake to Sayward Road and turn left at the traffic lights. Make a second left onto Hamsterly Road and a right onto Brookleigh Road to the park entrance at Hamsterly Beach. Parking is also available at Brookleigh Boat Launch, Waterski Beach and the fishing float on Elk Lake's west side (disabled parking only). Check with CRD parks for seasonal restrictions and closures (see p.226).

To Beaver Lake   From Victoria, take Highway #17 (Pat Bay) north, then take the Royal Oak exit and turn left on Royal Oak Drive. Cross the highway overpass and follow Royal Oak Drive to Elk Lake Drive. Turn right at the lights and continue to the park entrance, up ahead on the left. There are several parking lots including North Beach, Beaver Beach and the one next to the old filter beds at the lake's southern tip.

From Victoria, allow around 20 minutes driving time. The park is open from sunrise to sunset. Beaver Beach, the 10K Trail, some shorter paths, Hamsterly Beach, Brookleigh Boat Launch and the Elk Lake fishing float are user-friendly/wheelchair accessible. See CRD's brochure on User-Friendly Trails for more information (p.227).

HIKE DESCRIPTION The *10K Trail* circles Beaver Lake and Elk Lake (224 ha combined size) and winds through forests, fields and wetlands. There are stands of crabapple, western redcedar, cottonwood, Pacific willow, bigleaf maple and alder. The trail has many access points along the way. Start at Beaver Beach, at Beaver Lake's south end, turn left and cross the Colquitz River footbridge. Stay on the trail closest to the lake. Paths on the left lead to the park's Equestrian Centre and the dog training area at the retriever ponds. Contact local clubs concerning access.

On the west side of Elk/Beaver Lake, the 10K Trail is a multi-use trail, used by cyclists, hikers and equestrians. It heads north following the relatively flat rail bed of the defunct Victoria and Sidney (V & S) Railroad. The trail passes a fishing platform and heads north alongside Bear Hill Road (south end) to Waterski Beach and the Brookleigh boat launch. Here the route turns east to skirt Elk Lake's north shore to Hamsterly Beach. This section is for hiking only.

Continue south from Hamsterly Beach—the trail narrows and becomes uneven, paralleling the Patricia Bay (Pat Bay) Highway. Eagle Beach, close to the Victoria Rowing Society boathouse and dock, is a favourite swimming area. The trail branches with one path keeping close to Elk Lake and the other running alongside an open, grassy field. Look for cascara trees in this area. Dogs are often trained here, where they are allowed off-leash. Both trails lead back to Beaver Beach and the parking lot. You can shorten your 10K Trail hike by half a kilometre by keeping to the lakeside paths.

WORTH NOTING

- The Nature Centre, located near the main Beaver Lake parking lot, is open June to September. Check CRD website for hours.
- Elk Lake is stocked with catchable Rainbow Trout.
- The lakes are home to Painted Turtle, frogs, River Otter, Mink, Canada Geese, mergansers, Belted Kingfisher, Bufflehead and other waterfowl.
- Dogs are welcome, but allowed off-leash only at certain times of the year and in specific areas. Check signage.

OF INTEREST

- The City of Victoria created Elk/Beaver Lake Park in 1923; in 1966 it became a regional park.
- In 1872, the Colquitz River was dammed across a natural outlet, creating Victoria's first domestic water reservoir. Filter beds were constructed in 1896 at Beaver Lake's south end. Victoria residents were heard complaining that tadpoles and fish were flowing from household taps. When Victoria changed to Sooke for its water supply in 1914, the filter beds were abandoned.
- On Beaver Lake's west side, the trail follows the bed of the old Victoria and Sidney Railroad that, between 1894 and 1919, ran from Victoria through Royal Oak, Keating and Saanichton. Steam-driven and fired by wood, the V & S was nicknamed the "Cordwood Limited".
- The Victoria Rowing Society boathouse is located near Eagle Beach, on Elk Lake's southeast corner. Built in 1986, the boathouse is an Olympic Rowing Centre used by rowers from the Canadian National Team, the Victoria Rowing Society, the Greater Victoria Youth Rowing Society and the University of Victoria. Elk Lake is an exceptional year-round training setting.

NEARBY

Bear Hill Regional Park (49 ha) is accessed as for Elk Lake to Brookleigh Road. Stay on Brookleigh Road and turn right on Oldfield Road. Swing right onto Bear Hill Road (north end) to the main park entrance. You can also reach this point on foot via the right-of-way that links to the southern part of Bear Hill Road or the hiking/bridle trail off Brookleigh Road just before the boat launch. There are a number of bridle trails shared with hikers. Note that this CRD park has no facilities and is not wheelchair accessible. The park is open sunrise to sunset.

Bear Hill (like Mount Work, Mount Douglas and Mount Tolmie) is a monadnock, an isolated rocky hill left behind by receding glaciers about 15,000 years ago. Here the ice was about 1000 metres thick. Striations (grooves and scratches on area rocks) are evidence of their passing.

Bear Hill Summit Trail   Moderate/1.5 km, one-way: The trail is steep, with loose gravel in some sections. Open rock faces become extremely slippery in wet weather. On your hike, notice how the forest changes

Bear Hill. JESSICA HARCOMBE FLEMING

from Douglas-fir to arbutus, then to dry, open grassy areas and Garry oak meadows. Be sure to climb every knoll and false summit in order to catch every one of the many views. The best is at the Bear Hill summit (220 m). The panorama of the Gulf Islands, Haro Strait, Saanich Peninsula and Sidney is definitely worth the climb, and you may see Turkey Vulture or Bald Eagle circling overhead. Bear Hill's spring wildflowers include satin flowers (in March) followed by blue camas, fawn lilies, sea blush and canary violet. Please do not pick any flowers. The park's denser woodlands are good places to look for the Varied Thrush or Spotted Towhee. Listen for the telltale thrum of hidden grouse.

2f. Broadmead MAP 2f

DIFFICULTY/DISTANCE Easy to moderate/1.5 km to 5 km or longer, one-way

HIGHLIGHTS Broadmead, an area in the municipality of Saanich, contains nearly 60 ha of parkland, comprised of a number of small parks (some with dense, mainly second-growth coniferous forest), marshland, and small hills that offer mountain and ocean views (e.g., from the reservoir on Cordova Ridge). Two main circular trails can be combined and augmented by additional loops for walks of several hours. Check the Saanich municipal website for maps and detailed descriptions of trails in this area.

Best time to go Spring and summer for the vibrant wildflowers that cover rocky outcrops, but any time of year can be a delight—the forests of Douglas-fir, bigleaf maple, alder, and arbutus provide a natural habitat for wildlife, and over 100 bird species have been noted.

CAUTIONS
- Some portions of the trails can be steep and slippery when wet.
- Wear appropriate clothing and footwear.

ACCESS From Victoria, travel north on the Pat Bay Highway (Hwy #17) to the Royal Oak Exit. Turn right to enter the Broadmead Shopping Centre on the east side of Hwy #17.

For access to *Rithet's Bog* from Victoria, follow Highway #17 (Pat Bay) north and take the Quadra Street Exit, turn right on Quadra Street, then left onto Chatterton Way. Continue about 1 km to Dalewood Lane and a small parking area across from the houses on the street's south side.

HIKE DESCRIPTIONS
Grant Park/McMinn Park Trail Starting at the Broadmead Shopping Centre, follow Falaise Drive then Falaise Crescent to Deventer Drive, and turn left (north) at the fork in the trail—the narrower winding trail on the left skirts the east edge of Royal Oak Burial Park. (The right fork takes you to the *Boulderwood Hill Park Trail*). The trail continues to the ridge top, some cement buildings (the reservoir), and some great views. A well-defined chip trail descends into Grant Park and heads east to Lochside Drive and McMinn Park. McMinn Park has a large grassy area in the middle of the park, ponds and streams, and trails

Map 2f Broadmead

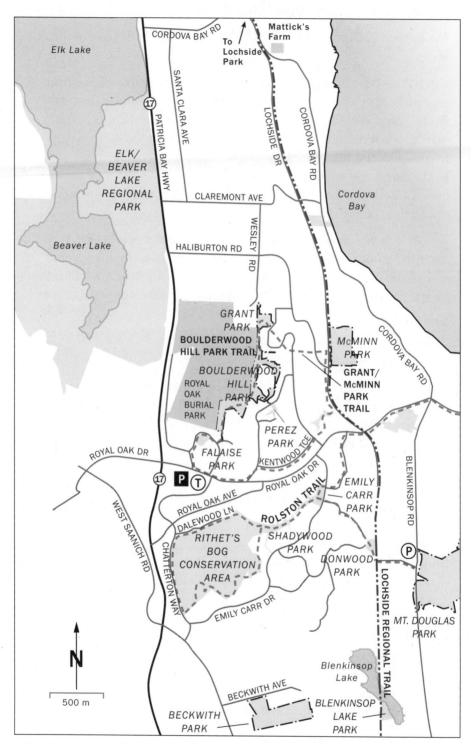

through the primarily western redcedar forest. You have several choices from here: retrace your steps to return to the shopping centre; before reaching Lochside Drive, turn right onto Amblewood and right again onto Boulderwood Drive and follow that to Royal Oak Drive and west to the shopping centre; follow Lochside Dr. south past Scottswood Lane and turn right on a short trail connecting to Royal Oak Drive. Cross Royal Oak Drive and join the marked *Rolston Trail.*

Boulderwood Hill Park Trail   There are two options for access: one about half-way between Falaise Park and Grant Park, and the other at the east end (dead end) of Deventer Drive, a path leads you through to Kentwood Lane and Boulderwood Drive. If you take the latter, climb Boulderwood to the summit. Directly opposite the Perez Park tennis courts, a trail marker shows the start of the Boulderwood Hill Park loop. Climb the hill and circle counter-clockwise—although the trail is a bit steep, wooden stairs and a metal bridge make it easier, and the sweeping views from Mount Tolmie and Mount Douglas, to the San Juan Islands (with Mount Baker as a backdrop) to the east, and north to James Island make it worth the effort. To the north is Grant Park and you could descend from here to Grant Park via Amblewood Drive, or continue around to the west side of the knoll (for expansive views of Saltspring Island and Little Saanich Mountain, west to the Malahat and Sooke Hills, Scafe Hill, and Mount Finlayson), and south to the Olympic Mountains. Descending south through a wooded area, you will cross the access road to the Boulderwood development and return to the trail (opposite Perez Park) that you first climbed.

Rolston Trail   The Rolston Trail, with the Gabo Creek bridge, runs through Shadywood and Emily Carr parks to link with other Broadmead area trails and urban walks (e.g., a portion of the Rolston Trail is part of the Rithet's Bog loop trail). You can connect to the Lochside Trail via Grant or Donwood parks.

Rithet's Bog   Saanich's 38.4 ha Rithet's Bog Conservation Area preserves the last of Greater Victoria's sphagnum bogs. An easy (3 km) meandering loop trail circles the perimeter of the marshland. The relatively flat trail is hard-packed gravel and chip bark. The southeast side has some moderate inclines. NOTE: Cyclists are not permitted on the trail. A bicycle rack is available by the Information Board. There are interpretive signs and benches en route, and a viewing platform is located on Dalewood Lane. Around the marshland are bulrushes, cattails, willows and scattered patches of shore pine, arbutus, aspen or cottonwood. Part of the perimeter trail follows Fir Tree Glen. **CAUTION** Stay on the trail at all times; the sphagnum bog conceals dangerous areas of deep water. On drier ground, arbutus, Douglas-fir and Garry oak dominate. This varied habitat makes Rithet's Bog a prime birdwatching destination (well over 100 species have been recorded in the area). It's also a great spot to observe seasonal butterflies, including the rare ringlet butterfly. Don't forget to bring insect repellent during mosquito season!

Rithet's Bog to Mattick's Farm   Mattick's Farm, next to Cordova Bay Golf Course, is a charming local shopping centre with a variety of specialty shops, including a garden centre, VQA wine shop, market and restaurant/tea room. Two options for routes, 5-7+ km one way: 1) from Rithet's east along the Rolston Trail to Lochside Drive, then north to the intersection with Cordova Bay Road. Mattick's is on the east side of Cordova Bay Road; 2) from the Rolston Trail, take the trail north to Kentwood Terrace and join the Boulderwood Hill trail. From the north side of the knoll, near the reservoir, take the trail to Wesley Road. Travel north on Wesley to Claremont Ave. Turn right on Claremont and left onto Lochside Drive. Continue north to the Cordova Bay Road intersection (as above).

Rithet's Bog to Mount Douglas Park   A mixture of sidewalks and chip trails will take you from Rithet's Bog to Mount Douglas Park (see p.79). Again, there are a number of options, as there are many trails connecting the winding streets. One option is to take the Rolston Trail east, turn right at Shadywood Drive, with a slight jog right then left onto Lohbrunner Road W. (There is also a trail—turn right—connecting the Rolston Trail to Emily Carr Drive, from which you can go left—east—then left onto Lohbrunner Road W,) Lohbrunner Rd W becomes Donwood Drive (stay left). At the trail marker, turn right and follow the trail to Lochside Regional Trail, where you turn left (south), then right onto Lohbrunner Road E. Continue east and cross Blenkinsop Road to enter Mount Douglas Park at the Mercer Trail.

WORTH NOTING
- Sections of the bog trail cross uneven ground where visitors in wheelchairs will require assistance.
- Dogs must be on leash and under control at all times to avoid

disturbing sensitive areas. Please remember to dispose of your dog's waste with the rest of your garbage.

NEARBY

Beckwith Park   This 9 ha community park has sports fields, a playground and a water park in the west half, and a natural area with trails, two lovely ponds, and a Garry oak forested area. It can be accessed by road via Quadra Street, then Beckwith Avenue, and via walking trails from Christmas Hill Nature Sanctuary (see p.75) and Lochside Regional Trail.

Blenkinsop Lake Park   A relatively small park, broken into several pieces, on the shores of Blenkinsop Lake, the park can be accessed from the Lochside Regional Trail (south of Lohbrunner Road).

OF INTEREST

- Broadmead was originally a 295 ha farm known as Rithet's Ranch and Broadmead Farm, and was named for the owner's favourite thoroughbred racehorse.
- The Rolston Trail is named to honour Gordon A. Rolston, a Broadmead community planner. Through his efforts in the 1960s, many natural areas were preserved as linear green spaces and now make up part of the Broadmead trail network.
- Rithet's Bog, named after Robert Patterson Rithet, was donated to Saanich in 1994 by the Guinness family of Britain, the brewers of Guinness stout. The Guinness cairn, located near the corner of Chatterton Way and Dalewood Lane, marks their generosity.

Map 2g   Swan Lake and Christmas Hill

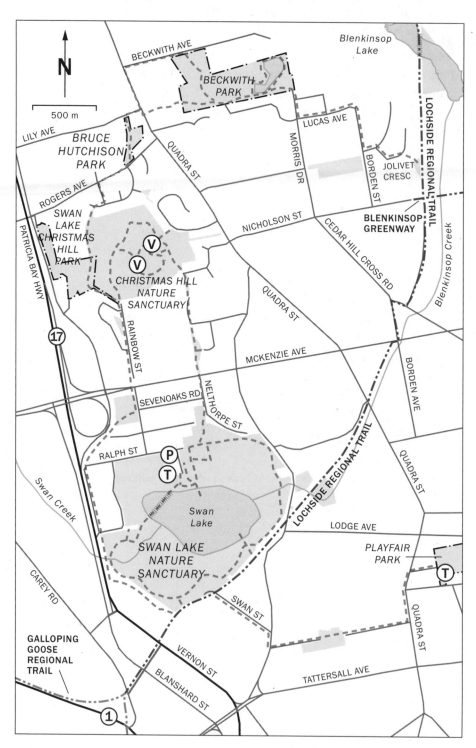

2g. Swan Lake and Christmas Hill   MAP 2g

DIFFICULTY/DISTANCE   Easy to moderate/1.3 km, one-way, to 2.5–10 km loops

HIGHLIGHTS   The Swan Lake/Christmas Hill Nature Sanctuary is located in Saanich and has 3.75 km of trails, 2.5 km loop trail around Swan Lake and 1.25 km in the Christmas Hill part of the sanctuary, forming two very different hikes. The Swan Lake Loop winds around picturesque Swan Lake (10 ha) on a partly chip bark, gravel and boardwalk trail. The marshland, fields and thickets surrounding the lake are perfect for birdwatching. The trail to Christmas Hill climbs to a protected Garry oak forest and rocky outcrops with seasonal wildflowers and several viewpoints. For a longer hike (10 km), add the loop from the nature house to Beckwith Park via the Lochside Regional Trail, and back to Swan Lake past Christmas Hill. The Swan Lake Nature House and information centre offers interpretive programs. Visit the nearby native garden. You can even purchase grain for feeding the ducks.

Best time to go   Spring for flowers, spring and fall for birds, but all times of the year for a variety of flora and fauna.

CAUTIONS
- Portions of the wooden bridges and boardwalk of the Swan Lake loop can be slippery when wet or frosty, and parts of the trail may be closed during peak flood periods. Contact the nature centre for current information.
- Christmas Hill trails are fairly steep and rocky.

ACCESS   *Swan Lake*: from Victoria take Blanshard Street then Highway #17 (Pat Bay) north to McKenzie Avenue. Turn right (east) to Rainbow Street. Swing right and continue to the intersection with Ralph Street. Turn left (east) at the sanctuary signpost. The parking area is near the end of Ralph Street. If traveling west along McKenzie Avenue, be aware there is no left turn at Rainbow Street. Instead, turn left at Nelthorpe Street and then right via Sevenoaks Road to Rainbow Street. Sections of the Swan Lake Loop are wheelchair-accessible.

To reach *Christmas Hill*, go to the end of Ralph Street. The marked trail starts at the northeast end of the parking lot. Both trails are open from sunrise to sunset.

HIKE DESCRIPTIONS

Swan Lake Loop   Easy/2.5 km loop: The trail begins at the Nature House as a wood chip path and encircles the lake. The path crosses Swan and Blenkinsop creeks en route. The floatingboardwalk, complete with benches is one highlight.

The trail accesses a bird blind and two wharves that allow visitors to more easily view the natural surroundings. Take your time and be observant. Many bird and duck species are found here, some resident, others migratory. The thick growth of cattails and duckweed around the lake is a perfect refuge. Painted Turtle, River Otter, and Muskrat are occasionally seen in and around Swan Lake. There is an impressive stand of giant cottonwoods on the south shore.

Christmas Hill   Moderate/1.25 km, one-way: The slightly more challenging hike to Christmas Hill from the Swan Lake Nature House leads to a fragile Garry oak forest and rocky outcrops. The surrounding areas are covered with lichens, mosses, ferns and seasonal wildflowers. Look for Red-tailed Hawk, Turkey Vulture and numerous songbirds, and a variety of butterflies from late spring through the summer.

From the Nature Centre parking lot, hike east, then north to a marked junction. Turn left and follow the Christmas Hill signposts. Take Nelthorpe Street to McKenzie Avenue and the pedestrian light. On McKenzie Avenue's north side, the path again briefly joins Nelthorpe Street. Continue north to cross Nicholson Street. Note the small stand of old-growth Douglas-fir. From this point on, the way is narrow, rocky and steep to the top, where the trail circles the summit. There are views

OF INTEREST

- The lake was formed 12,000 years ago when the last glacier receded. During most of its recent history, Swan Lake was a dumping ground for raw sewage, dairy farms and a winery. Cleanup began in the 1970s, and today the lake is rich with a variety of wildlife.
- Swan Lake is fed by Blenkinsop Lake, via Blenkinsop Creek. The lake is drained by Swan Creek, which flows under Douglas Street and McKenzie Avenue to join Colquitz Creek near Hyacinth Park.
- Swan Creek and Lake are named after James Gilchrist Swan, a well-known early ethnologist.

Swan Lake. SWAN LAKE CHRISTMAS HILL NATURE SANCTUARY

of Swan Lake, Central Saanich, and the spectacular 360-degree vista from the Christmas Hill summit (122 m) that takes in all of Victoria and environs. The walk will probably take you about 45 minutes but it is worth it.

Grand Loop—Swan Lake/Lochside/Beckwith/Hutchison Park/Christmas Hill/Swan Lake   Easy to moderate/approx. 10 km loop: Starting at Swan Lake Nature House, go down the path to the left, toward the lakeshore. Turn left onto a paved path. After about 20 metres, turn right onto a chip trail. Follow the signs for the "Loop Trail", keeping the lake on your right. Near where the trail crosses Blenkinsop Creek, you can access the Lochside Regional Trail. Turn left and follow the trail north past Nicholson Street junction. The next trail to the left (then right at the fork) will take you to Jolivet Crescent. Turn left, to Bracken Ave, and turn left again onto Borden Street. At Borden Street, turn right, then left to access Lucas Avenue (at the edge of Lake Hill Elementary school grounds). Turn right on Morris Drive and go north to join the trails in Beckwith Park. A mixture of trails and streets lead west then south to the northwest side of Christmas Hill. Follow the trail, then a short section of Beckwith Avenue, then turn left (south) onto Quadra Street. Turn right (west) on Lily Avenue, left (south) onto Rockhome Gardens past Hutchison Park, take the trail to Rogers Avenue, cross Rogers Avenue to Rogers Way. Follow Rogers Way to the end and join the trail to Christmas Hill, where you can either hike around Christmas Hill to the Nelthorpe trail or continue down Rainbow Road, left on Ralph Street back, to Swan Lake Nature Sanctuary.

Swan Lake boardwalk.   NEIL BURROUGHS

WORTH NOTING

- Stay on the trails to minimize damage to the area's fragile ecosystems.
- NO dogs and no bicycles are permitted on the trails.
- A wide variety of interpretive programs are offered at the Swan Lake Nature House, including bird watches, junior naturalist programs, and topics about everything from archaeology to reptiles. Contact www.swanlake.bc.ca for information.
- Along Swan Lake's south side you can connect with the Lochside Regional Trail and then the Galloping Goose Trail (see pp.193 and 198).

NEARBY

Playfair Park (3.7 ha) is "a jewel" within the Saanich Parks system. Over 250 species of plants grow here, including a seasonal display of magnificent rhododendrons. The parking lot is at the end of Rock Street, accessed off Quadra Street. The park has several trails, a picnic area and toilets.

Beckwith Park (9 ha)   This park features a winding wood chip trail along its perimeter, Garry oak trees and two lovely ponds. There are opportunities to observe birds and other wildlife. The large parking lot on Beckwith Avenue is accessed off Quadra Street. There are wheelchair-accessible toilets and a picnic area.

2h. Mount Douglas   MAP 2h

DIFFICULTY/DISTANCE   Easy to strenuous/200 m to 3.8+ km, one-way

HIGHLIGHTS   Mount Douglas Park (188 ha), in Gordon Head, is Saanich's largest park. Named PQ'ÁLS by the Tsawout First Nation, it has over 21 km of interconnecting trails, of varying degrees of difficulty, that lead hikers to sandy ocean beaches, down shady, fern-lined paths within Douglas-fir and western redcedar forests, and on more challenging routes that climb to Garry oak hilltop viewpoints. The park's spring wildflowers are a delight and the birdwatching unequalled. The 360-degree panorama at the Mount Douglas summit is one of southern Vancouver Island's best and one of Victoria's most popular year-round destinations.

Best time to go   Any time of year!

CAUTIONS

- Signage is incomplete at many trail junctions. Carry up-to-date maps.
- Cycling is permitted on paved roads only.
- Dogs must be kept under control at all times.
- Contact Saanich Parks for horse restrictions and seasonal dog regulations (see p.226).

ACCESS   Mount Douglas Park has several designated parking areas. Trails may also be reached from numerous points around the park's perimeter. There are marked trailheads along Cordova Bay Road. No parking is allowed on Cordova Bay Road. From downtown Victoria, allow 20 minutes driving time.

Main Parking Lot   From Victoria, travel north on Shelbourne Street, stay right at T-junction onto Cedar Hill Road, north to the intersection of Cordova Bay and Ash roads. Drive straight ahead and to the right to the main parking lot. Washrooms (wheelchair accessible), a children's playground and picnic areas are close by. A short path (200 m) and a set of steps lead from the parking area down to Cordova Bay and the sandy beach.

Churchill Drive   Note that the paved road is closed to vehicle traffic in the mornings until noon, seven days a week, and there is no parking 11 pm–6 am. A small roadside parking area is located at the

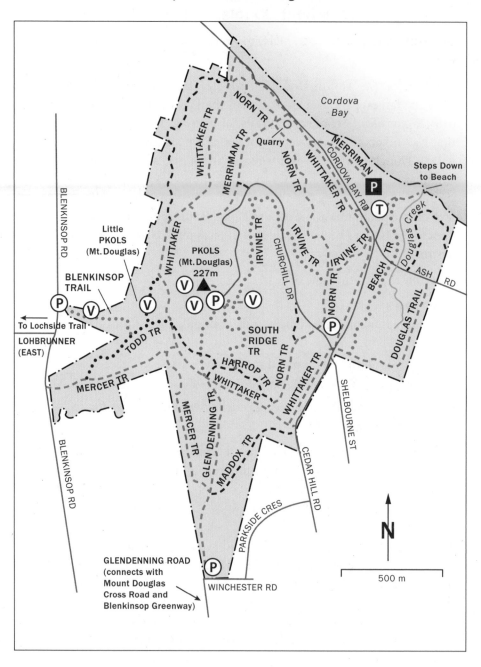

bottom of Churchill Drive, at the north end of Cedar Hill Road, near Shelbourne Street. You can drive another 1.5 km up the steep and winding Churchill Drive to the Summit parking lot that overlooks the Blenkinsop Valley.

Glendenning Road   Very limited roadside parking is available at the north end of Glendenning Road, accessed from Mount Douglas Cross Road.

Blenkinsop Road   A small parking lot on the Blenkinsop Road side of Mount Douglas Park, just north of Lohbrunner Road, is the trailhead for a rugged trail that passes through Garry oak and Douglas-fir forests, and offers sweeping views of the Blenkinsop Valley.

HIKE DESCRIPTIONS

Irvine Trail   Moderate/1.6 km, one-way: This signposted trail begins on Cordova Bay Road's west side, just south of the main parking lot, near Ash Road. At the Norn Trail junction, a detour north leads to a fine viewpoint on Irvine Hill that overlooks Cordova Bay. The trail soon steepens and crosses Churchill Drive and continues to rise steadily. It leaves the lower elevation forest behind to enter a craggy Garry oak and arbutus hilltop. On the approach to the Mount Douglas summit, the trail becomes rough and traverses open rock, which can be slippery at times. Some short scrambling may be required. Finally the trail reaches the summit area, near the radio antenna. Allow 45 minutes to 1 hour to reach the summit.

There are three viewpoints at the top. One is on the east side, next to the radio antenna; another is at the end of Churchill Drive, at the parking area overlook. The main viewpoint is just to the west, accessed along a paved, steep path. The Mount Douglas summit (227 m) features a 360-degree vista of the Saanich Peninsula, Victoria, Washington State's Cascade and Olympic Mountains, the Malahat, the Sooke Hills and the Gulf Islands.

Whittaker Trail   Moderate/3.8 km loop: One of the longest trails in the park, the Whittaker Trail winds completely around Mount Douglas, under a thick canopy of western redcedar, Douglas-fir, grand fir, Pacific dogwood and bigleaf maple. The route follows generally rolling terrain with some grades but nothing really strenuous. You can access the trail from the main parking lot by crossing Cordova Bay Road. The trail can be picked up at various other points along Cedar Hill Road and Cadboro Bay Road. Allow about 2 hours to complete the loop.

The Whittaker Trail connects with all of the major Mount Douglas trails. Figuring out exactly where you are, though, can be puzzling due to many unmarked and confusing trail intersections and side paths. You can stay on track by using the Mount Douglas summit as a reference point. For example, if you hike in a counter-clockwise direction, the summit will always be to your left.

An interesting section of the Whittaker Trail runs between the Mount Douglas summit and that of Little Mount Doug, on the park's northwest side. Side trails lead to the top of Little Mount Doug where there are excellent views and spring wildflowers. Old mine workings are located at the junction with the Harrop Trail and the Tod Trail (a strenuous route off the Mercer Trail). The *Mercer Trail*, a link to the Lochside Trail, comes in from Blenkinsop Road. Near this junction, look for a blowdown caused by a typhoon in the mid-1950s (started in Guam). From the Harrop Trail, just north of where the Whittaker and Glendenning trails meet, a short but arduous scramble over steep, exposed, rocky bluffs will bring you to the viewpoint at the summit parking area (see also *South Ridge Trail* description).

Merriman Trail   Moderate/1.3 km, one-way: From the north end of the main parking lot take the Merriman Trail along the bluff, cross Cordova Bay Road and turn right, briefly sharing the route with the Whittaker Trail, to a quarry (on the left), where you cut left. The trail is obvious at the beginning, with easy hiking in the lower section. The route crosses the Norn Trail and then narrows and starts to climb, passing close to Churchill Drive (near a connecting link to the Irvine Trail) and then turns west to the Whittaker Trail.

Norn Trail   Moderate/1.7 km, one-way: This trail is well defined and provides easy hiking on fairly level ground with some slight grades. It roughly parallels Cordova Bay Road passing through tall timber. Access is just north of the bottom parking area on Churchill Drive, at several points along the Whittaker Trail or via the Irvine Trail.

Beach Trail   Easy/860 m, one-way: From the parking area at the base of Churchill Drive you can follow this delightful trail that parallels Douglas Creek, crosses Ash Road and ends at the sandy Cordova Bay beach, below the main parking lot. During periods of extremely low tides, it's possible to extend your hike another 10 km north to Island View Beach (see p.197). The Beach Trail accesses the Douglas Trail, which runs through the forest on the park's eastern boundary to Ash Road.

Blenkinsop Trail Strenuous/600 m: Starting at the parking lot on the Blenkinsop Road side of Mount Douglas Park is the trailhead for a rugged trail that passes through Garry oak and Douglas-fir forests, and offers sweeping views of the Blenkinsop Valley. At the top end, it connects with the Tod Trail. At the bottom end, a new crosswalk connects the Blenkinsop Trail with Lohbrunner Road and the Lochside Regional Trail.

South Ridge Trail Moderate to strenuous/300+ m loop: A loop near the summit, this trail rewards hikers with marvelous views. It can be accessed from the parking lot, and has one strenuous section about 1/2 way around. It is also accessible from the Harrop Trail via a steep and strenuous section about 300 m). Another longer strenuous trail—the Glendenning Trail—can also be accessed from the South Ridge loop southwest of the parking lot.

WORTH NOTING

- The thick forests of Mount Douglas are home to a variety of birds. Watch for Anna's Hummingbird, woodpeckers, and Varied Thrush. Mount Douglas is one of Vancouver Island's major stopovers for migratory birds, including warblers, Spotted Towhee, Western Tanager, White-crowned Sparrow and Lazuli Bunting.
- In the spring, the forests, meadows and rocky outcrops on Mount Douglas offer a brilliant display of native wildflowers. Look for Hooker's onion, spring gold, camas, satin flowers, shooting stars, western buttercup, white fawn lilies, chocolate lilies and others. Mount Douglas is one of only 21 sites in B.C. where the rare purple sanicle grows. This "red-listed" species suffers from competition from invasive plants (like Scotch broom) and habitat loss.
- Please stay on designated trails to protect sensitive vegetation. Do not pick any wildflowers.
- Use caution when crossing Cordova Bay Road.
- The Friends of Mount Douglas is a society formed to ensure the park's natural state and to preserve the original park boundaries as set out by Sir James Douglas in 1889.
- The signed Mercer Trail links Mount Douglas with the Lochside Trail via Blenkinsop Road and Lohbrunner Road (east).

NEARBY Two tiny Saanich parks east of Mount Douglas Park are worth a visit. Both are excellent birdwatching destinations. Short trails lead to spectacular Haro Strait and San Juan Islands views. The parks have limited parking and toilets. No cyclists are permitted.

Glencoe Cove-Kwatsech Park (3.6 ha)   Glencoe Cove is a beautiful park tucked away in Gordon Point. The name ¿Kwatsech¿ is the Songhees name for Gordon Head. This tranquil shore was once the site of a prehistoric village or summer camp inhabited as long ago as 500 AD. It is accessed off Ferndale Road, and Gordon Point Drive. Parking is limited on Gordon Point Drive. There are aboriginal burial cairns, shell middens, rare plants (including prickly pear and bearded owl-clover), Garry oaks, a cormorant rookery, two small, secluded beaches and a pocket cove. Ferndale Forest, on Vantreight Drive's east side, is also part of the park. The Friends of Glencoe Cove-Kwatsech Park was established in 1995 to protect, preserve and restore the native plants and archeological sites at Glencoe Cove. For an easy, 1.5 hour loop walk, go from the park along Leyns Road, loop through Vantreight Park and right on Vantreight Drive, then right on Ferndale, left (south) on Pomona Way, and then right on Grandview Drive to Tyndall Avenue. South on Tyndall to Hillcrest Avenue, right on Hillcrest, left on Houlihan Place, left on Ferndale, right on Evergreen Place, along a short trail to Shore Way, and onto the trail to Glencoe Cove-Kwatsech Park.

Arbutus Cove Park (1.8 ha)   Accessed off Gordon Head Road (or via Finnerty to Hollydene/ Arbutus/Hollydene to Hollydene Park). Parking is limited on Arbutus Cove Lane. (See p.115 for more detail).

Not quite as close, but a good choice for an easy to moderate walk, is Mount Douglas to Rithet's Bog (see p.72).

OF INTEREST

- Originally called "Cedar Hill", Mount Douglas was set aside and renamed in 1858 by Governor Sir James Douglas as a Government Reserve and has been protected as a Crown Trust since 1889. We can credit early Victoria mayor, Bert Todd, with the foresight to construct an "auto road" to the summit as a tourist attraction. In late 1992, the park was transferred to Saanich.
- Several of the Mount Douglas trails are named after local pioneer families.
- Mount Douglas is an example of a "monadnock"—an isolated hill that has not eroded as quickly as the surrounding area.

2i. Colquitz River MAP 2i

DIFFICULTY/DISTANCE Easy/2 km loop to 5 km, one-way

HIGHLIGHTS Saanich's Colquitz River Linear Park and adjoining Cuthbert Holmes Park connect urban and rural parks stretching from Portage Inlet north to the Elk Lake area. Hikers can explore the scenic trail that parallels the Colquitz River through working farmland, commercial areas, residential housing and greenbelts. This fragile environment includes open forests, delicate wetlands, Garry oak hilltops, sensitive ecosystems and streams with spawning populations of trout and salmon. The trails within Cuthbert Holmes Park wind through an urban mixed forest to a river estuary, grassy fields and open meadows along the Colquitz River. Birdwatching and nature viewing opportunities are endless.

Best time to go From spring to fall for birds and botany.

CAUTIONS
- Use caution at all street crossings.
- Keep dogs on a leash and under control at all times. Please clean up after your pet. See Saanich Parks for specific seasonal restrictions.

ACCESS

To *Colquitz River Linear Park* From Victoria, take Highway #1 (Trans-Canada) to Tillicum Road intersection and turn left. At the Burnside Road West traffic lights, turn right and then make an immediate left into the Tillicum Mall. Park in the northwest corner of the lot (on the right) close to the Cuthbert Holmes Park trailhead. The Colquitz River Linear Park can be accessed at a number of points along its length. Parking is extremely limited at the Colquitz River Trail's north end. Most of the trail from Tillicum Mall north to Hyacinth Park is wheelchair accessible. From downtown Victoria, allow 15 minutes driving time.

To *Cuthbert Holmes Park* From Victoria, take Highway #1 (Trans-Canada) west to the Admirals Road lights. Turn left (south) onto Admirals Road. The parking lot is on the left, as soon as you turn off the highway. Another entry to the park is off Dysart Road at Ker Avenue, from behind the G.R. Pearkes Community Recreation Centre (off Arena Road) or at the trailhead at the Tillicum Mall parking lot. The paved main trail is wheelchair accessible. From downtown Victoria, allow 15 minutes driving time.

Map 2i Colquitz River

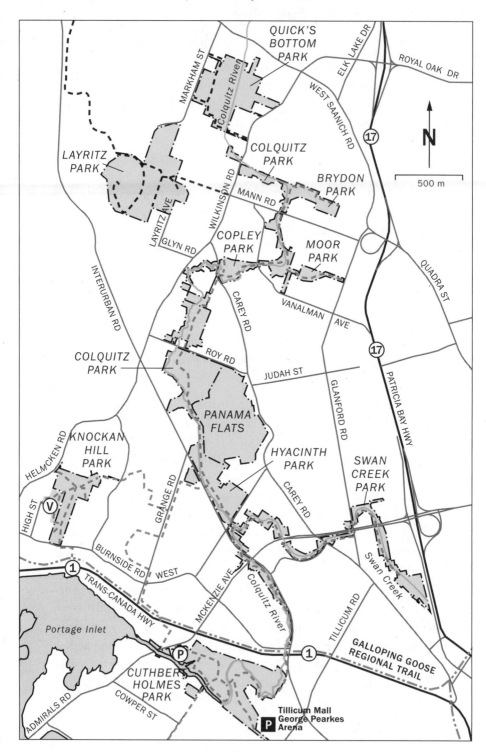

HIKE DESCRIPTIONS

The Colquitz River Trail was envisaged in 1967 and was one of Saanich's first efforts to protect urban streams. The southern portion is more scenic and shaded, as it follows the meandering creek. Unusual components of the trail are the rectangular "stepping stones" along the bank and in some places, across the creek. A number of pebble mosaics embedded in the path make the trail even more interesting. This trail passes through a complex of parks, from Cuthbert Holmes Park to the Royal Oak Trail, which takes you east of the highway and accesses Rithet's Bog (see p.71).

Colquitz River Linear Park   Easy/approximately 5 km, one-way: From the Tillicum Mall parking lot, take the Cuthbert Holmes Park access trail north to a fork. Ignore the path to the left that crosses the Colquitz River on a sturdy bridge; instead, keep north, under the Highway #1 overpass and the Galloping Goose Trail bridge, to cross Burnside Road West. A side path, on the left, climbs to the Pacific Forestry Centre. The gravel trail winds alongside the Colquitz River and in this stretch, small bridges and stepping stones assist with some creek crossings. You will pass under McKenzie Avenue and cross Interurban Road.

At the confluence of the Colquitz River and Swan Creek, near Violet Avenue, the *Swan Creek Trail* cuts off, to the right (see Nearby). Cross Marigold Road to enter Hyacinth Park (5 ha). The trail skirts the Panama Flats wetland, which always seems to attract birds, and climbs a bit to pass Panama Hill and Pond, both within Panama Hill Park (9 ha).

North of Roy Road, turn right and follow a short stretch of Gerda Road to Grange Road, then turn left and continue north to Carey Road. Across the street, look for the hard-to-see entrance to Copley Park (5.4 ha). This park is divided into east and west sections, on opposite sides of Vanalman Road.

At the east end of Copley Park East, the trail divides. If you turn east and enter Moor Park (1 ha), just over a metal bridge that spans the Colquitz River, the trail continues through Industrial Buffer Park (3.4 ha) to Glanford Avenue. You can follow Glanford north and access the Royal Oak Trail, which crosses the Pat Bay Hwy to access Rithet's Bog and Swan Lake Christmas Hill for longer hikes (see pp.71 and 75).

If you go north to Mann Road, the trail again divides. You can choose to go east to Glanford (see above), west along Mann Road to

Layritz Park (see Nearby), or continue north to Lindsay Street. Turn left on Lindsay to get to Wilkinson Road. Two trailheads for Quick's Bottom are just north of here, along Wilkinson Road (see Nearby). Turn east onto the Royal Oak Trail that leads to Glanford Avenue and on to the Royal Oak Shopping Centre and Rithet's Bog (see p.71).

Cuthbert Holmes Park   Easy/2 km loop: The area commonly referred to as Cuthbert Holmes Park is actually a combination of Cuthbert Holmes Park and Tillicum Park (total 25.6 ha). From the Admirals Road parking area, follow the paved main trail to a fork. The main trail runs through the centre of the park to a bridge on the Colquitz River. Turn right onto the narrower bark-mulch trail, which enters the woods dominated by Douglas-fir and grand fir and eventually meets and runs alongside the Colquitz River. A side path, on the right, angles off to the river estuary and tidal marsh. Walk quietly and you might see a Great Blue Heron stalking the tidal shallows.

Continue east along the riverbank, avoiding any paths on the left as there are many unmarked side paths, and soon you will reach Heron Bridge and foot access to Dysart Road. The river trail passes a disused heron rookery and curves north to rejoin the main trail near the previously mentioned Colquitz River bridge. Turn right onto the main trail and cross the bridge. Near the George Pearkes Arena access trail, which comes in on the right, the path enters an open, bushy area and then swings north, close to Tillicum Mall. Just past the mall parking lot trail access and a little before the highway overpass, turn left to cross the concrete bridge over the Colquitz River. The Colquitz River Linear Trail begins nearby. To return to the Admirals Road parking area, hike west parallel to Hwy #1 with a large meadow on the left.

Colquitz to Panama Flats to Knockan Hill Park Loop   Easy/5 km loop: As above for Colquitz Linear Park to Panama Flats. Bordered on the western edge by the Colquitz River, Panama Flats (approx. 26.6 ha) was used for agriculture for many years. It is a popular birdwatching area as it is used by many species, some of which are at risk. Take time to enjoy this section of the trail. There is a fork to the left (west) from the main Colquitz Linear Park trail about halfway along Panama Flats. This takes you to Interurban Road, where you can turn left (south) to Chesterfield Road. A trail connects Chesterfield Road to South Valley Drive, which becomes Helen Road, then Carmichael Terrace, then

Lianne Place, where it enters the park. You can take a slightly longer but quieter route by taking the left fork of the trail before it meets Interurban. This leads to Meadowview Place, crosses the road and joins the north end of Grange Road. Turn right at the intersection of Grange and Interurban, then left onto Chesterfield. From there to Knockan Hill Park is as above.

Colquitz to Knockan Hill Park   Easy/2.5 km one-way: As above for Colquitz Linear Park, up to the confluence of the Colquitz River and Swan Creek, near Violet Avenue. Turn left onto Violet Avenue. Follow Violet Avenue to the T-junction with Grange Road and turn left. Turn right onto Tulip Avenue and follow this to Wilkinson Road—there is a short section of trail joining the east and west sections of Tulip Avenue. Right on Wilkinson, left on the trail that leads to Mildred Street and a short jog right onto Knockan Place. Left on Knockan Place, left on Jean Place to enter the north end of the park.

Cuthbert Holmes Park–Hyacinth Park loop   Easy/5+ km: As above for Colquitz Linear Park from the Tillicum Mall parking lot to Hyacinth Park. From the park, cross Interurban Road onto Edge Place. Follow the trail from the end of Edge Place to Grange Road and turn right. At the intersection of Grange Road and Iris Avenue, turn right and follow Iris Avenue to skirt Marigold Park (one of Saanich's many small neighbourhood parks with playgrounds and natural spaces). A trail connects to Laburnum Road—go east to Grange. Turn right (south) on Grange, cross Burnside Road W to the Galloping Goose Regional Trail. Go east on the 'Goose" and turn left to the Esson Road access. Once on the south side of Hwy #1, go south on Esson, turn left on Admirals Road then right on Hunter Street. Follow the trail from the end of Hunter Street back to Cuthbert Holmes Park.

WORTH NOTING
- Do not remove any native vegetation and avoid trampling stream-side areas. Panama Pond and Panama Hill are sensitive regions.
- At Cuthbert Holmes Park, look for native grasses and a variety of shrubs such as wild rose, hawthorn and blackberry. Spring wild-flowers include white fawn lilies, lady slippers, Easter lilies, western trillium and camas. At the Colquitz River estuary, you might see Hooded Merganser, Mallard, teal, Great Blue Heron or Green Heron.

Swan Creek Park (10.3 ha)   From along the Colquitz River Trail at Hyacinth Park (near the confluence of the Colquitz River and Swan Creek) you can access the Swan Creek Trail. Turn east to follow tiny Swan Creek all the way to the Ralph Street allotment gardens. This involves a short section along the heavily travelled McKenzie Avenue.

Knockan Hill Park (9.3 ha)   Accessed along Burnside Road West, the trailhead is next to a 1930s stucco house called Stranton Lodge, a designated heritage house. Park on High Street near the Strawberry Vale Community Hall. The 0.5 km (one-way) trail climbs the driveway, past Stranton Lodge (Hall Cottage) to hilltop meadows and an open rocky summit with good views to the north and east. Spring wildflowers such as camas, white fawn lilies and chocolate lilies are abundant. There are a few benches. The Friends of Knockan Hill Park was established to preserve the park's natural character and its flora and fauna.

Quick's Bottom (15 ha)   NO dogs allowed here. This wildlife sanctuary, intersected by the Colquitz River, is one of the few remaining marshlands close to Victoria. Quick's Bottom is accessed off Markham Street or Wilkinson Road. Limited roadside parking is found on Greenlea Drive, off Wilkinson Road. A 1.5 km (35-minute) trail loops through the marsh and provides a close look at area birds, wildlife and wetland vegetation. The Victoria Natural History Society constructed the birdwatching blind at the marsh's southwest end, near the Saanich municipal nursery. There are benches en route. Take your time. More than one birder has added to a life list here. This bottomland is a depression remaining from the glacial age.

Layritz Park (29 ha)   The park is accessed off Wilkinson Road, then via Glyn Road and Layritz Avenue, via the pedestrian right-of-way off Wilkinson Road and Mann Avenue, or off Markham Street. Trails wind through Garry oak meadows on the park's wooded west side. Layritz Park and nearby Quick's Bottom are great spots to observe early spring migratory birds.

2j. Francis/King Regional Park   MAP 2j

DIFFICULTY/DISTANCE   Easy to moderate/up to 2.8 km, or longer, one-way

HIGHLIGHTS   There are approximately 11 km of year-round hiking trails at the CRD's Francis/King Regional Park (109 ha). This woodland and nature park, within which can be found a variety of terrain, has paths that are well signed and groomed, so are perfect for family outings. The Elsie King Interpretive Trail is specially designed for wheelchair accessibility. The park has bigleaf maple, red alder, western flowering dogwood, towering western redcedars, grand fir and some of Saanich's tallest and oldest old-growth Douglas-fir. Splashes of spring wildflowers carpet the forest floor. The Nature House features displays of the park's flora and fauna and offers interpretive programs.

Best time to go   Anytime, but in spring, the park is particularly beautiful.

CAUTIONS
- Some park trails have slight elevation changes with moderate grades.
- Rock outcrops and boardwalks may be slippery in wet weather.
- There are muddy sections and exposed roots so tread carefully and wear proper footgear.

ACCESS   **From Victoria**, take Highway #1 (Trans-Canada) and cut off at the Helmcken Road interchange (Exit 8). Head north to Burnside Road West and turn left. Continue to Prospect Lake Road and turn right. One kilometre along swing left on Munn Road. The parking lot is just ahead, on the right. From Victoria, allow 20 minutes driving time. The park is open 8 am to 9 pm (April to October)/8 am to 5 pm (October to April). The Elsie King Trail, toilets and Nature House are wheelchair accessible. For information on the Nature House hours and interpretive programs offered, contact CRD Parks.

HIKE DESCRIPTIONS

Elsie King Interpretive Trail   Easy/800 m loop: Starting near the Nature House, this self-guiding interpretive trail is wheelchair-friendly (an accessible toilet and water fountain are near the Nature House). The trail consists of hard-packed gravel and cedar boardwalks that cross sensitive areas. There are benches and rest areas, interpretive signposts and a shelter. The trail through stately Douglas-fir and grand fir is great for hikers of all ages. **NO dogs on this trail.**

Map 2j Francis/King Regional Park

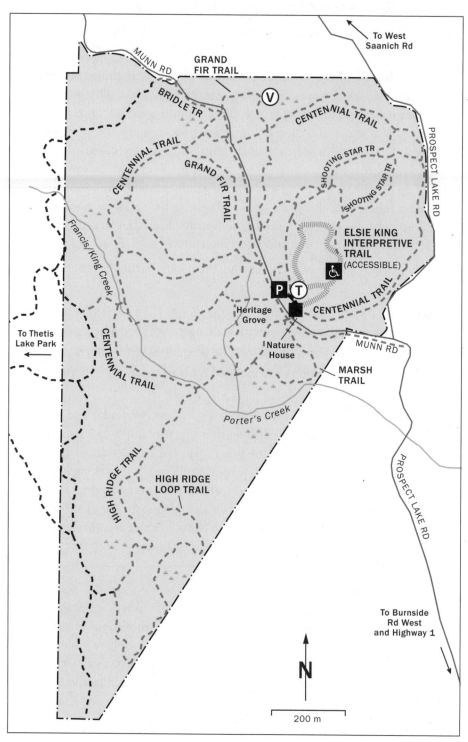

Access to Heritage Grove   Easy/200 m, one-way: The park's Heritage Grove features 500-year-old Douglas-fir up to 3 m in circumference and 75 m tall. From the parking lot, cross Munn Road to the west side and turn right at the fence gate and follow the *Bridle Trail* north, along Munn Road, to a second fence gate. Turn left and go through. The largest diameter Douglas-fir (3 m) is on the right, just before the creek.

Continue down a steep grade and cross the creek. Near the *Grand Fir Trail* junction, look for the tallest Douglas-fir (75 m), estimated at 500 years old.

Some trees here bear the scars of a forest fire that surged through the area in the 1950s. To extend your hike, bear left (south) to the *Centennial Trail* junction and return via that route, with the 15-minute *Marsh Trail* as an added option, or simply retrace your steps.

High Ridge Trail   Moderate/2.8 km, one-way: From the parking lot cross Munn Road to the west side and go through the fence gate onto the Centennial Trail and down a hill. At the first junction, swing left for a side trip onto the Marsh Trail, a 0.6 km loop (15 minutes) through area lowlands. A profusion of swamp lantern (skunk cabbage) is evident in the spring. Alder and Indian plum are also abundant. Watch for protruding roots and expect muddy sections.

Back on the Centennial Trail, continue straight ahead to cross another stream. The trail starts a climb to the ridge. At the next signpost where the Centennial Trail swings off to the right, keep left onto the High Ridge Trail. At the next fork you can go either way since the ridge trail circles back to this point. Expect some up and down stretches with moderate grades. You will pass rock outcrops (look for glacial scouring marks), open areas and some southeast views. Avoid the trail that runs west to connect with Thetis Lake. Backtrack to the Centennial Trail and out to the parking lot.

Other trail options (about 30 minutes) include the *Grand Fir* and *Shooting Star* trails (both are 1.3 km in length and link to the Centennial Trail) or the longer (1 hour) Centennial Trail (2.7 km) that loops around the park.

WORTH NOTING

- Dogs must be on leash at all times. No horses or vehicles (including bicycles) are allowed on trails, with the exception of the bridle path that parallels Munn Road and cuts through the park. The park provides important habitat for many resident and migrating birds. Please do not let your dog chase the birds.

- Please remember to dispose of your dog's waste with the rest of your garbage.
- No bicycles, motorized vehicles, camping or open fires are allowed in the Park.
- The park features spring wildflowers (including shooting stars, spring gold, white fawn lilies and camas), ferns, lichens and mosses. In the fall, various types of fungi appear.
- Some park bird species to look for are woodpeckers (Pileated, Hairy and Downy), Steller's Jay, Pacific Wren, chickadees, Cedar Waxwing and warblers. Hawks and Turkey Vulture may be visible overhead.
- Red Squirrel, the introduced Eastern Grey Squirrel, bats, snakes, Black-tailed Deer, and Raccoon all live in the park. Hard-to-spot Pacific Treefrogs may be heard near swampy bottomlands at certain times of year.
- In the drier uplands, where arbutus and Garry oak dominate the hilltops, you'll find oceanspray, salal and snowberry.

NEARBY Multi-use trails (hiking, biking and equestrian) link Francis/King Park with Thetis Lake Regional Park. These routes run generally north/south along Francis/King Regional Park's western boundary and may be accessed from Munn Road, the Centennial Trail or the High Ridge Trail. You can also hike from Thetis Lake to Mill Hill Regional Park (See also 2k. Thetis Lake and 2l. Mill Hill).

OF INTEREST

Francis/King Park consists of two properties, one on each side of Munn Road. The eastern sector was donated to the province in 1960 by Thomas Francis and became Thomas Francis Park. The land on the west side was transferred from the City of Victoria to the province in 1967 and became Freeman King Park. Freeman King, "Skipper", was a well-known naturalist, conservationist and Boy Scout leader. The Elsie King Trail is named after his wife, a well-liked leader of Victoria's Girl Guides. At one time the Victoria Natural History Society looked after both parks.

2k. Thetis Lake   MAP 2k

DIFFICULTY/DISTANCE   Easy to strenuous/1.3 km to 7 km and up, one-way

HIGHLIGHTS Thetis Lake Regional Park (831 ha) became Canada's first nature sanctuary in 1958 and was transferred from the City of Victoria to CRD Parks in 1993. Located in View Royal/Langford, this CRD Park has 47 km of trails with varying degrees of difficulty that can be hiked any time of the year. Many paths interconnect (described by some as a "spiderweb of trails") so it is easy to plot your own circular hike. The park offers brilliant displays of spring wildflowers, outcrops of moss-covered bedrock and mixed forests of Douglas-fir, arbutus and Garry oak. There are excellent opportunities for nature appreciation and wildlife viewing, all within a natural lake and swamp ecosystem.

Best time to go   Any time of year, but spring and summer can be spectacular for wildflowers, and swimming, canoeing and fishing are popular activities in summer.

CAUTIONS   Seymour Hill, north side has very steep sections. Parts of the trail are narrow and rocky.

ACCESS   **From Victoria**, take Highway #1 (Trans-Canada) west and turn off at Exit 10 (Colwood) and follow the Old Island Highway to the Six Mile Road traffic lights. Turn right and continue straight ahead to the main parking lot. Additional parking is available at the smaller West Beach lot. Contact CRD Parks for current information on fees and season passes. Limited roadside parking is available off Highland Road near Prior Lake, at the eastern trailhead for the Trillium Trail. From Victoria, allow 20 minutes driving time. The park is open from sunrise to sunset.

HIKE DESCRIPTIONS
Lewis J. Clark Trail   Moderate/1.4 km, one-way: This trail to one of the park's best viewpoints starts at the main parking lot kiosk. Take the trail on the right and follow the signposts. The route climbs, first through a Douglas-fir forest, then up through drier woodlands of Garry oak and arbutus. Expect some up and down hiking en route. At the junction with the Seymour Hill Trail, swing right (north) and hike the final pitch to the top.

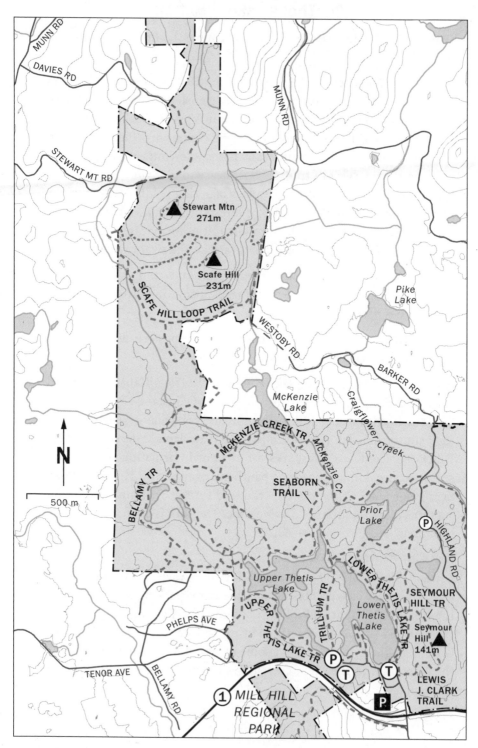

Map 2k Thetis Lake

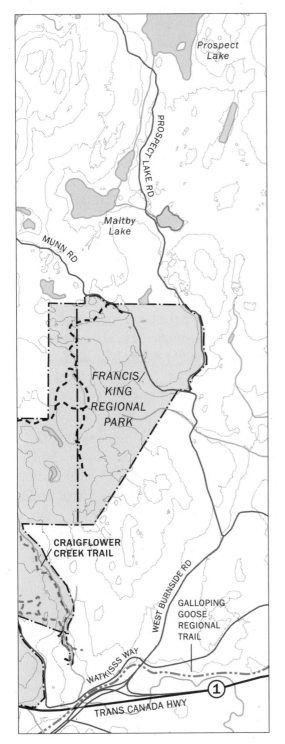

At the Seymour Hill summit (141 m) the view over Thetis Lake is spectacular. A directional cairn constructed by the Thetis Lake Nature Sanctuary Association in 1968 pinpoints local hills and mountains, including Mount Work and Mount Finlayson. Spring wildflowers abound on this hilltop.

To return to the starting point, retrace your steps or take the southern section of the Seymour Hill Trail. A third option is to tackle the rugged trail down Seymour Hill's north side. Hike with caution if you choose the latter. On your descent keep left until, at the bottom, you reach the trail along Lower Thetis Lake's east side leading south and back to the parking lot. Allow approximately 1 to 1.5 hours for a return hike.

Seymour Hill Trail Moderate/1.3 km, one-way: This is another way to the top of Seymour Hill. Take the middle trail from the main parking lot and climb to the summit viewpoint, just beyond the junction with the Lewis J. Clark Trail. See the Lewis J. Clark Trail description for additional details.

The Seymour Hill Trail continues north, down several steep inclines. Keep left at any junctions and you will eventually reach the lakeside trail that parallels Lower Thetis Lake's east shore. Swing left (south) for the parking lot. A return hike takes about 1 to 1.5 hours.

Two Lake Loop   Easy to moderate/4.5 km loop: The most popular hike at the park snakes around both Upper and Lower Thetis Lake. From the main parking lot, head north on the trail that parallels Lower Thetis Lake's east side. Halfway to Upper Thetis Lake's west end you can cut your hike short by turning left (south) onto the Trillium Trail, crossing the culvert bridge between the lakes and returning to the start.

Trillium Trail   Easy/2 km, one-way: The trail follows a fire access road from Highland Road, just south of Prior Lake, to the West Beach parking lot. It is a multi-use hiking, cycling and equestrian trail.

To continue the Two Lake Loop, take the trail around Upper Thetis Lake to the west end and weave back along the lake's southern shore. Take the time to investigate some of the numerous side paths that sneak down to the lakeside. Watch for waterfowl. The lakes are haunts for mallards, Canada Geese, Great Blue Heron and other resident and migratory species. Allow about 1.5 to 2 hours to complete the loop around the lakes.

Craigflower Creek Trail   Moderate/2 km, one-way: From the limited parking area on Highland Road walk north to the Craigflower Creek trailhead, on the right a little before the next bridge. A scenic trail winds through forests and wetlands along Craigflower Creek and loops south back to Highland Road. Parts of the route may be muddy in wet weather. The stream was once called Deadman Creek.

McKenzie Creek Trail   Easy to moderate/2.9 km, one-way: An east/west hiking corridor stretching from Highland Road, north of Prior Lake to the Bellamy Trail, the McKenzie Creek Trail is the fire access/trail to Scafe Hill and Stewart Mountain. The trail twists and turns along McKenzie Lake's outlet stream. Spring brings forth a profusion of swamp lantern (skunk cabbage) in low-lying wetter areas. In the shady forest look for western red cedar and hemlock and savour the verdant hues of the lichens and mosses. Near McKenzie Lake, there are numerous gullies to negotiate.

Thetis Lake to Scafe Hill   Moderate to strenuous/7 km, one-way: Trails access the park's more remote spots, but if you venture into these regions, know your directions. This isolated part of the park, northwest of the lakes, has numerous confusing old roads, side paths and unmarked trails and junctions. Some lead to private property. Please keep to the designated trails.

From the main parking lot, follow the lake loop trail along Lower Thetis Lake's east side, cross the Trillium Trail to the Seaborn Trail junction and turn right (north) to the McKenzie Creek Trail junction. For Scafe Hill, turn left from the Seaborn Trail onto the McKenzie Creek Trail and head west to the fire access road (Bellamy Trail) that roughly parallels the park's western boundary. At a T-junction, you can go either left or right on the (unsigned) Scafe Hill Loop Trail. If you turn left, a little way along the trail there will be a fork—take the right fork to the summit of Scafe Hill. If you turn right, you can take a longer route around the eastern side of the hill, and access the summit (231 m) from the north side.

Thetis Lake to Stewart Mountain   Moderate to strenuous/8 km one-way: For Stewart Mountain (271 m), start as for Scafe Hill. Once you are on the north side of Scafe Hill, follow the fire road/trail west. Follow the markers for Stewart Mountain Road (the fire road forms part of the Stewart Mountain Trail). After about 15–20 minutes on this road/trail, you will see a large unmarked 8x8 post on your right, which marks the trail to Stewart Mountain summit. Head up this trail (north) toward the power lines. Soon after the power lines (about 50 m), there is a side trail on your left, ascending to the peak (note that there are multiple routes to the top with line of sight to the peak). Once at the peak, you can retrace your steps (keeping to the left) or, for a much longer hike, descend the trail on the north side of the mountain. Following this trail will quickly drop down to a fire road, where you can turn left and access Stewart Mountain Road. Turning right takes you to Davies Road and out to Munn Road.

WORTH NOTING

- Spring wildflowers on rocky hilltops include satin flowers, camas, shooting stars, lilies, stonecrop and field chickweed. Do not pick wildflowers and stay on the marked trails.
- The park has swimming beaches, picnic areas and toilets. The main beaches are very busy in the summer.

- Bicycles and horses are permitted only on designated routes. These include the Trillium Trail, the fire access road/trail extending north to south along the Thetis Lake Park's western boundary and the trail off Highland Road that links to Francis/King Park.

- Dogs are generally welcome, but must be under control at all times. June 1 to September 15, dogs are not permitted in the Prior Lake beach and dock area. Dogs on leash are allowed to pass through the Thetis Lake main beach and picnic area but are not allowed to stay. Keep pets on the trails and pick up droppings.

NEARBY A short 1 km hiking trail runs south from Thetis Lake to link via Six Mile Road to the Calypso Trail in Mill Hill Regional Park (see p. 103), and Francis/King Regional Park (see p.91) can be accessed from Thetis Lake Park via the Panhandle Trail.

The Thetis-Langford Connector Trail, a 1.3-kilometre pedestrian/cycling trail, allows access to the park independently of hiking trails, and connects with other cycling routes such as the Galloping Goose Regional Trail. The Galloping Goose Trail can also be accessed from Six Mile Road or Watkiss Way.

OF INTEREST

The Thetis Park Nature Sanctuary Association was formed in 1957 to protect Thetis Lake and environs from encroaching postwar development. The Lewis J. Clark Trail bears the name of founding member and naturalist Dr. Lewis J. Clark, writer of a series of field guides to wildflowers of the Pacific Northwest. Ron Seaborn, for whom another trail is named, is credited with the early mapping of the park's trails. Thetis Lake Park became Canada's first nature sanctuary in 1958 and was transferred from the City of Victoria to CRD Parks in 1993.

21. Mill Hill   MAP 21

DIFFICULTY/DISTANCE   Moderate to strenuous/two trails, about 1 km, one-way

HIGHLIGHTS   Mill Hill Regional Park (61 ha) is noted for its seasonal wildflowers. There are over 100 varieties here, including 14 rare species, the most of any CRD park. Two well-marked trails climb to the top of Mill Hill where you will discover an excellent panorama of Mt. Baker to the Olympics, Victoria, Esquimalt Harbour, and environs. A part of one trail meanders along the cedar wetlands near Millstream Creek.

Best time to go   Spring and summer.

CAUTIONS
- Marked with yellow metal trail markers, the summit trails are steep in places and made up of loose gravel and rock, which may be slippery and difficult for young children. There are open rock sections that can be slick in wet weather. Watch for protruding roots.
- The Calypso Trail connects to Thetis Lake Regional Park via Six Mile Road. Access from Thetis Lake parking lot goes under the Trans-Canada Highway.

ACCESS   **From Victoria**, take the Colwood exit (Exit 10) from the Trans-Canada Highway onto the Old Island Highway. Turn right onto Six Mile Road, and then left onto Atkins Avenue*. Follow Atkins Avenue to the park entrance (about 3 km). Or take Exit 14 to Langford and drive south on Veterans Memorial Parkway. Turn left onto Hoffman Avenue to a four-way-stop. Turn right on Winster Road then left onto Atkins Avenue. Continue approximately 1 km to cross Millstream Creek and past the entrance to CRD Park Headquarters; watch for the sign-posted park entrance on the left. The gate is open 8 am–8 pm, April to October, 8 am–5 pm, October to April. Park trails are not wheelchair accessible but the picnic area and toilets near the parking lot are.

HIKE DESCRIPTIONS
Auburn Trail   Moderate/800 m, one-way: This trail, shorter and less of a grade than the Calypso Trail, begins at the parking lot's north end.

*Atkins is known as both Atkins Road and Atkins Avenue, depending on the map.

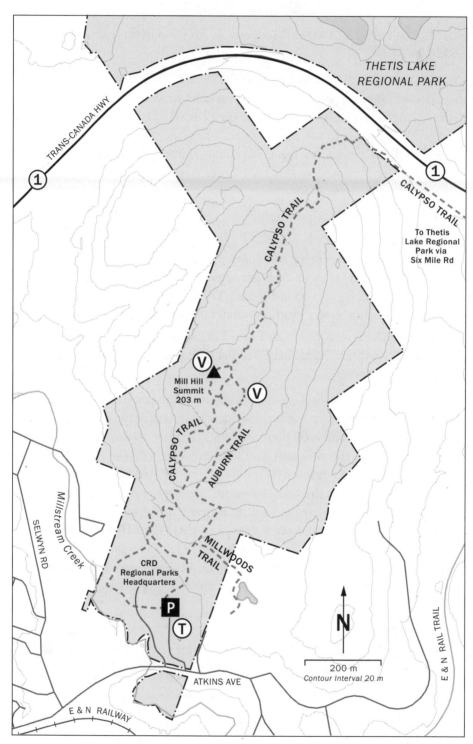

THETIS LAKE
REGIONAL PARK

TRANS-CANADA HWY

①

① CALYPSO TRAIL

To Thetis
Lake Regional
Park via
Six Mile Rd

CALYPSO TRAIL

CALYPSO TRAIL

Ⓥ
Mill Hill
Summit
203 m

Ⓥ

CALYPSO TRAIL

AUBURN TRAIL

Millstream Creek

SELWYN RD

MILLWOODS
TRAIL

CRD
Regional Parks
Headquarters

P

Ⓣ

N

200 m
Contour Interval 20 m

E & N RAIL TRAIL

ATKINS AVE

E & N RAILWAY

Keep right at the fork a short distance in. A left down this side path connects with the Calypso Trail. A short distance beyond on the right is the *Millwoods Trail*, connecting to the road Millwoods Court. Beyond this point, the trail rises steadily to several striking viewpoints before it joins the Calypso Trail, near the summit.

Calypso Trail Moderate/1.2 km, one-way: From the southwest end of the parking lot, the Calypso Trail drops down to Millstream Creek and a picturesque ravine. Look for trillium in the spring. The route then passes a side path on the right that links with the parking lot and climbs via a series of switchbacks to the summit, close to the junction with the Auburn Trail.

The viewpoint at the Mill Hill summit (203 m) offers a magnificent vista sweeping from Mt. Baker, past Race Rocks to the Olympics, not to mention Victoria, the Highlands, Esquimalt Harbour, and surrounding hills and seascapes.

WORTH NOTING

- Mill Hill's lower forest consists mainly of western redcedar, Douglas-fir and hemlock. The summit is predominately Garry oak and arbutus. From April through June, you will find the tiny calypso orchid or fairy slipper growing in the park's more forested, shady regions.
- The summit cairn, built on the remains of an old forestry lookout tower, commemorates the CRD's 35th anniversary.
- Keep to designated trails and do not pick any flowers.
- No bicycles or motorized vehicles on the park trails, no camping or open fires
- Dogs are permitted but must be kept under control at all times. Please remember to dispose of your dog's waste with the rest of your garbage.
- Before European contact, the Songhees people camped along Millstream Creek, and evidence of shell middens can be found in the park. Later, as early as 1848, the creek (also referred to as the Mill Stream and Rowe's Stream) supplied power for Vancouver Island's first sawmill, located at Esquimalt Harbour.

NEARBY For a longer hike, from the summit continue about 1 km down Mill Hill's north side on the Calypso Trail to connect with the network of trails in Thetis Lake Regional Park (see p.95) or with the Galloping Goose Regional Trail (see p.198) via Six Mile Road.

Map 2m Cedar Hill Golf Course Trail

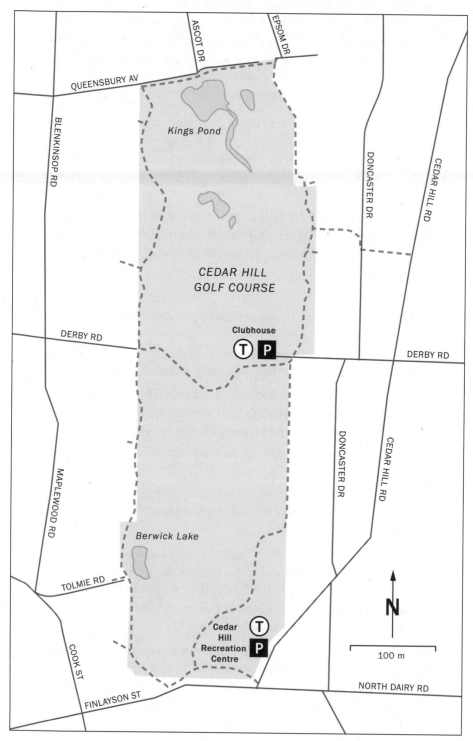

2m. Cedar Hill Golf Course Trail   MAP 2m

DIFFICULTY/DISTANCE   Moderate/3.6 km loop

HIGHLIGHTS   In the heart of Saanich, there is a delightful, somewhat hilly loop trail around the Cedar Hill Golf Course. Originally a dairy farm, Cedar Hill Golf Course was built in the 1920s as a 9-hole private course, and expanded in the 1950s to 18 holes. It was bought by Saanich in 1967 and reopened a few years later as Vancouver Island's very first municipal golf course. The trail passes two small lakes popular with birdwatchers and the higher points of land along the way provide captivating views of Victoria and Juan de Fuca Strait. Hikers and joggers use this path.

Best time to go   Good anytime of the year, but more birds and flowers are to be found along the way in the spring and fall.

ACCESS   About 3 km northeast of downtown Victoria, parking is available at the Cedar Hill Community Recreation Centre, near the intersection of Cedar Hill Road and Finlayson Street, or go north at the intersection on Cedar Hill Road, turn left onto Doncaster Drive and left again on Derby Road to the Cedar Hill Golf Course clubhouse parking lot. The trail is open sunrise to sunset and can be reached from many access points around the perimeter of the golf course.

HIKE DESCRIPTION   This 3.6 km trail combination hiking and jogging path, made up of chip bark, gravel and a paved section, circles the Cedar Hill Golf Course and winds through gently rolling hills, open terrain and wooded areas with scattered patches of Douglas-fir trees and gnarled Garry oaks. Roughly the shape of a figure eight, you can hike the northern or southern loops, each a little over 2 km, or hike the longer loop trail around the perimeter. The northern loop leads to King's Pond, with its abundant wildlife. Along the southern loop you will encounter some hills, including a sharp grade near beautiful Berwick Lake. The highest points along the trail offer great views of Victoria, the Juan de Fuca Strait and, on clear days, the stunning backdrop of the Olympic Mountains.

WORTH NOTING
- King's Pond and Berwick Lake have viewing areas—watch for Virginia Rail, Red-winged Blackbird, Mallard, American Widgeon, and other waterfowl.

Playfair Park. PATRICE SNOPKOWSKI

- There are numerous benches along the trail to watch the golfing action or just enjoy the scenery.
- The Cedar Hill Golf Course clubhouse food service is open to golfers and the general public.
- Dogs are permitted but must be on leash at all times. Please remember to dispose of your dog's waste with the rest of your garbage.

NEARBY Mount Tolmie and trails to its spectacular summit viewpoint are just a few blocks east of Cedar Hill Golf Course (see p.105).

Playfair Park (known for the beautiful colours and variety of rhododendrons in spring and early summer) can be accessed from the trail at Judge Place and Blenkinsop Road. A number of small, neighbourhood parks are within 2–4 km and the Swan Lake Christmas Hill Nature Sanctuary is about 5 km distant.

2n. University of Victoria and Vicinity MAP 2n

DIFFICULTY/DISTANCE Easy to moderate/0.5 km to 6 km loop, depending on route chosen

HIGHLIGHTS The many wooded areas and open fields and grasslands at the University of Victoria form the setting for a 4.5 km loop hike that winds around the campus perimeter. From the Alumni Trail, you may visit the magnificent rhododendrons and plant displays at Finnerty Gardens or explore Mystic Vale, an ecological protection area on the university's east side. Extend your walk with a climb up Mount Tolmie, one of Victoria's best viewpoints, into the 8.5 ha Henderson Park with its kilometer-long chip trail winding through the woods adjacent to the golf greens, or even further, to Ten Mile Point. There are great opportunities for nature appreciation and birdwatching.

Best time to go Year-round; springtime is best for Ten Mile Point camas, and April and May are the best times to view the flowers in Finnerty Gardens; late spring/early summer and late summer/early fall for birds.

CAUTION From May 1 to August 31, dogs are not permitted after 9:00 am on any day, in Cadboro Bay/Cadboro-Gyro Park and the public beach at Cadboro Bay lying between the easterly boundary of Cadboro-Gyro Park and the boundary of the Municipality of Oak Bay.

ACCESS The starting point for the *Alumni Trail* is near Parking Lot 10, reached via West Campus Gate off Gordon Head Road or the Ring Road (University Drive). Parking fees are in place—check information carefully. The trail may also be accessed at numerous places along its route. Most of the level sections of the Alumni Trail are wheelchair accessible, though on some grades one may require assistance.

To Mount Tolmie

By Foot As for the Alumni Trail to the Mount Tolmie Trail cut-off, on UVic's southwest corner. Walk to pedestrian light at the corner of Cedar Hill Cross Road and Gordon Head Road and cross Cedar Hill Road. The Mount Tolmie trailhead is on the south side.

By Road In Victoria, travel north on Shelbourne Street and turn right at the Cedar Hill Cross Road lights. Continue past Richmond Road to Mayfair Drive. Turn right, and park at any of the small roadside parking spots along Mayfair Drive, or in the larger area at the summit. Only the level sections of the trails are wheelchair accessible. Mount Tolmie trails are open sunrise to sunset.

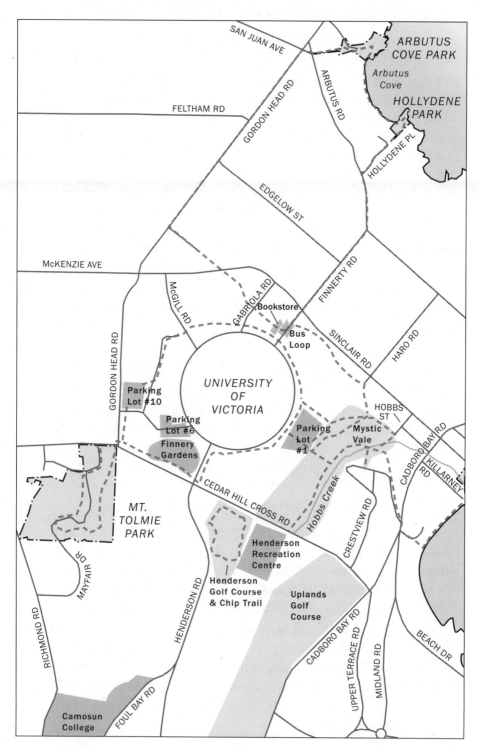

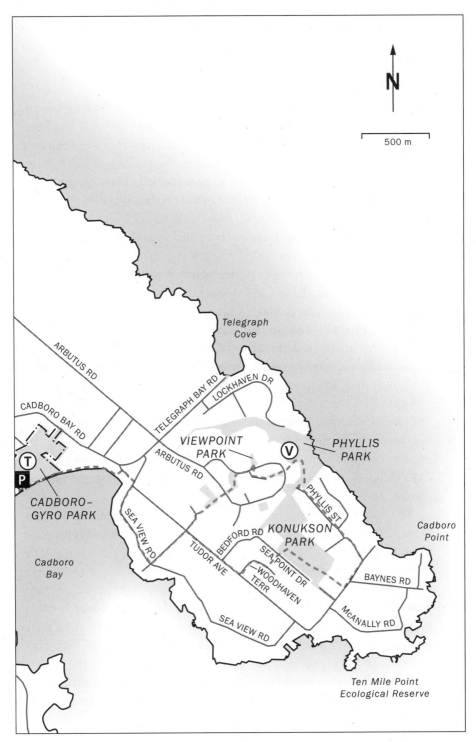

To Mystic Vale/Ten Mile Point

In Victoria, follow Cadboro Bay Road north (NE). From the intersection of Cadboro Bay Road and Sinclair, continue on Sinclair to Gyro Park, where you will find free parking and washrooms.

HIKE DESCRIPTION

Alumni Trail   Easy to moderate/4.5 km loop: Near Parking Lot 10, find the trail where it crosses the parking lot entrance road and head south. At the Garry oak meadow, near the university's southwest corner, is the cutoff trail to Mount Tolmie.

Keep left at the Mount Tolmie junction and follow the Alumni Trail through the field. The route parallels Cedar Hill Cross Road to the signed trail (on the left) to Finnerty Gardens (2.6 ha with numerous trails through the garden). There are resting benches and three quiet ponds. The garden contains over 4000 different trees and shrubs with more than 1500 rhododendron and azalea plants (one of Canada's best collections of rhododendrons) and is spectacular at any time of the year. Walk through the beauty and tranquility of the garden, past the pond and the University Interfaith Chapel and exit at University Drive. The gardens are open daily during daylight hours and there is no admission charge. Allow at least an hour to tour the gardens. Parking Lot 6, near the chapel and closest to the gardens, is wheelchair accessible.

From the Finnerty Gardens exit, head east at the Alumni Trail sign, and cross University Drive to the dense forest of South Woods. Next are two junctions fairly close together. Keep left at both by following the signs. One of the right trails leads across Cedar Hill Cross Road to Oak Bay's Henderson Park (8.5 ha) and a 1 km forested trail around the golf course.

The Alumni Trail swings towards Ring Road and then turns right along the southwest fringe of large Parking Lot 1. At the Mystic Vale signpost there is a choice of routes. The left path is the Mystic Vale bypass, which skirts Parking Lot 1 through the adjacent forest and runs past campus housing to Sinclair Road. Keep right at the junction to reach Mystic Vale (4.6 ha), accessed via a long, steep set of wooden steps. This ecological protection area within the University of Victoria property features a lush wooded ravine harbouring one of Victoria's last remaining moist Douglas-fir forests. The firs share the ravine with bigleaf maples, dogwood, yew trees and a plethora of shrubs and mosses. Be alert. Wandering Cougars have been spotted in and around Mystic Vale.

At the bottom of the steps swing left along Hobbs Creek to the ravine's north end, near Hobbs Street. Climb the bank and walk a short distance along the road to locate the trail up a steep hill. At the top, walk along the pavement to a trail on the right, follow it and then cut through a small parking area and past university residences to Sinclair Road. Turn left and take the sidewalk up the hill.

At Finnerty Road swing left and walk behind the bookstore and McKinnon Gym on a paved sidewalk and cross Gabriola Road. Beyond a sports field the path curves north to parallel McKenzie Avenue and passes Centennial Stadium. Turn south and cross McGill Road to a grassy field. The trail enters a wooded area near Bowker Creek, an important habitat for songbirds, woodpeckers and owls, and winds up a slight grade to Parking Lot 10.

WORTH NOTING

- The Alumni Trail, a popular jogging route, is partly chip, gravel and pavement.
- Campus woodlands include Douglas-fir, Garry oak, arbutus and bigleaf maple trees.
- Look for spring wildflowers like trillium, camas, shooting stars and vanilla leaf in the grassy fields and along the boulevards.
- Hutton's Vireo reside on the fringe of Mystic Vale. Listen and search for these elusive birds in the spring through early summer and again in the late summer through early fall. The ravine is home to Barred Owl, Great-horned Owl, Common Raven, Bald Eagle, Cooper's Hawk, and a variety of woodpeckers.

HIKE DESCRIPTION

Mount Tolmie Trails   Moderate/0.5 km to 2 km loop: Saanich's Mount Tolmie Park (18.3 ha) has several groomed trails that wind through a Garry oak and arbutus hilltop. You can create your own loop hike through wildflower meadows to the 120-m summit. Begin at the bottom, on Cedar Hill Cross Road, or higher up along Mayfair Drive. Trails on Mount Tolmie's east slope are slightly less steep than those on the west side. The magnificent view at the top offers a 360-degree panorama that includes Victoria, the Juan de Fuca Strait, the Olympic Mountains, the Sooke Hills, Mount Douglas, the Saanich Peninsula and the San Juan Islands. On a clear day you can see Mount Baker. The sunset here is unsurpassed.

WORTH NOTING

- Bicycles are not allowed on the Mount Tolmie trails.
- The park has picnic tables but no other facilities.
- Enjoy the seasonal meadow wildflowers but stay on the trails to protect fragile vegetation.
- Spring flowers include camas, fawn lilies and satin flowers (sometimes called grass widows).
- Watch for woodpeckers, Bewick's Wren, Anna's Hummingbird, Olive-sided Flycatcher, raptors and a variety of other birds. Early spring mornings are the best times for spotting migrant species. Golden-crowned Sparrow winter in the area.
- The park's drier terrain is habitat for Northern Alligator Lizards. These creatures blend in perfectly with their surroundings, even when they are basking in summer sunlight on a rock outcrop.
- Mount Tolmie's open rock faces display evidence of striation (grooving) caused by glacier scouring thousands of years ago.
- Mount Tolmie was named in 1934 after biologist Dr. William Fraser Tolmie, physician, botanist, linguist, ethnologist and legislator.

HIKE DESCRIPTION

Mystic Vale and Mystic Pond Loop   Easy, 2.9 km loop: This loop (portions of which are wheelchair accessible) takes approx. 1 hour, which allows time for looking at two natural ponds, one with heron rookery. Allow more time if exploring other Mystic Vale and University of Victoria trails and beyond. This loop may be combined with Ten Mile Point hike for a longer hike.

Start at Gyro Park, which has ample parking and washroom and picnic facilities. Turn right (west) along the beach from Gyro Park. After approx. 1/2 km, turn right and climb a flight of first stone, then wooden steps (approx. 100). At the top admire the view of Cadboro Bay over to Ten Mile Point. Take Hibbens Close to Cadboro Bay Road. Cross with caution to Vista Bay Road, just off to the right. Just past #2560 Vista Bay Road, turn right down a narrow trail. This may be obscured in spring and summer with new growth, but leads to a well-used trail after a few steps. A steep trail leads down to Mystic Creek. At the bottom there are several places to cross the creek, often dry in summer. At the base of the valley, there are several options. Turn left to explore Mystic Vale and head out to Cedar Hill Cross Road and across to Henderson

Ten Mile Point. NEIL BURROUGHS

Park Recreation Centre in Oak Bay, or, after having turned left, use one of the trails that lead up the embankment on the right to the University of Victoria. There are trails around the university, including to Finnerty Gardens. Beyond Finnerty Gardens, trails extend up to Mt. Tolmie with its breathtaking views over much of Victoria and over to the Olympic mountains.

The trail to the right takes you back to Gyro Park. As the trail exits on Hobbs St., there is another trail to the left leading up to the University of Victoria. From Hobbs St., turn right (SE) on Killarney Road. The safest crossing of Cadboro Bay Road is at the crosswalk and stop sign at Sinclair Road to your left. After crossing, walk back to Killarney, turn left then 1st right on Mystic Lane. The first natural pond is two houses in, on the right. Read about the legend of Mystic Spring on Google.

Continue down Killarney. The second pond is off Waring Place before #3764 and is sign posted "Mystic Pond". This one is bigger and herons can sometimes be seen perched on their nests in the tall trees. Walk back to Killarney Road and along the beach to Gyro Park, just steps to the left.

HIKE DESCRIPTION

Ten Mile Point Loop   Easy to moderate/6.1 km loop: Highlights of this delightful loop trail include breathtaking views of San Juan Island, Haro Straight, and Mount Baker, and literally carpets of camas in spring. The wooded peninsula which forms one side of Cadboro Bay, has many beaches and coves, one of which was the location of a dynamite factory in the 19th century, and another—"Smuggler's Cove"—was used in prohibition years. Cadboro Point, just south of Ten Mile Point, is the actual location of the 11 ha Ten Mile Point Ecological Reserve #66, so please respect the intertidal life in this area.

Begin the walk at Gyro Park. Turn left along the beach, which is easy walking except at high tide. Turn left onto Tudor Road. At the stop sign, turn right on Tudor Avenue. Walk up a steep path and turn right on Sea View Road. Where Cadboro View Road goes right, turn left at trail marker (copious amounts of blackberries in late summer!). Back out on Tudor Avenue and turn right. Pass Bedford, turn left on Woodhaven Terrace. Pass #3918, turn left onto tiny trail immediately before white house (at time of writing). Turn right at Sea Point Drive. About 30 metres (unmarked), turn left at fire hydrant into Konukson Park. Stay on the main path, keeping right at 1st and 2nd major forks and again at junction. Out on Tudor Ave. Turn left and left again onto Phyllis Street.

At the top of the hill, turn right before barrier. See footpath marker leading downhill into the woods. Keep left at fork. Here is the carpet of camas in spring. Follow the slightly rougher trail and climb up the steps to Phyllis Point, where you will find benches and a fenced lookout with spectacular views of San Juan Island, Haro Straight, and Mount Baker. Descend the steps to the street. Cross the road and enter Wedgepoint Park. Exit Wedgepoint Park onto an unmarked street (Wedgewood Terrace). Proceed to T-intersection, and turn right for about 10 metres. Cross the road and climb up six steps into Viewpoint Park. Follow the short trail to a bench. Views of Mount Doug, Cordova Bay to the east, Oak Bay and Sooke Hills to the west. Retrace steps to street. Turn right. Cross road and turn left opposite #2825 Wedgepoint Road into Arbutus Park. The trail crosses an unmarked road (Arbutus). Enter Benson Park (unmarked). Turn left at fork and exit on Benson. Cross over Tudor Avenue to trail marker.

Retrace your steps by turning right on Sea View Road, then left down a steep pathway. Left at the stop sign and proceed to the beach. Walk back along the beach to Gyro Park. At high tide there may be some scrambling over rocks but nothing serious. Consider having lunch at Gyro Park and continuing round the Mystic Vale Loop, (another 2.9 km) and/or a side trip to the University of Victoria.

NEARBY

Mount Douglas Park's many trails are fairly close to the University of Victoria (see p. 79).

Arbutus Cove Park   A loop route taking about 50-60 minutes, this park can be accessed either off Gordon Head Road or via Finnerty Road. Parking is limited on Arbutus Cove Lane. The Hollydene Park route takes you from UVic (start at Ring Road near the UVic Bus loop) along first Finnerty Road then left on Arbutus Road and right on Hollydene Place to Hollydene Park. There is a picnic site and benches along the bluff. The paved paths are wheelchair accessible. Take the stairs down to the beach and, at the other side of the cove, take the stairs back up to Arbutus Cove Park. Stay on the path, and if you don't want to get your feet wet, check local tide tables before you go. To return to UVic, you can shorten the route by using Arbutus Road to Finnerty Road, or you can go back the "long way" along Gordon Head Road to McCoy Road and onto the UVic campus.

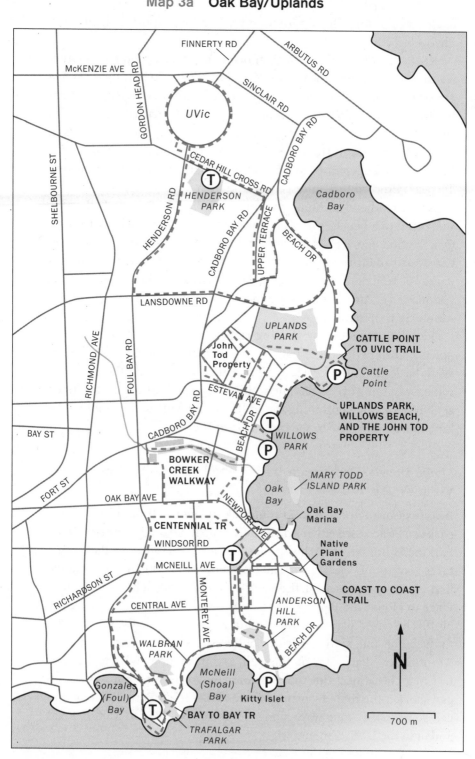

McKENZIE AVE

FINNERTY RD

ARBUTUS RD

GORDON HEAD RD

SINCLAIR RD

UVic

SHELBOURNE ST

CEDAR HILL CROSS RD

(T)

HENDERSON PARK

HENDERSON RD

CADBORO BAY RD

UPPER TERRACE

BEACH DR

CADBORO BAY RD

Cadboro Bay

LANSDOWNE RD

UPLANDS PARK

John Tod Property

RICHMOND AVE

FOUL BAY RD

CADBORO BAY RD

ESTEVAN AVE

BEACH DR

(P) *Cattle Point*

CATTLE POINT TO UVIC TRAIL

UPLANDS PARK, WILLOWS BEACH, AND THE JOHN TOD PROPERTY

BAY ST

(T)
Willows Park
(P)

BOWKER CREEK WALKWAY

FORT ST

OAK BAY AVE

Oak Bay

MARY TODD ISLAND PARK

Oak Bay Marina

CENTENNIAL TR

NEWPORT AVE

WINDSOR RD

RICHARDSON ST

MCNEILL AVE

(T)

MONTEREY AVE

Native Plant Gardens

COAST TO COAST TRAIL

CENTRAL AVE

ANDERSON HILL PARK

BEACH DR

WALBRAN PARK

McNeill (Shoal) Bay

(P)

Kitty Islet

N

Gonzales (Foul) Bay

(T)

BAY TO BAY TR

TRAFALGAR PARK

700 m

3

Victoria, Oak Bay and Esquimalt

3a. Oak Bay/Uplands Area   MAP 3a

DIFFICULTY/DISTANCE   Easy to moderate (some slightly steeper hills)/3.2–10.2 km loop routes

HIGHLIGHTS   Travelling east along the waterfront on Beach Drive you enter the municipality of Oak Bay. Some of the most beautiful streetscapes in the world, frequently lined by canopies of mature trees and lovely gardens, can be found in the municipality of Oak Bay. A complex of routes takes you through lanes, beside beaches, and to viewpoints for amazing views. Don't miss Gonzales Hill, Walbran and Anderson Hill parks, Willows Beach and Cattle Point.

Best time to go   Springtime for wildflowers but you can enjoy the views, gardens and "streetscapes" anytime of year.

CAUTIONS
- Bicycles are not permitted in Uplands Park, but bike racks are available at the Beach Drive and Dorset Road entrances.
- Depending on the park and which area along the waterfront, dogs may be permitted off-leash at specific times of the year. Watch for signs and remember to clean up after your pet.

ACCESS
Centennial Trail   From downtown Victoria, travel east on Beach Drive to the intersection with Foul Bay Road. On-street parking is limited.

Bowker Creek Walkway   From downtown Victoria, travel northeast on Fort Street. One block east of Foul Bay /road, turn right onto Bee Street and park at the recreation centre.

Coast to Coast Trail   From downtown Victoria, travel east/northeast on Beach Drive to the Oak Bay Marina. Some parking is available. Check rates.

Bay to Bay Trail   From downtown Victoria, travel east on Beach Drive to the intersection with Inglewood Terrace. On-street parking is limited.

Uplands Park/Cattle Point   From downtown Victoria, travel east/northeast on Beach Drive to the intersection of Beach Drive and Scenic Drive. One can access the point from Beach Drive. Main park entrances are on Beach Drive, Dorset Road, and Midland Road.

HIKE DESCRIPTIONS

Centennial Trail   The 6.8 km circuit takes you through Windsor Park, and later in the route, through Walbran Park, known to locals as "Gonzales Hill".

The 6.8 km Centennial Trail through south Oak Bay opened in 2006, and is marked by 14 carved posts and special trail markers between those posts to guide you as you explore. Starting at Foul Bay Road and Beach Drive, travel north on Foul Bay Rd and follow the trail markers, enjoying such highlights as:

Windsor Park   Originally called Oak Bay Park and site of sporting events since 1906, where you might see rugby or cricket being played. It also has a lovely rose garden.

The Oak Bay Native Plant Garden   At the junction of Beach Drive and Margate Avenue, this 2.1 ha natural area features mature trees and native plants indigenous to Oak Bay. The garden has benches and picnic tables, and there are two ponds built into the natural rock that are circled by a short loop trail.

Anderson Hill Park (Blueberry Hill)   Carpeted in spring with wildflowers, this 2.55 ha park is primarily Garry oak ecosystem, and there are benches along the numerous trails and walkways with incredible views of Mt. Baker and the Olympic Peninsula.

Walbran Park and Gonzales Hill observatory (a weather station for 75 years and now a heritage building) featuring unparalleled views from the highest point of land (66 m) on the south coast of Vancouver Island, these rocky knolls with Garry oaks and wildflowers are home to California Quail. This portion of the trail has some steeper sections— be careful on the steep stairs.

Bowker Creek Walkway This 3.2 km trail takes you through the heart of Oak Bay, with heritage areas containing a wealth of historically significant architecture, parks and tree-lined streets. Starting at the Oak Bay Recreation Centre, on Bee Street (off Caboro Bay Road just east of the Fort and Foul Bay roads intersection), the trail goes east between the Rec Centre and Oak Bay High School, following Bowker Creek into Fireman's Park. After you pass the Fire Hall, continue to Monteith Street and turn left (north). A very short distance later, turn right onto Cranmore Road. Right again at Beach Drive to take you south for a short way, then another right on San Carlos has you heading into the heritage area. Turn left on Prospect Place and right on Oak Bay Avenue to Elgin Road. Turn right on Elgin and follow the road and trail to Goldsmith Street and then right on Bee Street to complete the loop.

Coast to Coast Trail This 4.6 km trail takes you from Oak Bay to McNeill Bay (Shoal Bay) and back, with spectacular views at both coasts. Refer to local maps for choice of routes. Generally, most start near the Oak Bay Marina, on Beach Drive, and go north a short distance and then turn left onto Currie Road. Once you return to Beach Drive near McNeill Bay, depending on tides, you could take a quick side trip to Kitty Islet on the east side of the bay.

Bay to Bay Trail This 6 km trail is a round trip starting at Beach Drive and Inglewood Terrace (near Kitty Islet access). Going along Beach Drive overlooking McNeill Bay, it takes you to Harling Point and back. You can choose a loop to Lafayette Park and around through residential streets to Walbran Park and back to Beach Drive (steep stairs down) and thence to your start, or include the Walbran Park loop but extend the hike all the way to the loop on Harling Point, returning along Beach Drive to the start. The loop around Harling Point can be travelled either direction. The trail starts on the Lorne Terrace side of Trafalgar Park, an 1.4 hectare undeveloped natural area with steeply sloping waterfront access, and a scenic viewpoint from the parking lot at the top of the hill. Travel northwest on Lorne Terrace, turn left (south) onto Crescent Road and follow the trail around Harling Point back to Trafalgar Park. Spring wildflowers, great views of Trial Island (ecological reserve) and across Juan de Fuca Strait to the Olympic Mountains, and the Chinese Cemetery (see description in Victoria Waterfront chapter, p.123) are highlights of this loop. Return to the start along King George Terrace and Beach Drive.

Uplands Park, Willows Beach, and the John Tod property This 5 km route can be travelled either direction. Depending on time of day and weather, one can either finish the walk along the white sand of Willows Beach or in the more shaded trail through Uplands Park.

Uplands Park (30.6 ha) has two parts, separated by the main access road, Beach Drive. Cattle Point is on the water side and Uplands Park is on the hillside. Uplands Park offers gravel and dirt walking trails, most of which are considered easy going, level (not all) and suitable for most fitness levels. Cattle Point trails (with benches) provides beach and ocean access. The winding trails offer great opportunities for birdwatching and observing native flora, and spectacular views are possible—Mt. Baker, the Olympic Peninsula, and even Mount Rainier on a clear day. Mary Tod Islet Park is just offshore (south of Cattle Point).

Park at Cattle Point and make your way to the Esplanade along Willows Beach. Head southwest to Willows Park, where there are a few stairs, and then take Path Way to Heron Street, where you turn left. Near the corner of Estevan Avenue and Heron Street is Tod House, one of the oldest houses in Victoria (built in 1850) and the longest continuously occupied residence in western Canada (house and surrounding properties are not open to the public). Backtrack to Estevan Avenue and turn right (west). Follow Estevan past the tiny Lokier Park to a laneway just past Topp Avenue. Turn right and go along the lane to the intersection with Nottingham Road and Thompson Avenue. Go northeast (right) on Nottingham to Camas Lane, and turn right. Camas Lane, an Oak Bay Heritage Byway runs from Nottingham Road to Willows Beach. Before you get to the beach, however, turn left onto Lincoln Road and follow the trail into Uplands Park. From there you can travel east, past the Uplands Cenotaph, across Beach Drive, and back to the starting point at Cattle Point.

Cattle Point to UVic (University of Victoria)—exploring the Up-lands area One of the longer trails in Oak Bay, this 10.2 km trail takes you northward from the scenic Cattle Point in Uplands Park to UVic (where you can enjoy Finnerty Gardens—see UVic, p.107) and back past Uplands Golf Club. Begin by travelling north along Beach Drive to Lansdowne Road. Turn left and remain on this road all the way to Henderson Road, where you turn right. Henderson Road crosses Cedar Hill Cross Road to get to UVic and Finnerty Gardens. To return to Cattle Point, leave UVic by going left (east) on Cedar Hill Cross Road and then right onto Upland Terrace Road to Lansdowne. Left on Lansdowne and right on Beach Drive and you are back to where you started. If you do not wish to go all the way to UVic, you can explore the area by continuing north on Beach Drive to Midland Road, where you turn left.

You can include a short loop (about 4.7 km) by taking the Cotswold Road exit at the roundabout and going right onto Upper Terrace Road, left onto Uplands Road, left onto Weald Road and left onto Cotswold Road, to return to the roundabout, or continue on Midland to Uplands Park. There is a trail that goes east through the park and joins Beach Drive just north of Cattle Point. Check local maps for detailed routes.

WORTH NOTING

- A pamphlet on "Scenic Walks" in the municipality is available from the Oak Bay Parks and Recreation (www.recreation.oakbaybc.org).

NEARBY

See Victoria Waterfront (p.123), and UVic (p.107).

OF INTEREST

- Uplands Park (30.6 ha) was established in 1946 and is one of North America's first natural urban parks. It is a protected park with a vast collection of native plants, herbs and trees, including arbutus, Garry oak, giant horsetail, Indian pipe, licorice fern, and Hooker's onion. Bird sightings in Uplands Park and from Cattle Point include such species as the Eared Grebe, Red Crossbill, Cedar Waxwing, Orange-crowned Warbler, sparrows and swallows, Black Oystercatcher, Bald Eagle, Turkey Vulture, and Great Blue Heron.
- The John Tod home has a number of still largely intact, interesting original features including the interior hand-hewn finish and the field stone fireplaces. A designated heritage property was the home of John Tod, Hudson's Bay Company (HBC) Factor, Chief Fur Trader at Kamloops, and one of the first appointed members of B.C.'s Legislative Council. It is supposed to be haunted.
- Camas Lane once separated John Tod's Willows Farm and Hudson's Bay Uplands Farm, providing access to the southern parts of the farm.

Map 3b   Victoria Waterfront

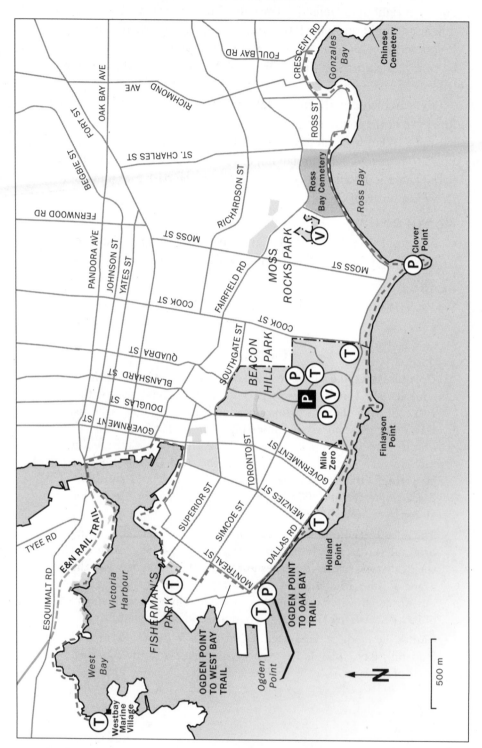

3b. Victoria Waterfront   MAP 3b

DIFFICULTY/DISTANCE   Easy/3 km, one-way

HIGHLIGHTS   This world-class stroll, along the Juan de Fuca Strait, begins at the 0.8 km-long Ogden Point breakwater. Two hikes—one to the east and one to the west of Ogden Point—together feature one of Victoria's most beautiful seascape walks. See the chapter on Esquimalt parks and waterfront (p.129) for more walks to the west, and Oak Bay (p.117) for additional walks to the east.

Best time to go   Springtime for wildflowers but the spectacular views, changing with the seasons, can be enjoyed at anytime of year.

CAUTIONS   Dogs are permitted off-leash on the south side of Dallas Road, from Douglas Street to (and including) Clover Point Park, but dogs must be on leash from Ogden Point to West Bay.

ACCESS

There is a pay parking lot near the Ogden Point breakwater (near Dallas Road and Dock Street in James Bay). Free parking is available along Dallas Road and at Clover Point.

If you are starting at the West Bay Marina end of the hike, there is a parking lot off Head Street.

Public toilets are available on Dallas Road in Holland Point Park, near the Harrison Yacht Pond at the foot of Government Street, and at the end of Cook Street in Beacon Hill Park. Restroom facilities are available to customers only at Ogden Point Café. From Ogden Point west, public toilets are available at Fisherman's Wharf, the Inner Harbour, and at WestBay Marine Village. Several restaurants are along the route, but restrooms are for clients only.

HIKE DESCRIPTIONS

Ogden Point to Oak Bay   Begin the walk at the Ogden Point breakwater, in James Bay. The 0.8-km-long breakwater dates back to 1913 and was constructed from rock quarried at Albert Head. The breakwater is a popular birdwatching spot and a great destination for just getting wind-blown. Offshore is Brotchie Ledge beacon, scene of many marine disasters. The light is a prominent geographical reference point for pilots, scuba divers, fishermen, and government agencies.

From the breakwater, head east along the seawall, past Holland Point Park (5 ha) and the Harrison model yacht pond, named after the mayor of Victoria in the 1950s. The cliff-side walk, with numerous beach access points, parallels Dallas Road and offers magnificent views of the Olympic Mountains and the Juan de Fuca Strait. Near Paddon Street, there is a bench in a sheltered nook. Offshore is Glimpse Reef. Nearby Fonyo Beach is named after Steve Fonyo, whose Journey for Lives run ended there in 1985.

At the foot of Douglas Street you have three choices. You could cross the road to visit the "Mile 0" monument, marking the western terminus of the Trans-Canada Highway and the Vancouver Island section of the Trans-Canada Trail. A bronze statue of Terry Fox was erected nearby in 2005 to commemorate his courageous Marathon of Hope run. From here detour up Douglas Street for a soft ice cream cone at the Beacon Drive-In Restaurant, and then cross Douglas Street to enter Beacon Hill Park. The park has trails meandering through it, and you can visit the petting zoo (summer only) or climb to the viewpoint for a spectacular view of the Olympic Mountains. Your second option is to take the stairs near the foot of Douglas Street and hike along the beach, or, thirdly, continue east on the cliff-side walk.

The bluffs, particularly near Holland Point, display evidence of the incessant erosion on the cliff face, and of the controversial attempts to stop that erosion by artificial berms, drains, and the planting of native shrubs. The latter include Nootka rose, snowberry, red currant, ocean spray, mock orange, Saskatoon berry and Garry oak.

Halfway to Clover Point you will reach a shelter, near Finlayson Point. There is a monument honouring Marilyn Bell, who swam the Juan de Fuca Strait in 1956. In the spring, you will see the yellow gorse and Scotch broom in bloom. Efforts to eradicate both of these two invasive species are ongoing, but have not yet been successful.

As you approach Clover Point, you are likely to see colourful kites overhead. Those really big kites, with humans attached, are paragliders, akin to hang-gliders. Take special note of the birds in the air and on the waves. Glaucous-winged Gull, Harlequin Duck and pigeons are common. Clover Point is one of the best places around Victoria to spot migrating species.

You have a choice once you reach Clover Point—walk the perimeter of the point or take the path across the grass and entrance road to the seawall. The route continues either as sidewalk on Dallas Road, or on the seawall below the road, past the Ross Bay Cemetery to the foot of St. Charles Street. *Ross Bay Cemetery* (11 ha) is a fine example of a typical

Victoria waterfront/view from Dallas Road. NEIL BURROUGHS

Victorian cemetery, with formal landscaping and a variety of interesting tombstones. This has been the final resting place of many of Victoria's prominent citizens since 1873. The section of the route east from Clover Point along the seawall (seaside promenade) can be spectacular and is sometimes closed during rough weather. Just west of the cemetery, the small Moss Rocks Park offers a lovely view across the Strait.

If you are at the end of the waterfront trail (along the beach), turn left to go up a slight incline to reach Hollywood Crescent. The route continues on Hollywood, with beautiful views—Hollywood becomes Robertson Street. At the intersection of Robertson and Ross streets, turn right to go along Crescent Road. Turn right again to drop down onto Gonzales Bay beach (or stay on Crescent Road, running parallel to the beach, if the tide is too high). Follow the beach to a set of concrete stairs up to Foul Bay Road. Foul Bay Road marks much of the boundary between Victoria and Oak Bay.

WORTH NOTING

- The trail is level and wide enough for wheelchairs or scooters.
- A special pet fountain is located on the Dallas Road Waterfront Trail, just east of the foot of Douglas Street.

- The Capital Bike and Walk Society publishes Walk Downtown Victoria, a pamphlet describing many of Victoria's urban walks. These range from 15 minutes to an hour. Contact http://www.capitalbikeandwalk.org for more details.
- NO dogs are allowed in Ross Bay Cemetery.

NEARBY

The *Chinese Cemetery* (1.4 ha)   Accessed off King George Terrace at the foot of Crescent Road is Canada's oldest Chinese cemetery. The Chinese Consolidated Benevolent Association originally purchased the land in 1903. In 1996, the cemetery was designated a National Historic Site. At Harling Point, there are spring wildflowers and great views across Juan de Fuca Strait to the Olympic Mountains.

Continuing along the waterfront to Beach Drive you enter the municipality of Oak Bay. Available from the Oak Bay Parks and Recreation is a pamphlet on "Scenic Walks" in the municipality (www.recreation.oakbaybc.org). Do not miss Gonzales Hill, Walbran and Anderson Hill Parks, Willows Beach and Cattle Point. This will end your eastward walk close to the University of Victoria. (See p.107.)

Ogden Point to West Bay   From Ogden Point breakwater, turn left and walk along Dallas Road to Montreal Street, where there is a blue and orange Walk Victoria sign. Follow the signs to Fisherman's Wharf— worth pausing to explore. Enjoy fish and chips or an ice cream cone at the popular Barb's Place. Look across the harbour to see where your walk will take you. Victoria Harbour is a busy working harbour. Float planes, "dancing" ferries (the Harbour Ferry Ballet in the Inner Harbour, started in 1993, delights onlookers every Saturday and Sunday morning May to September), dragon boat racing, whale- watching zodiacs, classic boat festivals and Swiftsure yacht racing all vie for the space and attention. Return to the street, turn left and continue to follow the signs, all around the Inner Harbour, past the Parliament buildings, the famous Empress Hotel, and the old Custom House to the Johnson Street Bridge. Cross the bridge to the Songhees lands, where the trail becomes Westsong Way and follows the contours of the coastline to West Bay (about 4 km from the Johnson Street Bridge to West Bay). Westsong Way connects a few small parks and is bordered by the Victoria harbour on one side and trees and greenery on the other. Portions of the walkway feature overhanging Douglas-fir and arbutus trees, as well as some Garry oak and wildflowers. One can also

- Sir James Douglas named Clover Point as he landed here in 1843, presumably because he saw reddish-purple flowers of springbank clover, a perennial native species and food source for local First Nations people.
- Beacon Hill Park (75 ha) features lawns, fields, flower garden and native and imported trees. A variety of paths intersect the park. Burial mounds, constructed of large granite rocks, may be seen on Beacon Hill's southern slope, below the flagpole. This area is carpeted with blue camas in May.
- Dallas Road was named for Alexander Grant Dallas, and Finlayson Point was named for Roderick Finlayson, both of whom were Chief Factor with the Hudson's Bay Company. A plaque advises that Finlayson Point was once the site of an ancient fortified village and also marks the site of a gun battery during the Russo-Turkish war (1878–1892).

see glacial score marks on some of the rocky outcrops. The walkway is made up of wooden boardwalk or concrete path, with a few spots with stairs to go down to the water's edge to check out tidal pools and small sand beaches. If you become tired at any point along the way, take one of the little ferries across the harbour to pick up the walkway again.

NEARBY   At West Bay, you are in Esquimalt, which has some real gems to explore. Look for Fleming Beach, Kinsmen Gorge and High-rock Park with the Royal Canadian Navy cairn, and Saxe Point, a beautiful bayside park with forest paths and ocean views (see Esquimalt parks and waterfront, p.129).

Map 3c Esquimalt Parks and Waterfront

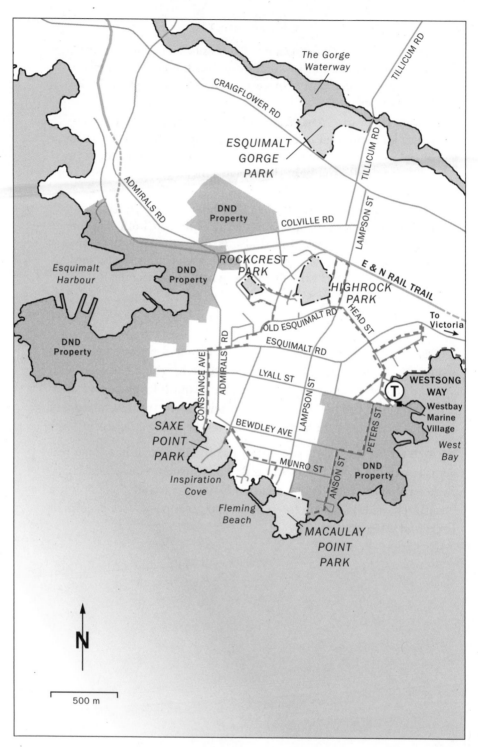

TILLICUM RD

The Gorge
Waterway

CRAIGFLOWER RD

ESQUIMALT
GORGE
PARK

TILLICUM RD

ADMIRALS RD

DND
Property

COLVILLE RD

LAMPSON ST

Esquimalt
Harbour

DND
Property

ROCKCREST
PARK

HIGHROCK
PARK

E & N RAIL TRAIL

HEAD ST

OLD ESQUIMALT RD

To
Victoria

DND
Property

ESQUIMALT RD

LYALL ST

ADMIRALS RD

CONSTANCE AVE

LAMPSON ST

WESTSONG
WAY

Westbay
Marine
Village

West
Bay

SAXE
POINT
PARK

BEWDLEY AVE

PETERS ST

Inspiration
Cove

MUNRO ST

ANSON ST

DND
Property

Fleming
Beach

MACAULAY
POINT
PARK

N

500 m

128

3c. Esquimalt Parks and Waterfront   MAP 3c

DIFFICULTY/DISTANCE   Easy to moderate/3–6 km, one-way

HIGHLIGHTS   Esquimalt is one of the municipalities in Greater Victoria (the word Esquimalt is the First Nations' name referring to the narrowing at the head of the harbour), and is a fascinating mix of interesting urban areas full of history, scenic coastline, and small parks, including a beautiful hilltop park and bayside parks with forest paths and ocean views.

Best time to go   Springtime for flowers, summer for picnics, and anytime of year for the views.

CAUTIONS
- Cycling is not permitted on the Westsong Way.
- Not all hikes are suitable for wheelchairs or scooters—several have steep sections and/or stairs.

ACCESS
Parking and public toilets are available at Westbay Marine Village. Additional parking can be found on Head Street opposite the Captain Jacobson Park.

HIKE DESCRIPTIONS
Westsong Way   Approximately 5 km long, the Westsong Way (combination of the Songhees Walkway and West Bay Walkway) is a walking path and boardwalk connecting Esquimalt (from Head Street at Westbay Marine Village) to downtown Victoria (Johnston Street Bridge). The walkway follows the contours of the coastline from the Johnson Street Bridge to West Bay, bordered by the Victoria harbour on one side and trees and greenery on the other. Portions of the walkway feature overhanging Douglas-fir, Garry oak, and arbutus trees, as well as wildflowers in spring and summer. There are a few spots with stairs to go down to the water's edge to check out tidal pools and small sand beaches. Watch the activity in the busy harbour, and maybe try birdwatching while on your walk.

Esquimalt Parks and Waterfront   This 5+ km loop walk takes you from Westbay Marine Village to Highrock Park, then west and south to Saxe Point and Macaulay Point on Esquimalt Harbour. Wheelchair access is limited. The last portion of the route takes you past Department of National Defense (DND) Work Point Barracks and then back to the marina.

West Bay to Highrock Park   Starting at the Head Street end (west end) of Westsong Way, travel north on Head Street to Old Esquimalt Road and turn left. A short distance along, cross Lampson Street and then turn right onto Cairn Road to access the park. Follow the paved path through a field to the cairn. You can also enter from Highrock Avenue, off Rockheights Avenue, or from Matheson Avenue.

Highrock Park (7.1 ha) (also called Cairn Park, referring to a cairn dedicated on the fiftieth anniversary of the Royal Canadian Navy) is the highest point of land (71 m) in Esquimalt. Offering fantastic views of downtown Victoria, the Sooke Hills and the Olympic Mountains, the park features glaciated knolls, stands of Garry oak, arbutus and Douglas-fir, and wildflowers such as blue camas. Very close by (accessible by foot from Rockcrest Avenue or Highrock Avenue) is the smallest natural area (1 ha) in the township, Rockcrest Park. Spring wildflowers such as camas and shooting star appear among Douglas-fir trees and in a small Garry oak meadow.

Highrock Park to Saxe Point Park   Leaving the cairn at Highrock Park, follow the paved path down and continue on when the trail become a somewhat rocky route. Descend the stairs to Highrock Avenue (west of the park). If you wish to visit Rockcrest Park, stay on Highrock, cross Rockheights Avenue and turn left into the park. Leave the park via Rockcrest Avenue and at the intersection of Rockheights and Rockcrest avenues, turn right (south) onto Rockheights Avenue. Turn right onto Old Esquimalt Road, and right again onto Park Terrace. After a short distance, turn left to enter Memorial Park. Go through the park, passing the cenotaph commemorating Esquimalt residents who died in WWI, to Esquimalt Road and turn right. After crossing Admirals Road, turn left onto Constance Avenue to head south. As you near the ocean, there is a narrow gravel footpath (on the left) connecting Constance Avenue and Admirals Road. The footpath emerges at the corner of Admirals and Bewdley Avenue. Having turned right, once on Bewdley Avenue, watch for the trail off to the right (off Saxe Place) and enter *Saxe Point Park*. The trail in the park may be hard to see, but keep the water on your right and go to the flagpole at the tip of the point. Saxe Point Park offers great variety: extensive herbaceous borders, beach accesses, forested trails with mature Douglas-fir and Grand fir, and spectacular views of the Olympic Mountains and Strait of Juan de Fuca.

Saxe Point Park to Fleming Beach, Buxton Green and Macaulay Point
Keeping the water on your right, follow the trail northeast to Munro
Street. Turn right and stay on Munro, crossing Kinver Street, until you
come to signs for Fleming Beach and the boat ramp. Fleming Beach is
one of the entrances to Buxton Green and Macaulay Point Park. The 0.9
hectare site has native plants and a small sandy beach. Rock faces and
cliffs in the park are well-used by rock climbers. A walkway adjacent
to the beach leads to the 1-ha Buxton Green Park and a breakwater,
from which views are amazing. Buxton Green adjoins Macaulay Point
Park, a 7.6 ha park popular with birdwatchers, hikers and dog walkers.
Views from the headland trail are of the Strait of Juan de Fuca, the
Olympic Mountains, Metchosin shoreline and East Sooke. "The
Bunkers" are the abandoned gun emplacements of the oldest coastal
defense battery in B.C. Within Macaulay Point Park are some fenced-
off areas containing species protected under Canada's Species At Risk
Act. Dogs are prohibited in the protected areas. Visitors and their dogs
are required to stay on designated paths to help protect this fragile area.

Macaulay Point Park to West Bay   The most scenic route by which to
leave Macaulay Point and return to West Bay is to follow the trail along
the headland to Anson Crescent. Here you turn left and go north, first
on Anson Crescent then on Anson Street. Stay on Anson Street until
you reach Bewdley Avenue. Turn right and then left onto Peters Street.
You will have now passed the DND property and Work Point Barracks.
Depending on your starting point, at the intersection of Peters and
Lyall Street, turn right toward the ocean and Westbay Marine Village,
or turn left to get to Gore Street.

WORTH NOTING
- The Township of Esquimalt has several Walking Tours brochures
  available (see p.227).

- There are four designated Leash Optional Areas in Esquimalt—
  check the Township website for details, and look for signs in Captain
  Jacobson Park (overlooking Westbay Marine Village), Highrock,
  Saxe Point, Macaulay Point and Esquimalt Gorge parks.

NEARBY
Esquimalt Gorge Park (13 ha)   The park is on Tillicum Road just south
of the Gorge Waterway, and has gardens, forested areas, and picnic
areas in the rolling landscape of the park, with benches dotted along

the waterway path (the park is wheelchair accessible). You can also enter on foot from Sioux Place, off Craigflower Road. Gorge Creek was restored in 2005 and is now home to native plants and wildfowl unique to the region. The Gorge Waterway Nature House is in the park, and a hands-on opportunity to explore the ecology of the area around the Gorge Waterway.

OF INTEREST

- *Highrock Park* (also known as Cairn Park) is one of the oldest parks in the township. Originally named Transfer Woods, it was there that horses owned by the Victoria Transfer Company were transferred from the south side to the north side of the township. In the 1960s, it was renamed in conjunction with the development of the Rockheights subdivision.
- *Macaulay Point* began as a Hudson Bay farm, then later became part of Fort Macaulay.
- *E & N Rail Trail* Currently under development, the trail will eventually stretch from Vic West to the West Shore communities. Constructed alongside a deactivated railroad, it will provide opportunities for walkers and cyclists to travel between communities.

4

Western Communities to Port Renfrew

4a. Royal Roads, Esquimalt Lagoon, and Fort Rodd Hill   MAP 4a

DIFFICULTY/DISTANCE   Easy to moderate/2–8 km and up, one-way

HIGHLIGHTS   Royal Roads University, established in 1995, was first Hatley Park estate (in the early 1900s), and then in 1940, became Royal Roads Military College, a degree-granting university for Canadian officers (purchased by the federal government for $75,000). In 1997, the campus and surrounding 202.4 ha of national defense property were declared a national historic site. The campus grounds, open to the public, are extensive and varied, with ponds and streams, formal gardens, open parkland and dense, oldgrowth forest. The saltmarsh estuary at the mouth of Colwood Creek, along the shores of Esquimalt Lagoon, is a rare ecosystem in the Victoria area. Highlights include spectacular views of Esquimalt Lagoon, Juan de Fuca Strait and the Olympic Mountains.

Best time to go   any time of year, but the gardens are best in spring and summer.

CAUTIONS

- Be aware that the campus is adjacent to Department of National Defense property, and access to some areas is limited. Watch for signs.
- Note that several of the roads are one way—please obey the signs.
- Check the Hatley Gardens website for information regarding the hours when open to the public.

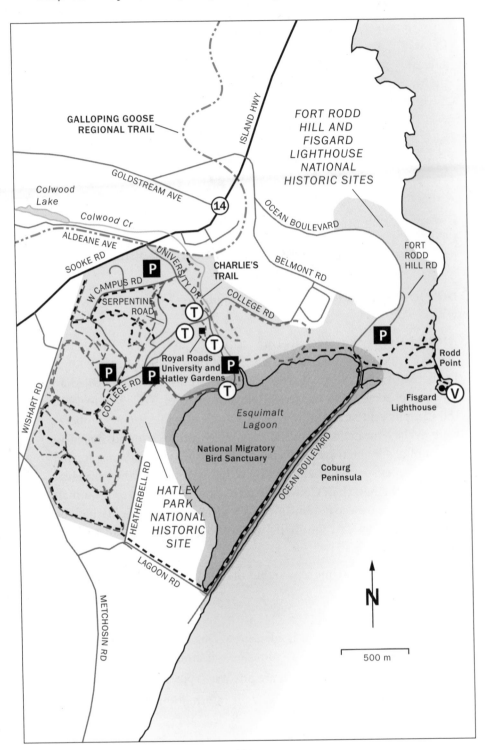

ACCESS

Royal Roads University   From Victoria, take the Trans-Canada Highway. After about 10 km, take the Colwood exit (Exit 10) and go under the Trans-Canada onto the Old Island Highway. The Old Island Highway will become Sooke Road. After about 3 km, turn left onto University Drive—the main entrance of Royal Roads University/Hatley Park. Pay parking is in effect at the lots off the main road—University Drive.

Esquimalt Lagoon   From Victoria, take the Trans-Canada Highway. After about 10 km, take the Colwood exit (Exit 10) and go under the Trans-Canada onto the Old Island Highway. Turn left onto Ocean Boulevard and follow it all the way the lagoon, or stay right onto Belmont Road, and follow it to Ocean Boulevard and turn right. Free parking is available along Ocean Boulevard—check the signs for restrictions.

Fort Rodd Hill   From Victoria, take the Trans-Canada Highway (Highway #1) for 5 km, then take the Colwood exit (Exit 10). Follow Highway #1A for 2 km then turn left at the third traffic light onto Ocean Boulevard. Follow the signs to Fort Rodd Hill.

HIKE DESCRIPTIONS   Several loop trails, ranging from 30 minutes to 3 hours, wind through the campus grounds. Note that the map in this book does not show all roads or trails for the site—check the Royal Roads University website for a free map showing many of the trails not described here.

The routes follow a combination of dirt trails, gravel or dirt roads, and some short paved sections. The longest starts near the junction of University Drive and College Road, just below the parking lot. *Charlie's Trail* winds along on the east side of University Drive, north along *Colwood Creek* and wraps back around to University Drive. Cross the creek at a small waterfall and again just before the trail goes through a treed gully, then climb a flight of stairs and continue climbing, following a chain-link fence. The creek (on your right) flows through a lovely rocky gorge. At the top of the climb, turn left at the fork in the trail (away from the creek), go down another set of stairs and then through a meadow until you get to University Drive. This is the end of Charlie's Trail. Continuing on your hike, a short distance west on West Campus Road (100 m), the trail heads south (left) opposite the tennis courts. At the fork, turn right and wind through a wooded area,

Esquimalt Lagoon. NEIL BURROUGHS

crossing a paved access road. Turn right at the next junction and then straight-ahead at the four-way intersection. Turning left at the next trail marker will take you down a steep path. Turn left onto the gravel roadway behind the recreation centre.

At this point, you can choose a shorter walk by following the gravel roadway to College Drive, turning left and circling back to your starting point. If you prefer a longer walk, turn right on the gravel path and then right again on West Campus Road. Continue along the road about 60 metres, and take the steeply climbing trail on the left. After about 75 metres, turn left at the top, then right along a wide gravel trail about 50 metres further. Reaching the perimeter fence (along Wishart Road), turn left and follow the wooded trail along the fence. The trail crosses a wide gravel trail; go left on a well-established trail that forks right at the top of a steep incline. Take the trail through a wooded section and descend a long hill to join a gravel road. Turning left on this road takes you through a marshy area, past a gate, to University Drive, where you turn right. There is a marked trail about 70 metres past the boathouse that drops down to Colwood Creek. After crossing a wooden bridge and bearing left up a slight hill past a small brick building, take the wide gated trail to the rocky bluff where you will be rewarded with spectacular views of Esquimalt Lagoon and the Olympic Mountains. Rising steadily, the trail goes past a pump house and along a chain-link fence, ending at College Drive. To return to the trailhead, turn left onto College Drive and after about 400 metres, turn left down a gravel road, then 300 metres further, take an unmarked trail on the right. Cross a wooden bridge and stay left until you reach University Drive.

WORTH NOTING Dogs must be kept on leash and on designated trails. They must be on leash at all times within the Esquimalt Lagoon National Migratory Bird Sanctuary in order to protect habit and nesting areas. Watch for signs.

Esquimalt Lagoon The 3 km Coburg Peninsula (Ocean Boulevard) is a delight to all—open ocean on one side and the sheltered waters of Esquimalt Lagoon on the other. The lagoon, where swans, herons, ducks, and even eagles are found, is one of seven National Migratory Bird Sanctuaries in B.C. Both sides of the peninsula offer great birdwatching, especially at times of migration. In the early fall, you might be lucky enough to see the huge "kettles" of Turkey Vultures as they cross the Strait to the Olympic Peninsula and beyond.

Fort Rodd Hill and Fisgard Lighthouse National Historic sites These national historic sites are great places to explore and have a picnic, not to mention enjoy the panoramic ocean views. Fort Rodd Hill has some lovely trails through the property (including a rare Garry oak meadow) and out to the 150-year-old Fisgard Lighthouse. Tour the original 19th century buildings—an artillery fortress active from 1895 to 1956. Check with Parks Canada regarding open hours and fees. (see p.227).

OF INTEREST

- Hatley Castle, the dominant building on the university grounds, was built as a home for James Dunsmuir, premier of B.C. 1900–1902 and lieutenant-governor of the province from 1906–1909. Samuel McClure, a well-known Victoria architect, was commissioned to design the home, which took 2.5 years and $4 million to build.
- The estate was self-supporting with kennels, slaughterhouse, horse stables, laundry smokehouse and even its own Chinese village.

4b. Metchosin Shoreline   MAP 4b

DIFFICULTY/DISTANCE   Easy to moderate/0.3–7.4 km one-way, 14+ km loop

HIGHLIGHTS   Metchosin features some of southern Vancouver Island's most picturesque hiking destinations. Popular trails at Albert Head, Witty's Lagoon, Sea Bluff Trail and Devonian parks lead through forests and grasslands to salt marshes, sandy beaches, quiet lagoons, rocky shorelines, seaside bluffs and breathtaking seascapes. The area is a mecca for birdwatchers and habitat for a variety of plants and animals.

Best time to go   Anytime of year—spring is particularly good for birds and flowers.

ACCESS

To Metchosin   From Victoria, follow Highway #1 (Trans-Canada) west. There are several options to access Metchosin Road: take Exit 10 (Colwood), travel through the business "strip" of View Royal and Colwood and follow Sooke Road to the Metchosin Road junction (take a left); or (probably a little faster) from Victoria, continue on Highway #1 and take Exit 14 through Langford on Veterans Memorial Parkway to its end at a rock face and T-junction. Turn left (Latoria Road) and continue to another T-junction. Turn right onto Metchosin Road.

To Albert Head Lagoon Regional Park   Take the next left off Metchosin Road onto Farhill Road, then make an immediate right turn onto Park Drive (lower) which becomes Delgada Road and leads to limited parking at the beach (gated in the evening). From Victoria, allow 30 minutes driving time. The park is open 7 am to sunset.

To Witty's Lagoon Regional Park

To Tower Point   For the Tower Point section of the park, continue west on Metchosin Road from Farhill Road, past Duke Road and Chapel Heights Drive to a second Duke Road junction (Duke Road is a loop). Turn left off Metchosin Road onto Duke Road, then right onto Olympic View Drive to the park entrance. (See map, p.140.) In winter, the limited parking area is closed, so you must park on the road. Tower Point facilities include toilets and a picnic area. From Victoria, allow 40 minutes driving time. The Lagoon Trail at the west end of Olympic View Drive leads to the main part of Witty's Lagoon Park.

Main Access The main entrance to Witty's Lagoon is farther down Metchosin Road, just past Pears Road, with the parking lot, small office and access trail across from the Metchosin Golf Club. This is the best parking area and the closest access to the Nature House and Sitting Lady Falls. One can hike between the beach, the waterfall and the Nature Centre. The Nature Centre, a picnic area and toilets are wheelchair accessible. From Victoria, allow 40 minutes driving time. The park is open 8 am to sunset. Note that the stairs off the end of Witty Beach Road are closed, and there is no longer any beach access from this point.

To Mitchell Park Sea Bluff Trail Next along Metchosin Road is Wooton Road, on the left, which leads to Sea Bluff Trail. The trail is accessed from Wooton Road and also from Parry Road (off William Head Road) and Parry Cross Road. Parking is very limited. From Victoria allow 45 minutes driving time.

To Devonian Regional Park For Devonian, the final shoreline park in the series, continue on Metchosin Road past Metchosin town centre (where Metchosin Road becomes William Head Road) to Devonian Park. The picnic area and toilets near the parking area are wheelchair accessible. From Victoria, allow 45 minutes driving time. The park is *open sunrise to sunset.*

To Lester B. Pearson United World College of the Pacific From downtown Victoria, drive along Metchosin Rd to the intersection of Metchosin, Happy Valley and William Head roads, and go straight ahead onto William Head Road, passing My-Chosen Café on the right (Metchosin Road becomes William Head Road). Continue on Williams Head Road past Weirs Beach and the RV Resort (on left), and turn right at Pearson College Drive. Continue on Pearson College Drive for 1.6 km—follow signs to Visitor Parking. Allow close to an hour driving time.

Albert Head Lagoon Regional Park

HIKE DESCRIPTION

Albert Head Lagoon Trail Easy/0.3 km, one-way: This small CRD park (7.1 ha) encircles a picture-perfect lagoon that is almost closed off by its gravel berm. A diversity of plants grows along the berm and the lagoon nature sanctuary is great for birdwatching. Keep an eye out for Mute Swan, ducks, geese and other migrating waterfowl. There is a short stretch of cobble beach.

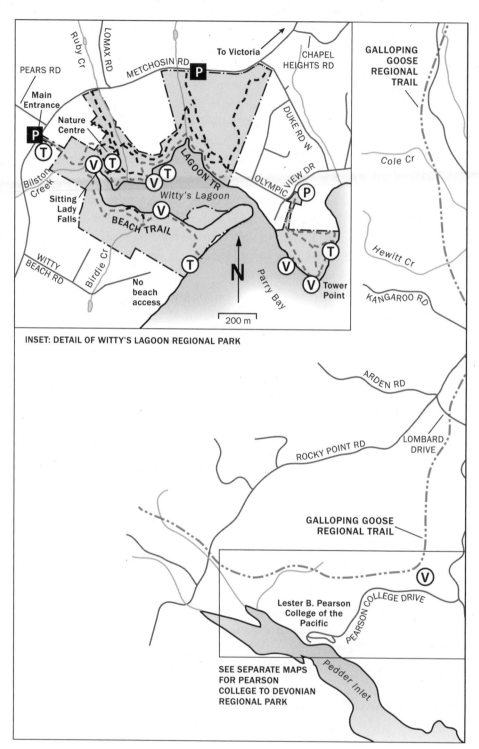

INSET: DETAIL OF WITTY'S LAGOON REGIONAL PARK

Map 4b   Metchosin Shoreline

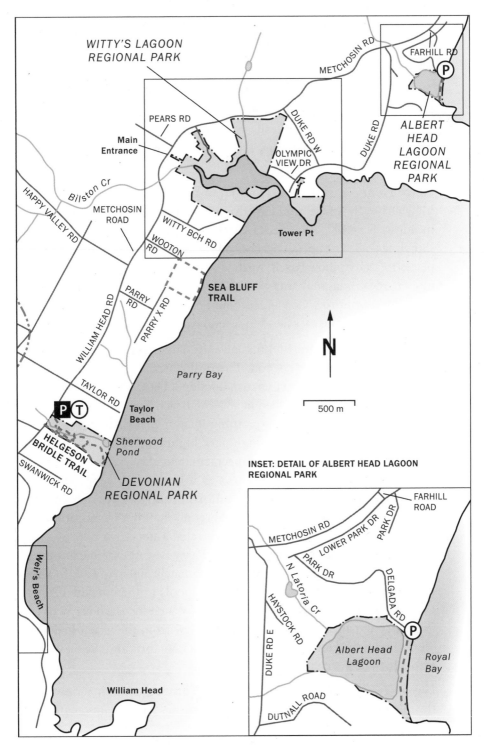

WITTY'S LAGOON
REGIONAL PARK

METCHOSIN RD

FARHILL RD

P

PEARS RD

DUKE RD W

DUKE RD

ALBERT
HEAD
LAGOON
REGIONAL
PARK

Main
Entrance

OLYMPIC
VIEW DR

HAPPY VALLEY RD

Bilston Cr

METCHOSIN
ROAD

WITTY BCH RD

WOOTON
RD

Tower Pt

PARRY
RD

PARRY X RD

WILLIAM HEAD RD

SEA BLUFF
TRAIL

N

TAYLOR RD

Parry Bay

500 m

P T

Taylor
Beach

HELGESON
BRIDLE TRAIL

Sherwood
Pond

SWANWICK RD

DEVONIAN
REGIONAL PARK

INSET: DETAIL OF ALBERT HEAD LAGOON
REGIONAL PARK

Weir's Beach

FARHILL
ROAD

METCHOSIN RD

LOWER PARK DR

PARK DR

N Latoria Cr

PARK DR

DELGADA RD

DUKE RD E

HAYSTOCK RD

P

Albert Head
Lagoon

Royal
Bay

William Head

DUTNALL ROAD

WORTH NOTING   In 1846, Captain Kellett named Albert Head after HRH Prince Albert, husband to Queen Victoria, because of its proximity to Victoria. Just north of the parking lot is the site of Vancouver Island's first steam-powered sawmills.

Witty's Lagoon Regional Park

HIKE DESCRIPTIONS   Metchosin's Witty's Lagoon Regional Park (58.2 ha) has over 5 km of trails to explore, including two that skirt the lagoon. Though not adjoining, a loop trail at Tower Point is also part of the park.

Tower Point   Easy/1.2 km loop: From the parking area on Olympic View Drive, the gravel trail cuts through a bushy area to a large, grassy meadow. Several paths crisscross the meadow. Continue along the shoreline trail. The pocket beaches on the point's west side are excellent places to study pillow basalt, formed about 55 million years ago when molten rock (magma) was cooled by ocean waters. Hike along the bluffs for a front-row view of Harbour Seals just off shore. Short, steep scrambles down the rocks lead to several tiny, rocky beaches.

Beach Trail   Moderate/1.5 km, one-way: The Beach Trail is the most popular hike at Witty's Lagoon. The trail starts at the Nature Centre and leads down a sharp incline to a junction. (The path to the left is the Lagoon Trail, briefly described next.) The Beach Trail follows the right fork to the well-built bridge spanning Bilston Creek. Cross the creek to Sitting Lady Falls, a 50-m-high park highlight. There is a viewing platform here. The waterfall is spectacular in the winter and spring after heavy rains. The trail narrows as it begins its steepest descent to sea level and skirts the lagoon and its estuary salt marsh. Watch for Great Blue Herons foraging in shoreline shallows. A multitude of shorebirds and ducks frequent these protected waters.

The trail ends at the sandy beach on Parry Bay. At extreme low tide, the beach and sandspit stretch out approximately 500 m in length. This is the best time to explore the many tide pools in the intertidal zone. Do not disturb or remove any marine life. Watch for Harbour Seals in Parry Bay at times of higher tides. The view from the beach includes Tower Point, the Haystack Islets, Race Rocks, Victoria and the seascapes across Juan de Fuca Strait.

Lagoon Trail   Moderate/1.7 km, one-way: From the trail junction near the Bilston Creek bridge the Lagoon Trail swings left and curves around

Witty's Lagoon was the site of the village of the Ka-Kyaakan band in the 1850s when the first settlers arrived. Through the Douglas Treaties, the Hudson's Bay Company purchased Metchosin from the band for the equivalent in blankets of less than 44 British pounds. The village was abandoned in the early 1860s. The few surviving members, practiced in Songhees ways and traditions, moved to Esquimalt to join the main Songhees tribe. The park is named after John Witty, a neighbouring landowner from 1867 on.

the lagoon's north side to access the park service road and Whitney-Griffiths Point (picnic area, toilets and viewpoint). The trail continues east to Olympic View Drive, which links to Tower Point.

WORTH NOTING

- At the end of Olympic View Drive, there are sign-posted hiking and equestrian trails leading to the main part of Witty's Lagoon Regional Park. Use the Tower Point parking lot, as parking at this trail access is very limited.
- There are several bridle paths on Witty's Lagoon's north side.
- Protect fragile vegetation by keeping to the paths.
- Witty's Lagoon is one place where cyclamen (in the primrose family) grows wild.
- Tides permitting, a 3 km one-way hike from Witty's Lagoon to Taylor Road or Devonian Park is possible. The hike follows the shelving, pebble beach.
- For information on the park's Nature Centre hours, interpretive programs and wheelchair access, contact CRD Parks (see p.226). A pamphlet is available detailing over 160 species of birds seen at Witty's Lagoon.

Mitchell Park Sea Bluff Trail

HIKE DESCRIPTION

Sea Bluff Trail Easy/1.2 km loop: Sea Bluff Trail winds around open fields, through woods and past an irrigation pond. Sea views along the 50-m-high bluffs look south across Parry Bay to William Head and the Olympic Mountains. Only the perimeter trail has public access. The open space in the centre is part of an operating farm. Please do not hike over this area and do not disturb the sheep. Dogs MUST be leashed at all times, and keep the gate closed. Public access depends on this.

WORTH NOTING   Geoff and Jacqueline Mitchell, long-time Metchosin residents, donated the property for the Sea Bluff Trail.

Devonian Regional Park

HIKE DESCRIPTION

Beach Trail, Devonian Park   Moderate/0.9 km, one-way: This trail at the CRD's Devonian Regional Park (14 ha) winds through a shady Douglas-fir and bigleaf maple forest carpeted in a lush, seasonal growth of ferns. The route twists and turns along Sherwood Creek (there are a few steep sections) to emerge at a cobble beach on Parry Bay. Here you will find an impressive view of Race Rocks, the Olympic Mountains and Juan de Fuca Strait. You might even spot a pod of Orca. Sherwood Pond is a year-round birdwatcher's delight.

WORTH NOTING   The Helgesen bridle trail contours down to the beach along the park's western boundary.

NEARBY   There are many other municipal parks, trails and green space corridors in Metchosin. (See the Western Metchosin section on p.149.)

Pearson College to Devonian Regional Park

HIKE DESCRIPTIONS   There are several options: a one-way route, which works if you can do a car shuttle from Devonian; and a loop route. Combinations of trails, including shorter loops (or same route out and back), e.g., from Pearson College to the ocean and back, or Devonian to Weir Beach, along the ocean and back, are also possibilities. There are a number of interesting forest trails in Pearson Woods that the general public are allowed to use. Parking is available at Devonian Regional Park and Pearson College, and limited parking is available at Weir's Beach (approx. 3.6 km from My-Chosen Café).

Pearson College to Devonian Regional Park   Easy-moderate/7.4 km one-way: Park one vehicle at Devonian and drive to Pearson College (see access above) and park in the visitor parking. Note that the only toilets are at Devonian Regional Park. There are no public toilets at the college.

At Pearson College, check out the 13 m skeleton of a Grey Whale at the front of the third building on the right. In 1990, over several months, the students cleaned the skeleton and assisted in preparing it for

- Captain Kellett of HMS Herald named Parry Bay and William Head after his friend, the noted Arctic explorer, Rear Admiral Sir William Edward Parry.
- Sherwood Pond used to be one of many lagoons found along the Metchosin coast. Its barrier spit eventually closed off the lagoon, leaving it, and a population of sea-run Cutthroat Trout, landlocked. Usually trout fry leave for the ocean in their second or third year and return to spawn in their fourth. This population adapted to fresh water for life. The cobble barrier is porous enough to allow some water passage, so the level of the pond can vary by as much as two metres.

display. A spectacular achievement! From here, start the hike at the south end of the parking lot by going over a little wooden bridge. From the little bridge, a 50 m trail climbs steeply to meet the steps up to the Godin/Newton Observatory. Take a right at the first connected trail, then a left, and take the steps up to the observatory for a great view of the Olympic Mountains. From here you can follow forest trails to Pearson College Drive, then the Ron Weir Trail to Weir Beach and on to Devonian (see directions below), or you can take a delightful loop inland, which includes the Barde Knockie Trail—the original route to Sooke, returning to Pearson College Drive and thence to Weir Beach and Devonian. If you choose the latter, going inland (north) from the observatory, follow the track down to a tree with a yellow marker (25 m) and turn left onto the narrow trail at the second yellow marker leading into the woods. Keep to the main trail towards Pedder Bay (Barde Knockie Trail), and stay on the right side of the creek. Right turn at the T-junction, and you will know you are on the right trail by the sections of wooden boardwalk. Travel northwest first along the shore then along the river, staying on the right side (keep the water on your left). The area near Pedder Creek is muddy and wet in winter but well worth the sudden cascade of Pearson Falls (a trickle in summer). Exquisite ferns!

Climb the trail up to the northwest corner of the soccer field and cross diagonally to the southwest corner. Look for the sign for the "Galloping Gosling", leading up (to the left) to the Galloping Goose Regional Trail. After approx. 1.25 km on the Goose, turn right onto

Map 4b
Metchosin
Shoreline (detail)

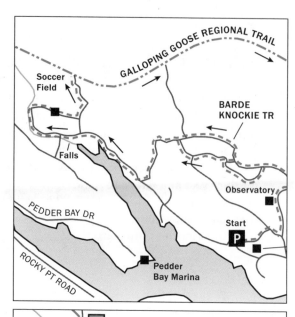

DETAIL OF TWO CAR OPTION
FROM PEARSON COLLEGE TO
DEVONIAN REGIONAL PARK

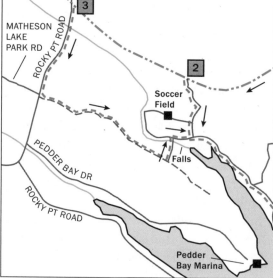

DETAIL OF RETURN LOOP TO
PEARSON COLLEGE VIA THE
GALLOPING GOOSE REGIONAL
TRAIL

the trail leading to Pearson College Drive—the turnoff back into the woods is clearly signed.

Once you reach Pearson College Drive, you have two choices—for a shorter hike, you can turn right to return to the parking lot, or you may continue to Devonian Regional Park. If you choose the longer route, turn left on Pearson College Drive, and about 0.5 km along the Drive, watch for a sign for the *Ron Weir Trail* (there is a cement barrier below

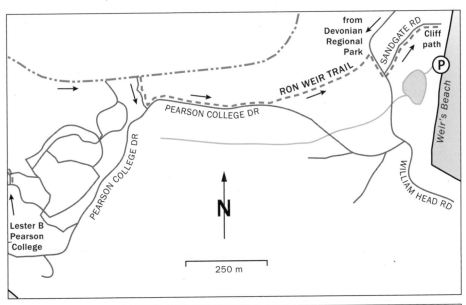

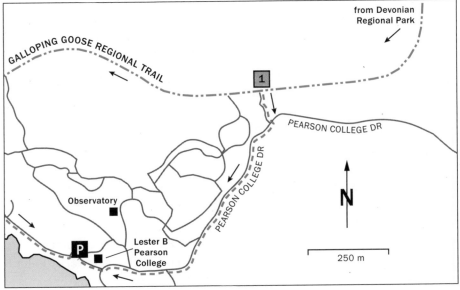

the sign). This 0.45 km trail through the woods is more pleasant than walking along the road.

Follow the trail to William Head Road and turn right (toward the ocean). Left on Sandgate (first street on the left) leads to north end of Weir Beach. The freshwater lagoon at the Weir's Beach RV Resort hosts many bird species in winter, some resident, some on migration. If you are lucky, you may also see deer and River Otter. Note that periodically, seaweed will build up on the beach and can be a VERY unpleasant smell (one that will linger on shoes and clothes). At the south end of Weir Beach, there is a steep bit of rock face that can be very slippery—use caution. This is where you leave the beach and walk along the cliffs—a path that has some beautiful views—to Devonian Regional Park. Once you reach Devonian, complete your trip by collecting your parked vehicle and driving back to Pearson College parking lot to retrieve your other vehicle.

If you have only one vehicle and want the longer walk, you could retrace your steps for an "out and back" route, or try the loop route described below.

Pearson College to Devonian Regional Park Loop   Easy-moderate/10+ km loop: As above from Pearson College to Devonian, but return to Pearson College on foot via a route that includes a longer portion of the Galloping Goose Trail. From Devonian, turn left onto William Head Road then right on Lombard, from which you can get onto the Galloping Goose Regional Trail (see p.146/147). Turn left (south) on the Goose, toward Sooke. Watch for the sign indicating the trail to Pearson College (#1 on inset map). Turn left onto the trail and follow it to Pearson College Drive, where you turn right to return to the parking lot and your vehicle. Alternatively (for a longer hike or if you miss that turn at #1), keep walking to a slight right turn in the Goose and a sign for the Galloping Gosling—a trail through the woods to the Pearson College soccer field (#2 on inset map). The walk down the hill takes you to the field near the marina, and then you can walk in the forest close to the shore of Pedder Bay (stay left at the first junction, and right at the next one) and emerge at the tennis courts in Pearson College. The parking lot (and your vehicle) is close by. If you miss both turns described above and cross Rocky Point Road, you have gone further than you need to, but can still get back to the college. Turn left (south) onto Rocky Point Road (#3 on inset map) and left at the trail across from the entrance to Matheson Lake Park Road. Go through the field toward Pedder Bay Marina (about 500 m). Turn left at the trail junction, cross Pedder Bay Creek and turn right. This will get you onto the trail that follows the shoreline to Pearson College.

4c. Western Metchosin   MAP 4c

DIFFICULTY/DISTANCE   Easy to strenuous/varies

HIGHLIGHTS   Metchosin has many delightful parks and trails, including some of the prettiest parts of the Galloping Goose Trail. Matheson Lake Regional Park (157 ha) features a loop trail that circles the lake and provides opportunities for hiking, nature appreciation and wildlife viewing. Roche Cove Regional Park (163 ha) offers over seven kilometres of hiking trails for you to enjoy the beauty and seclusion of the cove. There are ocean and hilltop viewpoints and the forests harbour groves of large oldgrowth cedars. Metchosin's lesser known rural hiking trails and parks are all worth exploring.

Best time to go   Anytime of year, but some hiking trails are better in summer or early fall (drier weather).

CAUTIONS

- Mosquitoes can be problematic in low-lying regions.
- In wet weather, or just after, trails near lakes, creeks and boggy areas can become extremely muddy and slippery.
- Dogs are prohibited at Ayum Creek Regional Park Reserve.

Ayum Creek.   TOD CARNAHAN

Map 4c Western Metchosin

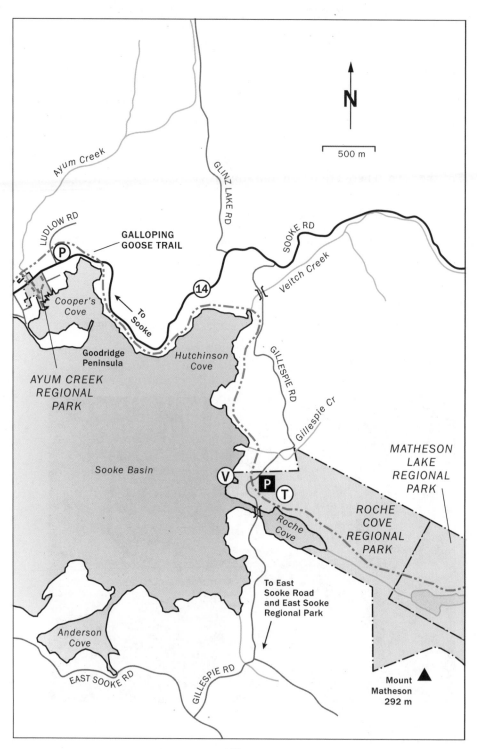

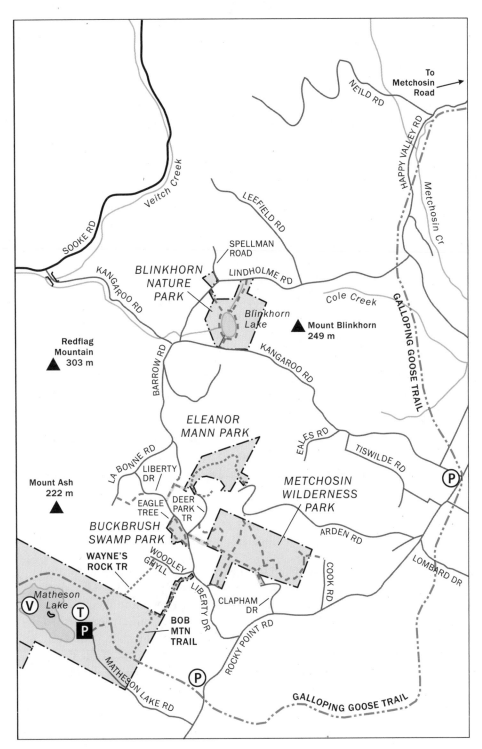

Matheson Lake Regional Park

ACCESS   Follow Highway #1 (Trans-Canada) west from Victoria and take Exit 14 to Langford. Drive south on Veterans Memorial Parkway to Sooke Road. Turn right and head west towards Sooke. From Sooke Road turn left on Happy Valley Road, then right on Rocky Point Road and right again onto Matheson Lake Park Road to the parking lot. From Victoria, allow 35 minutes driving time. This CRD park is open sunrise to sunset.

HIKE DESCRIPTION

Matheson Lake Loop   Moderate/3.8 km loop: Start from the beach and picnic area, a short walk from the parking lot, with Matheson Lake on your left. Hike the trail to Wildwood Creek and continue around the lake's north side. Be prepared for some up and down hiking. Avoid any trails on the right that lead away from the lake. Watch for cyclists and equestrians at the junction with the Galloping Goose Trail.

At Matheson Lake's west end, cross Matheson Creek on a bridge near an old dam and backtrack east to your starting point. The seasonal trail west along Matheson Creek passes a waterfall and roughly parallels the Galloping Goose Trail to Roche Cove (see p.154). About halfway along the lake's south side, take the side trail to a small point of land and lake viewpoint.

WORTH NOTING

* Western redcedar and Douglas-fir dominate the low-lying forest. You can identify lodgepole pine on the rocky outcrops. Willow and dogwood prefer areas near the lakeshore. In the spring, listen and watch for woodpeckers.

OF INTEREST

The trail along the creek from Matheson Lake to Roche Cove was an "old-timers'" portage trail in the 1850s and '60s. The route was part of the Lake Passe (to Pedder Bay) and on to Weir's Beach (which became known as the Barde Knockie Trail), from Sooke to Bilston Farm and on to Victoria. The part of the Lake Passe Trail along Matheson Creek is still in use, as is that part of the Barde Knockie Trail within the Lester B. Pearson College of the Pacific property.

Map 4c Matheson Lake

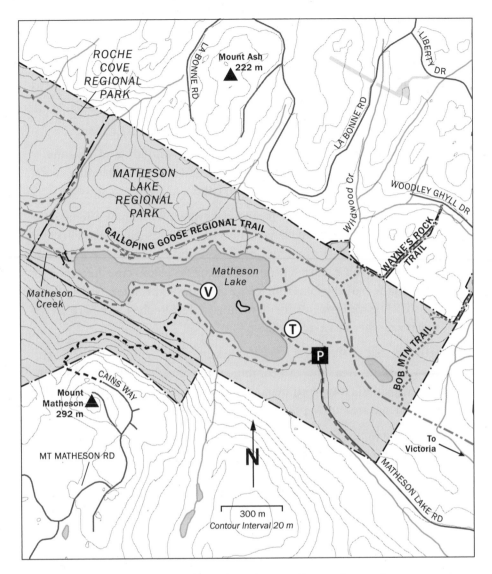

- Matheson Lake is a popular swimming, angling and canoeing destination.
- Bicycles and horses are restricted to the Galloping Goose Trail.

NEARBY The Galloping Goose Trail intersects the park and connects with Roche Cove Regional Park. From the Galloping Goose at Wildwood Creek a trail leads up to Wayne's Rock and also accesses the steep *Bob Mountain Trail* and other district trails and parks (e.g., Eleanor Mann Park). *Wayne's Rock Trail* and *Bob Mountain Trail* can also be accessed from the Matheson Lake Loop Trail by taking a short trail from the parking lot to the Galloping Goose and heading left to Wayne's Rock Trail, which can be part of a loop through Buckbrush Swamp and back to the Galloping Goose (see below), or right to Bob Mountain Trail. See also West Shore Parks and Recreation for maps and detailed information http://www.westshorerecreation.ca/

Roche Cove Regional Park

CAUTIONS Low-lying areas may be wet, muddy and seasonally impassable. On the Matheson Creek Trail beware of protruding roots. This trail is steepest nearer Matheson Lake.

ACCESS From Victoria follow Highway #1 (Trans-Canada) and take Exit 14 to Langford. Drive south on Veterans Memorial Parkway to Sooke Road. Turn right and head west towards Sooke. Shortly after the 17 Mile House, turn left onto Gillespie Road and continue another 3 km to the parking lot. From Victoria, allow 45 minutes driving time. This CRD park is open sunrise to sunset. The Roche Cove parking lot toilets are wheelchair-accessible.

HIKE DESCRIPTIONS Several hiking trails begin near the Roche Cove parking area. You can combine some of these with the Galloping Goose Trail to create your own loop hike. It is a short walk to the park's small picnic area and a pocket beach on Roche Cove.

Galloping Goose Trail Easy/4.5 km to Matheson Lake, one way: Take the Galloping Goose east to Matheson Lake along a relatively flat, wide, gravel trail. As you travel through the old railway rock cuts, look for the splashy yellow flowers of stonecrop, a succulent that blooms in the late spring. Near the 34 km marker, a short, steep side trail (which also links with the Matheson Creek Trail to Matheson Lake) descends to the head of Roche Cove. This protected cove, near the mouth of Matheson Creek, has a tidal mud flat beach and rocky shoreline.

Cedar Grove Trail Moderate/1.9 km, one-way: At the north end of the parking area the trail winds uphill past mossy rock outcrops and through a forest of large bigleaf maple trees. Follow the Cedar Grove Trail signposts. There are confusing junctions and cross paths on the way. One marked trail goes to a former viewpoint, now obscured by trees.

Swing east at a major fork to a grove of cedars. A few trees here are over 500 years old. Continue east to pass an alder forest on the left.

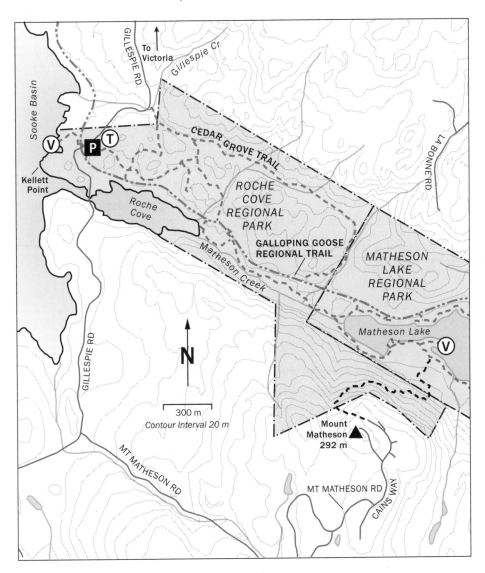

This is a good birdwatching area in the spring or fall. The trail, now less distinct, eventually drops down to the Galloping Goose Trail, near Matheson Lake Regional Park's western boundary. Take the Galloping Goose back to the starting point. Just before the parking lot is a great view of Roche Cove.

Matheson Creek Trail   Moderate/seasonal: From the parking area, follow the Galloping Goose Trail to Roche Cove's east end (near the

34 km marker) and the start of a seasonal trail through a lush forest to Matheson Lake. High water may render the route impassable in the winter. There are two creek crossings (one on stones, the other on a log) and some changes in elevation. Watch your step carefully.

The bracken fern is profuse in this temperate rainforest. One highlight is a grove of western redcedars. Maintain a stealthy pace through the low-lying, often muddy areas. You will have a better chance of catching a fleeting glimpse of a salamander, particularly near rotten logs.

Kellett Point   Easy/150 m, one way: On the west side of Gillespie Road, a trail leads from the Roche Cove parking lot to Kellett Point, three tiny beaches, lovely grassy slopes and beautiful views of Sooke Basin and the Olympic Mountains. Kellett Point is an excellent picnic area.

WORTH NOTING

- Watch for Belted Kingfisher and River Otter at Kellett Point and Roche Cove.
- Migrating ducks and shorebirds frequent area waters in the early spring and late summer.
- Bicycles and horses are restricted to the Galloping Goose Trail.

Roche Cove to Ayum Creek Regional Park Reserve

DIFFICULTY/DISTANCE   Easy, mostly level paths /10 km round trip.

CAUTIONS   There are two dangerous street crossings. There are no services at Ayum Creek.

ACCESS   Free parking is available at Roche Cove Regional Park off Gillespie Road, where toilets are located. Limited parking is also available at the Ayum Creek end, roadside just south of the creek, and some on Ludlow Road.

OF INTEREST

Roche Cove (and Roche Harbour, San Juan Island, USA) is named after Richard Roche (later Captain), RN, who served as midshipman under Captain Henry Kellett (for whom Kellett Point is named) aboard the Herald. In 1845, Captain Kellett first had to take the Herald to the Arctic in search of Sir John Franklin before undertaking a survey of Victoria and Esquimalt harbours and Sooke Inlet, a year later. Roche also served as mate (again with Captain Kellett) on the Arctic exploring ship Resolute, 1852–54.

HIKE DESCRIPTION The hike begins across Gillespie Road on the Galloping Goose trail. The route goes north following the shore of Sooke Basin with some splendid views over the water to East Sooke Park and the Olympic mountains beyond. The Salish people referred to this stretch as Saseenos or " the sunny land sloping gently up from the sea". Except for two ravines, the trail is mostly flat and wide. Where the trail passes over Veitch Creek, there is an interesting sign telling the story of the first Vancouver Island sawmill built there by Walter Colquhoun Grant in 1849. Beside the trail, especially in spring, there are numerous wildflowers such as common camas, death camas, fawn lily, Hooker's onion, stonecrop, thimbleberry, larkspur and Nootka rose. At Cooper's Cove, there is a dangerous street crossing of Sooke Road, which has been made less hazardous with a traffic stoplight. The Galloping Goose trail continues to Ludlow Road where the route leaves the Goose and turns left towards Sooke Road where the access to Ayum Creek Reserve is located to the right. The route recrosses Sooke Road near the Shell gas station and proceeds along the south side of the road to the bridge over Ayum Creek. A trail into the reserve begins on the west side of the bridge and proceeds alongside the creek out to the estuary before looping back. By crossing a narrow channel at low tide, a further trail can be accessed. This is a favourite birdwatching spot for shorebirds and raptors. Nest boxes have been built for the uncommon purple martin and during nesting season their melodious gurgling calls can be heard. The route can then be retraced back to the Galloping Goose at the pedestrian crossing, either via Ludlow Road, or by carefully walking alongside Sooke Road. It is worth noting that excellent ice-cream is available at the Shell station on Sooke Road.

NEARBY   Matheson Lake is directly east of Roche Cove. The Galloping Goose Trail intersects both regional parks.

Blinkhorn Lake Nature Park

ACCESS   From Victoria, proceed as for Matheson Lake to Sooke Road. Head west on Highway #14 (Sooke Road) and turn left on Kangaroo Road. Continue a little past Lindholm Road and watch for the trailhead on the left. There is very little roadside parking.

HIKE DESCRIPTION
Blinkhorn Lake Nature Park (18.2 ha) is a pleasant spot to visit, with a woodland trail encircling a picturesque lake and lowland. There are opportunities for birdwatching and nature appreciation. Side trails lead to Lindholm Road trailheads. Hiking is fine all year-round; other uses are best in dry weather.

OF INTEREST

Blinkhorn Lake and mountain are named after Thomas Blinkhorn. He and his wife, Anne, arrived in 1851 as independent settlers to manage Captain James Cooper's Metchosin farm. Years earlier, as a stockman in Australia, Blinkhorn had rescued Captain Sir John Franklin, lost in the bush. Thomas Blinkhorn served as magistrate from 1853 to his death in 1856.

Metchosin Wilderness Park, Buckbrush Swamp, Eleanor Mann Park, Bob Mountain Trail and Wayne's Rock Trail

CAUTIONS

- Roadside parking is very limited at most trailheads. The best place to park is at either of two designated Galloping Goose Trail lots: one at the junction of Rocky Point and Kangaroo roads; the other farther along Rocky Point Road, about 4 km past Kangaroo Road. From these parking lots, you can walk to several area trailheads (see map p.151).

- Eleanor Mann Park trails and the Bob Mountain Trail are very steep and challenging.

ACCESS   Follow Highway #1 (Trans-Canada) west from Victoria and take Exit 14 to Langford. Drive south on Veterans Memorial Parkway to Sooke Road. Turn right and head west towards Sooke. From Sooke Road (Highway #14) turn left on Happy Valley Road, then right on Rocky Point Road to the signed Galloping Goose parking lots. From Victoria, allow 35 minutes driving time. The trails are open sunrise to sunset.

HIKE DESCRIPTIONS

Metchosin Wilderness Park (40.5 ha)   This park is situated between Arden Road and Clapham Drive and is also known as 100 Acre Wood. On a hot day, the park is an excellent destination for a cool, shady hike. There are quiet woods, small creeks and great opportunities for nature appreciation and birdwatching. Trailheads are located on Liberty Drive, Deer Park Trail Road, Arden Road, and at the main signposted entrance on Clapham Drive. Various corridors and bridle paths link the park with Eleanor Mann Park and neighbourhood trails.

From the Clapham Road entrance (limited roadside parking), follow the main trail through a stand of alders. At a major trail junction, bear left, cross a wooden bridge and hike west through the park to Liberty Drive, directly opposite the Buckbrush Swamp Trail. Or turn right at the junction on a 3 km circular hike that winds through the deep forest and around marshland.

In the shadows of tall western redcedars, gigantic sword fern thrive on the forest floor. You will also see bracken fern, salal and ocean spray. Thickets pervade around the marsh and in the spring, its east end is rife with swamp lantern (skunk cabbage). Part of the loop trail traverses drier terrain where the forest has more Douglas-fir mixed with the cedars, and Oregon grape mingles with trailside salal.

Buckbrush Swamp Trail   The trailhead is located on Liberty Drive at Eagle Tree Place. Trails link with Metchosin Wilderness Park and Matheson Lake Regional Park. An easy, signposted loop trail circles Buckbrush Swamp and provides opportunities for wetland observation and birdwatching.

Eleanor Mann Park (17 ha)   Trailheads are located on Arden Road and Deer Park Trail Road. Trails connect to Metchosin Wilderness Park. The steep trail to a viewpoint off Deer Park Trail Road is for hiking only. A variety of forested hiking trails and bridle paths snake through the park.

Bob Mountain Trail   The north end trailhead is on Liberty Drive, near Woodley Ghyll Drive. Located within Bob Mountain Park (1.3 ha), the Bob Mountain links Metchosin Wilderness Park with the Galloping Goose Trail, near Matheson Lake. The Bob Mountain Trail is challenging—very steep and strenuous.

It follows a narrow park corridor south to Matheson Lake Park's northern boundary, turns west and then descends south to the Galloping Goose Trail. Expect numerous confusing side paths and places where the route is indistinct.

Wayne's Rock Trail   Access is off Woodley Ghyll Drive. The trail runs south to Matheson Lake Park and connects with the Galloping Goose Trail, just east of Wildwood Creek.

WORTH NOTING

- Many unmarked old roads, bridle paths and side trails lead to private property. Please stay on the main routes and do not trespass.
- Equestrians share many area trails. Be courteous to all trail-users.
- Cycling is only permitted on the Galloping Goose Trail.
- For more information on Metchosin trails contact the District of Metchosin (see p.226).

NEARBY   Four Metchosin shoreline parks along Metchosin Road (Albert Head, Witty's Lagoon, Sea Bluff Trail and Devonian) are close by (see p.138). The Galloping Goose Trail (see p.198) intersects the region and is accessed at several points, notably along Rocky Point Road and at Matheson Lake Park.

4d. East Sooke   MAP 4d

DIFFICULTY/DISTANCE   Easy to strenuous/400 m to 10+ km, one-way

HIGHLIGHTS   The CRD's East Sooke Regional Park (1435 ha) is a hiker's paradise. Acquired in 1966 as a regional park, the park has 50 km of spectacular wilderness trails that offer a diversity of day hikes from short walks to longer, more challenging treks. Many trails intersect so you can create your own loop hike. East Sooke Park features breathtaking seascapes, dense rainforests, panoramic mountain viewpoints and superlative opportunities for wildlife viewing, birdwatching and nature appreciation.

Best time to go   Anytime of year, as each season brings different things to see (summer is generally good for whales, among other things), but remember that many of the trails become treacherous in wet weather, and can be dangerous in the heat of summer if hikers are not prepared.

HIKING DISTANCES   Hiking distances at East Sooke Park can be deceptive because of rough terrain and the surprising amount of up and down travel. Many trail intersections, overgrown old roads, side paths and game trails are unmarked and confusing. It is wise to begin your hike early in the day and not overestimate your capabilities. Always allow more than enough time to return to your vehicle before dark.

The major interconnecting trails are all well cut and signposted at key junctions. It is possible to shorten a hike and use one of these trails to return early, if necessary. Our map depicts officially signposted trails. Stick to the marked routes; more than one hiker has unintentionally spent an unexpected night in East Sooke Park.

CAUTIONS

- Most park trails are uneven and rocky. Expect protruding roots, loose rocks and steep sections. Wear adequate footwear and dress warmly. Chilling sea breezes, sea fog and strong winds are prevalent along the coast. Prepare for capricious weather.
- When hiking in coastal areas beware of dangerous rogue waves. Use extreme caution along cliff edges, bluffs and open rock faces.
- The Mount Maguire routes cross rough terrain and may not be suitable for children. Expect a lot of laborious up-and-down hiking. The hills get steeper the higher you climb.

Map 4d East Sooke

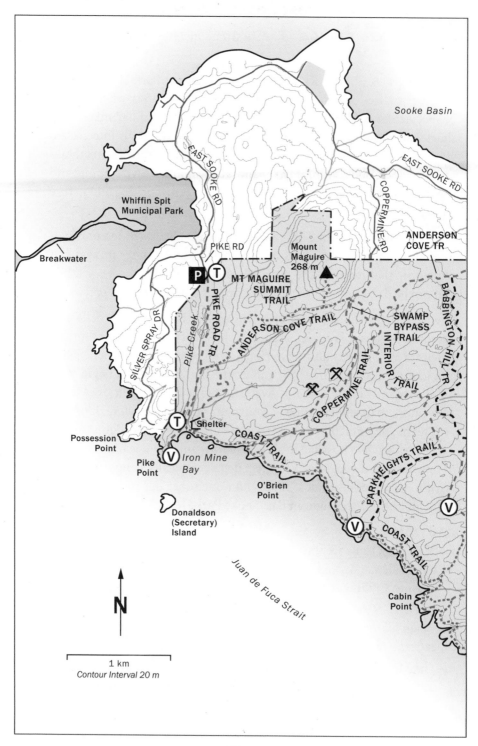

Sooke Basin

EAST SOOKE RD

EAST SOOKE RD

COPPERMINE RD

Whiffin Spit
Municipal Park

PIKE RD

Mount
Maguire
268 m

ANDERSON
COVE TR

Breakwater

P T MT MAGUIRE
SUMMIT
TRAIL

SWAMP
BYPASS
TRAIL

BABBINGTON HILL TR

SILVER SPRAY DR

Pike Creek

PIKE ROAD TR

ANDERSON COVE TRAIL

COPPERMINE TRAIL

INTERIOR TRAIL

Possession
Point

T Shelter

COAST TRAIL

PARKHEIGHTS TRAIL

Pike
Point

V Iron Mine
Bay

O'Brien
Point

V

COAST TRAIL

Donaldson
(Secretary)
Island

V

Juan de Fuca Strait

Cabin
Point

N

1 km
Contour Interval 20 m

162

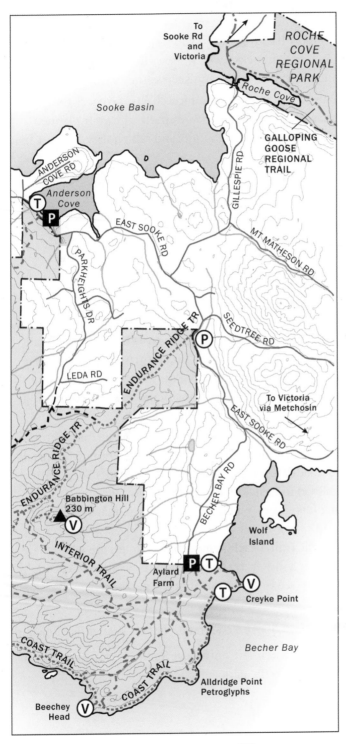

- Much of the Coast Trail traverses rocky ground and is sometimes hard to locate. If you become momentarily disoriented, to regain your bearings, simply backtrack until you locate a Coast Trail indicator (yellow markers on rocks), which shows the designated route. In general, avoid any inland paths and keep to the coast.
- Carry good maps (consider a topographical chart) and check the park information boards closely. Familiarize yourself with your planned destination prior to your hike. GPS units and cell phones may not work in all parts of the park.
- Never hike alone and allow ample time for a return journey. If hiking the complete Coast Trail, consider leaving a second vehicle at your destination parking lot or arrange for a ride back to your starting point.
- Low-lying sections of the inland trails may flood over the winter. Carry an adequate supply of water. Do not rely on creeks.

ACCESS

The park is open 8 am to sunset.

A) To reach the park, take the Old Island Highway (#1A) to Sooke Road. Follow Sooke Road (#7) to Happy Valley Road, turn left and continue down Happy Valley. Turn right on Rocky Point Road, which becomes East Sooke Road, and leads to park entrances and designated parking lots at Aylard Farm, Anderson Cove, and Pike Road.

B) Alternatively, follow Highway #1 (Trans-Canada) west from Victoria and take Exit 14 to Langford. Drive south on Veterans Memorial Parkway to Sooke Road. Turn right and head west towards Sooke. Turn left onto Gillespie Road to East Sooke Road. See below for how to access designated parking lots. From Victoria, allow approximately an hour's driving time (34 km).

At Aylard Farm, the trail, beach approach and toilets are wheelchair accessible. Customized hiker transportation is available through Trailhead Taxi Service (see Information Sources, p.226).

ACCESS to *Aylard Farm*

A) From Rocky Point/East Sooke Road, take a left on Becher Bay Road.

B) From Gillespie Road, turn left onto East Sooke Road, then take a right on Becher Bay Road to the park entrance.

HIKE DESCRIPTIONS

Aylard Farm to Becher Bay   Easy/400 m, one-way: With nearby park facilities (picnic sites, toilets), good access to sandy beaches and other hiking options, Aylard Farm is a popular destination for a family outing. A short, mostly flat 10-minute hike from the parking lot leads through the remains of old apple orchards and open meadows to the sandy Becher Bay beach. A set of stairs drops down to the beach. From here, take a side trip to the Creyke Point lookout (with a view of the coast from Metchosin to Victoria) and the strange rock formations at the headland. From Aylard Farm, you can follow the *Interior Trail* to access Babbington Hill (230 m). The steep route to the summit is tiring but worth the effort. The view across Juan de Fuca Strait to the Olympic Mountains is spectacular.

Aylard Farm to Beechey Head   Moderate/3 km, one-way: From the parking area, hike through the old Aylard farm site to Becher Bay. Turn right and follow the Coast Trail for about 30 minutes to Alldridge Point, which features Coast Salish petroglyphs and was designated a Provincial Heritage Site in 1927. At this point take a shortcut inland trail back to Aylard Farm or continue along the coast to Beechey Head, a popular fishing spot and excellent viewpoint. This headland is one of the best places on southern Vancouver Island to observe the annual "Hawk Watch" or Turkey Vulture migration (see p.18). Retrace your steps along the coast or return to the parking lot on the slightly shorter inland trail.

ACCESS to *Anderson Cove*
As per Aylard Farm access to East Sooke Road.

A) From Rocky Point/East Sooke Road, continue past Gillespie Road to the parking area on the left.

B) From Gillespie Road, turn right onto East Sooke Road to the parking area, on the left. A beautiful picnic site (with toilets) is located across the road on Anderson Cove.

HIKE DESCRIPTION

Anderson Cove Trail to Mount Maguire   Moderate to strenuous/3 to 3.5 km, one-way: Begin your hike up Mount Maguire from either the Pike Road or Anderson Cove trailheads (there is also a connecting trail from the end of Coppermine Road). Both main sign-posted routes lead to the Mount Maguire summit trail, but the Pike Road access is slightly shorter. Initially fairly easy, the difficulty increases as you gain altitude. There are portions of the trail that might be flooded in the winter, and in wet conditions, the already slippery trail up Mount Maguire, particularly the open rock faces, could become dangerously slick. In the summer, this area is very dry and the fire hazard extreme.

From Anderson Cove, the trail negotiates a steep grade and follows a meandering southwest course through the shady forest. There are links to several of the park's less-travelled inland connectors, including the Babbington Hill and the Interior trails. Near a swampy area you will reach the junction with the Coppermine Trail. A little south down the Coppermine Trail are some old mine workings.

Keep west along the Anderson Cove Trail and soon you will reach the marked turnoff for Mount Maguire. Swing north for the summit. The short but strenuous final pitch to the top includes a dried-up creek bed with loose rock, which may be slippery. You can rest on a bench at the summit—the viewpoint at the Mount Maguire summit (268 m) takes in the surrounding hills, Juan de Fuca Strait, the Olympic Peninsula, Donaldson Island, Iron Mine Bay and Possession Point.

ACCESS to *Pike Road*

As per Aylard Farm access to East Sooke Road.

A) From Rocky Point/East Sooke Road, continue past Gillespie Road to Pike Road. Turn left to small parking lot.

B) From Gillespie Road, turn right onto East Sooke Road, drive past Anderson Cove and turn left onto Pike Road to one of two small parking areas.

HIKE DESCRIPTIONS

Pike Road Trail   Easy/1.5 km, one-way: From the parking lot, wind your way south on the level, smooth gravel path, an old logging road, through forest to meadow and beach. Part way to the coast, the Anderson Cove Trail comes in on the left, near Pike Creek. This is the cutoff for Mount Maguire, for those hiking in from the west. Turn left onto the Anderson Cove Trail and continue east to the Mount Maguire cutoff (see description above). The difficulty increases as you gain altitude (200+m elevation gain).

The Pike Road Trail makes a short descent as it nears the sea. Just before Iron Mine Bay, a trail on the right leads past old mine workings to a viewpoint at Pike Point, a small isthmus of land that juts out into the strait. The bay's name is a reminder of the iron and copper mining enterprises that operated in the area between 1863 and 1971.

Iron Mine Bay features a beautiful pebble beach and views of the bay, Juan de Fuca Strait, Donaldson (Secretary) Island and Pike Point. At low tide, explore the intertidal zones at Iron Mine Bay. You will discover a myriad of marine life and seaweeds. A small shelter is located above Iron Mine Bay at the west end of the Coast Trail.

Coast Trail   Strenuous/10 km, one-way, 6 hours: The most challenging trail at East Sooke Park is the 10 km route from Iron Mine Bay to Aylard Farm—a true west coast wilderness experience. Recommended for energetic and experienced hikers only, the trail has magnificent seascapes, views of the Olympic Peninsula, secluded coves and bays, cliffs, rocky bluffs, seaside chasms, deep ravines and an atmosphere of remoteness and adventure.

Start at either end of the Coast Trail, but the CRD recommends you begin at the Pike Road trailhead and travel east to Aylard Farm.

From the parking lot take the wide Pike Road Trail south to Iron Mine Bay. Turn east to follow the Coast Trail signpost. The first trail junction you reach, on the left, loops north to the Anderson Cove Trail. Near O'Brien Point you can choose from two trails that branch off onto the Coppermine Trail.

Halfway down the Coast Trail, where sharp, jagged cliffs thrust up from the waters of the strait, pelagic cormorants roost along the rocky bluffs. The birds are often seen diving for food. The Parkheights Trail junction is close by. Near Cabin Point, several paths swing inland to join the Interior Trail in the vicinity of Babbington Hill. A particularly confusing section is on the descent from the bluffs as you approach Cabin Point. Here, near an open area just before the headland, watch closely for the correct turn, to the right, where the trail drops into a steep gully. Avoid the false trail straight ahead.

The restored trap shack near Cabin Point dates back to the early 1900s and is testimony to East Sooke's rich fishing history. Take the time to explore the wide pebble beach on the nearby shallow bay. This sheltered cove is a great choice for a rest stop. Continue east along the rugged coastline bluffs toward Beechey Head. The lookout is a popular place during the annual fall hawk migration (Hawk Watch). From Beechey Head, you can take one of two inland paths to Aylard Farm or keep along the coast via Alldridge Point. Check out the petroglyphs while you are at the Point.

Endurance Ridge Trail   Strenuous/2.9 km, one-way: Along the west side of East Sooke Road (between Becher Bay Road and Gillespie Road and close to Seedtree Road) watch for a small roadside parking area. This is the trailhead for the Endurance Ridge Trail, a rough alternate route to Babbington Hill and Cabin Point. It starts with a long, grueling 2.9 km climb up Endurance Ridge. The trail runs southwest to connect with the routes to Babbington Hill, the Interior Trail and the Coast Trail, near Cabin Point.

WORTH NOTING

- The Aylard Farm area and toilets are the only part of the park suitable for wheelchair use.
- Please do not disturb or remove any plants, animals or marine life.
- Bicycles are not permitted on East Sooke Park trails.
- Dogs must be under control at all times. From June 1 to September 15, dogs must be on leash when passing through beach and picnic areas and are not allowed to stay. The park provides important habitat for many resident and migrating birds. Please do not let your dog chase the birds, and remember to dispose of your dog's waste with the rest of your garbage.

NEARBY   Roche Cove and the Galloping Goose Trail are situated just to the northeast, off Gillespie Road (see pp.154 and 198).

HIKING DISTANCES

Approximate minimum hiking times in East Sooke Park, one-way:
Coast Trail (Iron Mine Bay to Aylard Farm, including Pike Road Trail) 6 to 7 hours
PLUS

Aylard Farm to Beechey Head (via coast)	1 hour
Aylard Farm to Beechey Head (via inland trail)	45 minutes
Aylard Farm to Babbington Hill	1 hour, 15 minutes
Beechey Head to Cabin Point	1.5 to 2 hours
Cabin Point to Iron Mine Bay	3.5 to 4 hours
Coppermine Trail to Interior Trail (from coast)	1 hour
Parkheights Trail to Interior Trail (from coast)	30 minutes
Pike Road to Iron Mine Bay	30 minutes
Pike Road to Mount Maguire	1.5 hours
Anderson Cove to Mount Maguire	2 hours
Anderson Cove to Babbington Hill	2 hours

Anderson Cove to Pike Road, via the Anderson Cove Trail	2 hours
Interior Trail, from Anderson Cove Trail, to Parkheights Trail	1 hour, 15 minutes
Interior Trail, from Anderson Cove Trail to Aylard Farm	3 hours
Endurance Ridge to Babbington Hill	1.5 to 2 hours

OF INTEREST

- East Sooke Park's flora and fauna is as diverse as the nature of its trails. The woodland floor in the shady, dense lowland forest (Douglas-fir, western redcedar, alder and hemlock, with Sitka spruce closer to the coast) is carpeted with a variety of ferns. Swamp lanterns (skunk cabbage) and fungi flourish in the wetter areas. The drier, upland forests are mainly comprised of arbutus, Garry oak, hairy manzanita and lodgepole pine. Near the windswept coast, the ubiquitous salal thrives alongside kinnikinnick and Oregon grape, despite a constant barrage from high winds and sea spray. In the spring and summer, flower enthusiasts may find a variety of species, including Indian paintbrush, fringe cup, orange honeysuckle, patches of stonecrop, monkey flower, hardtack, blue camas, death camas, western buttercup, red columbine, Queen Anne's lace, seaside woolly sunflower, hedge nettle, fairy orchids, sea blush, Columbia tiger lily and many more.

- Offshore you may spot seals, sea lions and River Otter. Orca are common from the middle of May through September. Watch for Grey Whale, February to April.

- The park is home to resident and migratory birds, Raccoon, squirrels, grouse, Black-tailed Deer, Pine Marten, Mink and the occasional Cougar and Black Bear. Beechey Head is a prime spot to witness the annual fall Turkey Vulture migration or "Hawk Watch". Each year, hundreds of these birds gather overhead, in final staging prior to their lengthy crossing of Juan de Fuca Strait. The migration starts in mid-September and runs through the end of October, peaking around the end of September. For best viewing, choose a sunny, warm day, in the late morning to early afternoon. That's when there are scores of birds wheeling and soaring high up in the daily thermals. As well as the Turkey Vulture, try to identify other raptors like Red-tailed Hawk, Merlin, Cooper's Hawk, Bald Eagle, Peregrine Falcon, Osprey and American Kestrel.

Map 4e Sooke Potholes

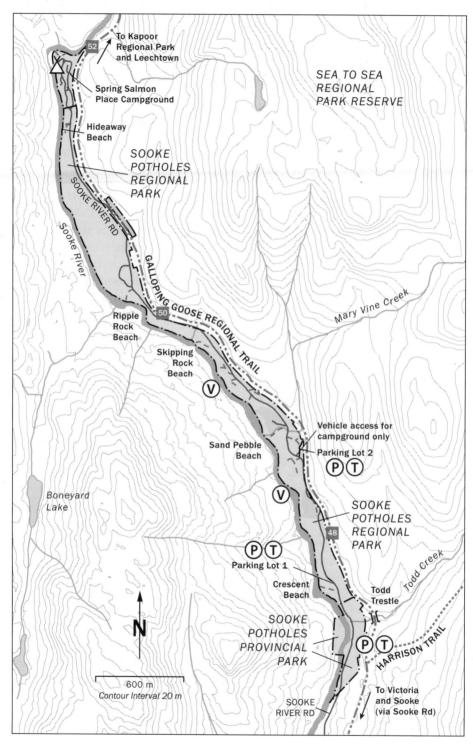

To Kapoor Regional Park and Leechtown

52

Spring Salmon Place Campground

Hideaway Beach

SOOKE POTHOLES REGIONAL PARK

SOOKE RIVER RD

SOOKE River

GALLOPING GOOSE REGIONAL TRAIL

SEA TO SEA REGIONAL PARK RESERVE

Mary Vine Creek

Ripple Rock Beach

50

Skipping Rock Beach

V

Sand Pebble Beach

Vehicle access for campground only

Parking Lot 2

P T

Boneyard Lake

V

SOOKE POTHOLES REGIONAL PARK

48

P T

Parking Lot 1

Crescent Beach

Todd Trestle

Todd Creek

N

SOOKE POTHOLES PROVINCIAL PARK

P T

HARRISON TRAIL

600 m
Contour Interval 20 m

SOOKE RIVER RD

To Victoria and Sooke (via Sooke Rd)

4e Sooke Potholes and Sooke Hills   MAP 4e

DIFFICULTY/DISTANCE   Easy to moderate/up to 5 km, one way

HIGHLIGHTS   There are two parks along the Sooke River: the Sooke Potholes Provincial Park (7.28 ha), and the CRD Sooke Potholes Regional Park (63.5 ha). Both are "must-see". The polished rock pools and potholes of Sooke Potholes Provincial Park were naturally carved by glacial action during the last ice age. The water in this very popular park is clean and clear, providing a wonderful swimming and picnicking destination. And since the Sooke River is an important Coho and Chinook salmon spawning river, this is a great place to view the annual salmon-spawning run. The regional park, north of the provincial park, was created in 2005. The park protects a 5 km corridor along the Sooke River's eastern banks and ensures public access to the spectacular upper canyon, river potholes and pocket beaches. Trails lead upriver to several bluff viewpoints. Both parks provide wildlife viewing opportunities and protect remnant oldgrowth Douglas-fir and associated sensitive plant communities that line Sooke River. The Sierra wood fern, a red-listed plant, is found in the provincial park.

Best time to go   All seasons provide a great experience, but summer is best for swimming and picnicking. Note that the Potholes parks and surrounding areas are largely undeveloped and care should be taken at all times when hiking.

CAUTIONS
- Avoid the cliff edges.
- After periods of heavy rain and in the off-season, beware of suddenly rising or falling water levels in the Sooke River. Dangerous, steep cliffs border the Sooke River. Wear proper footwear, exercise extreme caution near slippery rock surfaces and stay away from the drop-offs. Be particularly attentive with children.

ACCESS   From Victoria, follow Highway #1 (Trans-Canada) and take Exit 14 to Langford. Drive south on Veterans Memorial Parkway to Sooke Road. Turn right and head west towards Sooke. Just before the Sooke River bridge, turn right onto Sooke River Road and continue north to the provincial park.

The first parking lot along Sooke River Road is approximately 2.5 km from the intersection of Hwy #14 and Sooke River Road, and is one of the places where the Galloping Goose Regional Trail crosses the road. There is a trail (2.3 km) from here to the provincial park. Travel north on Sooke River Road another 2+ km north to the gate for the Sooke Potholes Provincial Park. There is no hiking at this location. This park provides good access to swimming pools just to the north and inside the regional park. From Victoria, allow 45 minutes travel time.

To enter the regional park, continue north on Sooke River Road and park in one of the two small parking lots. Summer hours are 8 am–9 pm. Near Parking Lot 1 in the regional park is where the main lodge of the failed Deertrail development once stood. You can follow short groomed trails to high bluffs that overlook dazzling green pools in the river canyon. Note that there is a road from Parking Lot 2 to the Spring Salmon Place Campground, but the gate is closed to vehicle traffic Oct–June.

HIKE DESCRIPTION   The majority of park trails are largely undeveloped, but a number of well-defined routes wander up the Sooke River Valley. There are short trails going down to the river at various points, often with steep sections closer to the river. Avoid cliff edges. Follow the Sooke River Road for a gentler grade, but remember cars will be travelling on this road as well.

Highlights are the river canyons, gorges, waterfalls, rapids, pocket beaches and potholes.

The Galloping Goose Regional Trail runs parallel to the park and provides a nice alternate hiking route. Watch for bicycles on this route and possibly horses.

WORTH NOTING

- Sooke Potholes Provincial Park is a day-use only park. Two pit toilets, located at the parking lot, are the only facilities.

- Camping is available at the Spring Salmon Place Campground. The campground, located at the north end of Sooke Potholes Regional Park and adjacent to the Galloping Goose Regional Trail, operates on a first-come, first-serviced basis. No online or phone reservations. It is operated by T'Sou-ke Nation (open July 10–October 5 under a pilot project with the CRD for the 2015 season). Contact T'Sou-ke Nation or CRD Regional Parks for current information (see p.226, 227). Dogs must be on-leash in campground.

- Dogs must be on leash when passing through beach and picnic areas and are not allowed to stay in these areas from June 1 to September 15. Keep dogs under control and on the trail, and clean up after your pet.

- The Sooke River is an important wildlife corridor for all species, including Black Bear and Roosevelt Elk, and the Sooke Potholes Regional Park connects the Sooke Hills and the CRD Sea to Sea Regional Park Reserve (3874 ha). The reserve stretches from Saanich Inlet to Juan de Fuca Strait.

- Together, the Sooke Potholes Provincial Park, the Sooke Potholes Regional Park, Sooke Mountain Provincial Park, and the Sea to Sea Regional Park Reserve protect more than 4300 ha of land.

NEARBY

Sooke Hills Area and Sooke Mountain Provincial Park With the exception of the provincial and regional parks, much of this area is included in CRD's Sea to Sea Regional Park Reserve. Sooke Mountain Provincial Park (435 ha) is also part of an extensive wilderness corridor preserving wildlife habitat and fragile watersheds. The park has been a backwoods recreation area since its creation in 1928. This part of the Sooke Hills is home to Black Bear, Grey Wolf, Cougar, Roosevelt Elk and Black-tailed Deer. You may hear grouse, squirrels or even owls. For further information and maps, contact CRD and BC Parks (see p.226).

CAUTIONS

- This is a backcountry area with no facilities. There are no maintained hiking trails.

- There is primarily walk-in access only, which involves strenuous hiking in a remote area.

- Carry appropriate maps, compass and/or GPS unit. Be prepared for all kinds of weather. You may encounter Black Bear or Cougar. Fire closures may apply.

- Cyclists use some portions of some trails.

- Motorized vehicles (public) are prohibited in the Sea to Sea Regional Park.

ACCESS

To Sooke Mountain Provincial Park, Sheilds Lake, Crabapple Lake and Empress Mountain Main access is from Harbour View Road, off Sooke Road. The first 2+ km from Sooke Road (Hwy #14) are paved and then give way to a somewhat rugged gravel/dirt road. Limited parking is available at the turnaround near the locked gate. Public entry over adjacent private lands has always been a contentious issue. Obey all posted notices and do not trespass.

Map 4e   Sooke Mountain Provincial Park

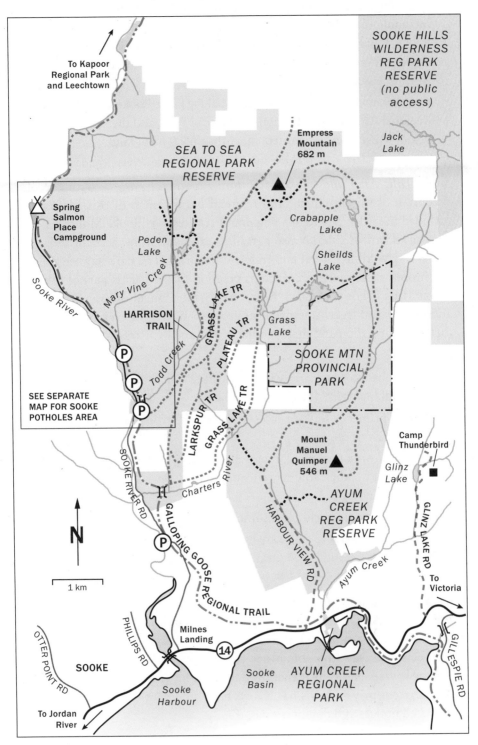

To Kapoor
Regional Park
and Leechtown

SOOKE HILLS
WILDERNESS
REG PARK
RESERVE
(no public
access)

SEA TO SEA
REGIONAL PARK
RESERVE

Empress
Mountain
682 m

Jack
Lake

Crabapple
Lake

Sheilds
Lake

Spring
Salmon
Place
Campground

Peden
Lake

Mary Vine Creek

Sooke River

HARRISON
TRAIL

GRASS LAKE TR

PLATEAU TR

Grass
Lake

SOOKE MTN
PROVINCIAL
PARK

Todd Creek

P

P

P

SEE SEPARATE
MAP FOR SOOKE
POTHOLES AREA

LARKSPUR TR

GRASS LAKE TR

Mount
Manuel
Quimper
546 m

Camp
Thunderbird

Glinz
Lake

SOOKE RIVER RD

Charters River

AYUM
CREEK
REG PARK
RESERVE

GLINZ LAKE RD

N

GALLOPING GOOSE REGIONAL TRAIL

P

HARBOUR VIEW RD

Ayum Creek

To
Victoria

1 km

PHILLIPS RD

Milnes
Landing

14

OTTER POINT RD

SOOKE

Sooke
Harbour

Sooke
Basin

AYUM CREEK
REGIONAL
PARK

GILLESPIE RD

To Jordan
River

The trail from the end of Harbour View Road to Sheilds Lake (approx. 13 km, with an overall elevation gain close to 500 m) is rugged, with many dips and bumps, as well as a number of river/stream crossings, some with remains of old bridges and even some with stepping stones.

To Grass Lake From Sooke River Road or the Galloping Goose at the Charters River trestle, take the old road along Charters River and climb up to Grass (Grassie) Lake.

To Peden Lake and Empress Mountain a rough, overgrown old road (known by locals as the Harrison Trail) off Sooke River Road, south of Todd Creek, provides trail access to Peden Lake and to the top of Empress Mountain from the west. From Peden Lake, you can reach Grass Lake, but the trails are very rough and have some steep sections through dense bush.

Both the Charters River and Harrison trails can also be accessed from the Galloping Goose Trail. In addition, there are rough, old trails connecting the Charters River and Harrison trails and the Harbour View Road and Charters River route, and others connecting Harrison Trail and the top end of Harbour View Road route, at Empress Mountain.

HIKE DESCRIPTIONS If you enjoy strenuous hiking on wilderness routes, this is the place for you. Expect a maze of old roads, indistinct side paths and game trails throughout this remote area. Most routes are poorly marked and not maintained. Some cross open rocky hillsides, others peter out and you may have to bushwhack. It is best to travel with someone familiar with the region. Contact local hiking clubs.

OF INTEREST

The Sooke River's unique potholes and smooth, deep pools were caused by glacial action 15,000 years ago. As the melting ice sheets passed by they scoured the soft sandstone and deposited large boulders, which wedged in the river. Strong, surging currents buffeted and twirled the rocks between canyon walls and on the river bottom, carving the geological formations we see today. The Sooke River, southern Vancouver Island's second largest and important spawning grounds for Chinook and Coho, is a great place to view the annual fall salmon run.

Harbour View Road is a rough, mostly uphill "route" with numerous washouts and loose rocks. Part-way up the steady ascent along Harbour View Road are several spur roads on the right. The old road in to Mount Manuel Quimper is on the right side about 2 km from the gate. The Quimper summit (540 m) is accessed via rough, obscure routes that travel mostly uphill. Closer to the top, the trail narrows and there are washouts and loose rocks. About 8 km in, and just outside the Sooke Mountain Provincial Park's northern boundary, the old road divides. Turn left and a steep climb up the old road base will take you to Sheilds Lake. Sheilds Lake has good water access, lots of spots for wilderness camping, and there is a boat you can use, old but still floats! Grass (Grassie) Lake lies further to the west. Keep straight on and you will end up at Crabapple Lake. Today they are good lakes to fish and popular camping spots. Continuing beyond Crabapple Lake, if you know the territory, you can journey all the way to the top of Empress Mountain (673 m). The summit views are unmatched.

Grass (Grassie) Lake (approx. 3 km)   From Sooke River Road or the Galloping Goose at the Charters River trestle, take the old road along Charters River and climb up to Grass Lake's west end. There is no beach access and at times, lots of bugs. There is a trail around the west and then northern tip of Grass Lake that will take you to Sheilds Lake. This trail is has some large elevation changes—somewhat easier trail down, tougher and uphill going from Sheilds to Grass Lake). You can return by retracing steps or take a longer loop back along Harbour View Road (see above and map p.174).

If you know the area, one might combine several trails for a longer hike and/or a loop (some of these trails are rough, overgrown and have big elevation changes): Harbour View Road past Crabapple Lake to Empress Mountain, returning west past Sheilds Lake on logging roads past Peden Lake to the Sooke River. From there, follow the Galloping Goose Trail to the Charters River.

NEARBY

Kapoor Regional Park, accessed on foot or by bicycle (there is no direct vehicle access) from the Galloping Goose Trail, lies along the Sooke River past Sooke Potholes Regional Park at the end of the Galloping Goose Regional Trail (7.3 km from the regional park). The park offers a bike rack, information kiosk and toilets at the rest area. Numerous old trails and roads wind through the property, which includes almost two kilometres of riverfront land, providing habitat for Golden and Bald eagles, as well as deer, Northern Alligator Lizards, and Pileated Woodpeckers.

Camp Thunderbird, a YM-YWCA camp has developed good bush trails around their facility. From Sooke Road, cut right (north) onto Glinz Lake Road (just west of Gillespie Road) and continue to the camp. The signed trails here are generally open to the public from mid-October to mid-April. The gate at the entrance to the private property is usually locked, but there is a sign on the gate with a number to call for access. You must obtain permission before hiking there. There is limited parking outside the gate. Contact the downtown Victoria Y for information and permission (www.victoriay.com or 250-386-7511 and ask for the Camp Manager).

Camp Barnard, a 101 ha camp west of Sooke Potholes, is used year-round by a variety of organizations. This is private property, but public access information is available at www.campbarnard.ca. The camp offers wilderness camping and residential camping, and day-use opportunities, including a great hike up a steep, rocky trail from the north end of Young Lake (the trailhead is inside the camp property) up to a hilltop viewpoint on Bluff Mountain (535 m) and a delightful loop trail around Young Lake (5.7 ha). In Sooke, turn right from Sooke Road onto Otter Point Road and continue for about 5 km to Young Lake Road. Turn right and follow the signposts to the camp. Parking and toilets (outhouses) are available.

OF INTEREST

- The Harrison Trail is named for the late Claude Harrison, a former Victoria mayor, who, along with the Alpine Club, lobbied for the creation of Sooke Mountain Provincial Park.
- Three lakes, Sheilds Lake (often misspelled) was called Smokehouse Lake by hunters who once smoked venison nearby, Grass (Grassie) Lake, named for its shoreline reeds, and Crabapple Lake, for the trees around its circumference, were watering stops for pack animals during the Leechtown gold rush in 1864.
- Kapoor Regional Park is adjacent to the historic site of Leechtown, a mid-19th century gold mining town, and is the site of former railway logging operations. Relic mining and logging equipment lies throughout the area.

4f. Whiffin Spit

DIFFICULTY/DISTANCE   Easy/1.2 km, one-way

HIGHLIGHTS   Whiffin Spit Park is a beautiful sandy breakwater that separates Sooke Harbour and the Juan de Fuca Strait. A seaside trail to the end of the spit rewards hikers with striking seascapes and mountain vistas. The spit extends out into Sooke Inlet and provides a semi-natural barrier that protects Sooke Harbour from the often-turbulent sea conditions out on more exposed waters. The spit has been reinforced at a couple of breach points to allow continued access to the spit's east end. Winter bird watching is popular here and there are opportunities to view marine mammals and intertidal marine life.

Best time to go   The park is delightful in any season, but October to April are best for birdwatching.

CAUTIONS   Dress warmly. The spit can be windy, the weather changeable.

ACCESS   **From Victoria**, take Highway #1 (Trans-Canada) west to Exit 14, (Langford). Turn left on Veterans Memorial Parkway, continue south to Sooke Road and turn right. From the traffic lights in Sooke (at the junction of Otter Point Road and West Coast Road (#14), travel west another 1.8 km on West Coast Road to Whiffin Spit Road. Turn left and continue all the way to the beach and the parking area. From Victoria, allow 45 minutes driving time.

HIKE DESCRIPTION   The 1.2-km trail along Whiffin Spit begins at the parking lot at the end of Whiffin Spit Road. It is a pleasant 25-minute hike, past sand and gravel beaches and grassy areas, to the east end of the winding spit. One narrow section is only nine metres wide. Along the way are majestic views of Sooke, the Sooke Hills, the Juan de Fuca Strait and the Olympic Mountains. An added bonus is the chance to observe the reversing tidal currents near the marine navigation light at the end of Whiffin Spit. Time your hike for lower tides and follow the trail one way and, on your way back, beachcomb along the shoreline.

WORTH NOTING
- Whiffin Spit, with its sandy shoreline and adjacent shallow waters, is an excellent destination for winter birdwatching (October to April).

Whiffin Spit. NEIL BURROUGHS

Among the shorebirds and migrant species to watch for are loons, scoters (diving ducks) and Western Grebes.

- Flocks of seagulls congregate in the offshore waters. Sightings may include Bonaparte's, Heermann's, Glaucous-winged and California gulls.
- Scan the skies for Bald Eagle and Turkey Vulture; the waters for otters and harbour seals.
- The spit is a popular dog-walking area—dogs are required to be leashed for the protection of the environment and for public safety.
- Situated beside Quimper Park, a heritage site commemorating the 1790 arrival of the first European ship in Sooke waters, the spit is named after John George Whiffin, a clerk aboard the Royal Navy vessel Herald. The name Whiffin Spit was adopted in 1846.

NEARBY   The Sooke Potholes, the Galloping Goose Trail and other Sooke area hiking destinations are close to Whiffin Spit (see pp.171 and 198).

4g. West Coast Road: Sooke to Port Renfrew
MAP 4g

DIFFICULTY/DISTANCE   Easy to strenuous/varies

HIGHLIGHTS   Highway #14 (West Coast Road) stretches almost 73 km from Sooke to Port Renfrew and is the gateway to the Juan de Fuca Trail (see p.203). The seascapes enroute are unforgettable and several wild west coast beaches can be accessed via scenic rainforest trails, offering opportunities for wildlife viewing, nature appreciation and birdwatching.

Best time to go   Spring and fall for views of the migrating Grey Whale. Summer for the best weather, although storms can occur anytime of the year. Several of the trails to the beaches are extremely muddy and open to the winds and weather. Get the most out of Botanical Beach's incredible tide pools by timing your visit to coincide with the lowest tides…spring is good.

CAUTIONS
* Area rainforests are prime habitat for Black Bear and Cougar. Be alert when hiking, particularly when travelling with small children. It is recommended you leave your pets at home.
* Be prepared for torrential rains, dense sea fog and severe, blustery winds, which may occur at any time of the year and with little warning.
* Kayaking and canoeing are not recommended due to strong ocean currents.
* When beach hiking, beware of unexpected rogue waves. Check the tide tables carefully to avoid becoming marooned by high water. Tidal knowledge is crucial along many trails as headlands may be impassable at high tide. Storms and steady winds may increase the heights of predicted high water.
* You may encounter logging trucks and other industrial traffic along the West Coast Road and area logging roads. Always yield the right-of-way and drive defensively. Use your headlights.
* Use precautions against wood ticks. Avoid low bushes and tall grasses. These parasites are most problematic between March and June.

ACCESS   From Victoria, take Highway #14 (West Coast Road) to Sooke. Using the intersection of the West Coast Road and Otter Point Road in Sooke as the Km 0 mark, continue west and enjoy (see map, p. 182).

Sooke to Port Renfrew (all distances approximate)

Km 0	West Coast Road (Highway #14)/Otter Point Road intersection in Sooke (traffic lights)
Km 1.7	Whiffin Spit Road (access to Whiffin Spit hiking) (See p.178 for more information)
Km 21.7	French Beach (trail to beach)
Km 28.7	Sandcut Creek Trail (trail to beach)
Km 32.5	Jordan River bridge
Km 35	China Beach campground (trail to beach)
Km 36.7	China Beach day-use area (trail to beach/Juan de Fuca Trail access #1)
Km 56.8	Sombrio Beach (trail to beach/Juan de Fuca Trail access #2)
Km 66.4	Parkinson Creek access road (trail to beach/Juan de Fuca Trail access #3)
Km 72.4	Port Renfrew Recreation Centre/Deering Road junction (right turn for Cowichan Lake, Fairy and Lizard lakes)
Km 74.3	Cerantes Road (keep left for Botanical Beach/Juan de Fuca Trail access #4)

Starting at the junction of the West Coast Road and Otter Point Road in Sooke, continue west. Whiffin Spit Road (Km 1.7) leads to great hiking at Whiffin Spit Park (see p.178). At Km 10.4, you will see the wide expanse of Gordon's Beach. Look for the Sheringham Point lighthouse in the distance. The Sheringham Point Lighthouse Preservation Society is working to ensure the lighthouse, surrounding property, and historic public access are preserved and protected for the years to come.

ACCESS to *French Beach* (Km 21.7)   French Beach Provincial Park (59 ha) is a serviced, 69-site campground along West Coast Road. From Victoria, allow 45 minutes driving time. The picnic/day-use area and toilets are wheelchair accessible.

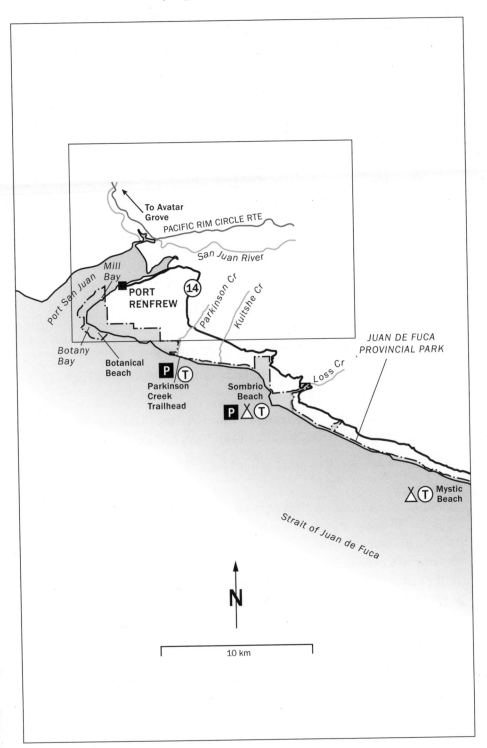

Map 4g West Coast Road

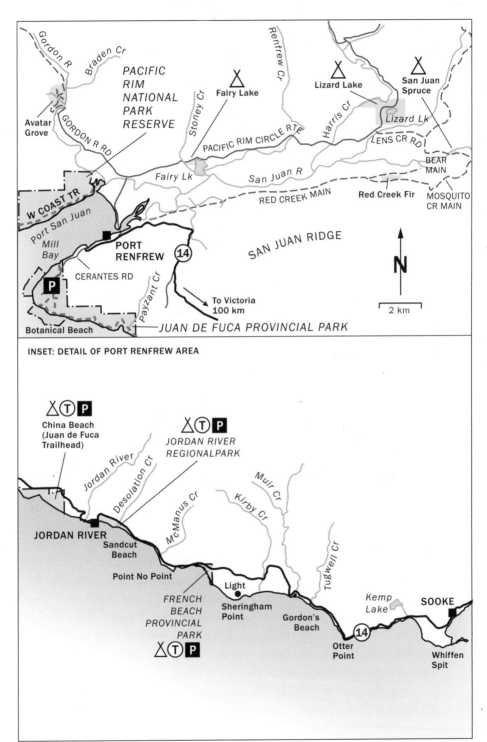

PACIFIC RIM NATIONAL PARK RESERVE

Gordon R
Braden Cr
Renfrew Cr

Fairy Lake

Lizard Lake

San Juan Spruce

Stoney Cr

Avatar Grove

GORDON R RD

Harris Cr

Lizard Lk

PACIFIC RIM CIRCLE RTE

LENS CR RD

Fairy Lk

San Juan R

BEAR MAIN

W COAST TR

RED CREEK MAIN

Red Creek Fir

MOSQUITO CR MAIN

Port San Juan

Mill Bay

PORT RENFREW (14)

SAN JUAN RIDGE

N

P

CERANTES RD

Payzant Cr

To Victoria 100 km

2 km

Botanical Beach

JUAN DE FUCA PROVINCIAL PARK

INSET: DETAIL OF PORT RENFREW AREA

China Beach (Juan de Fuca Trailhead)

JORDAN RIVER REGIONALPARK

Jordan River

Desolation Cr

McManus Cr

Kirby Cr

Muir Cr

Tugwell Cr

JORDAN RIVER

Sandcut Beach

Point No Point

Light

FRENCH BEACH PROVINCIAL PARK

Sheringham Point

Gordon's Beach

Kemp Lake

SOOKE

(14)

Otter Point

Whiffen Spit

HIKE DESCRIPTION

French Beach Trail Easy/100 m, one-way: From the parking lot, a short (5 to 10 minutes), easy trail leads to French Beach. The shoreline view from the beautiful pebble and sand beach takes in Juan de Fuca Strait and the Olympic Mountains. The surf on this somewhat exposed shoreline can be impressive. Explore the 1.6 km beach from the north end, near the group camping area, all the way south, to where a trail curves inland at Goudie Creek. See BC Parks website for detailed maps of the area.

Other trails wind through the park's second-growth forest (Douglas-fir, western redcedar, western hemlock and Sitka spruce) and salt marsh. One trail, close to the parking lot, parallels Frenchome Creek and connects the beach with the West Coast Road. French Beach is a good spot to watch for Ospreys, eagles, and seabirds.

WORTH NOTING

* The French Beach campground is open year-round, but from October 12–March 1, when lower winter fees are in effect, no water, firewood or sani-station is available.
* No beach fires are allowed.
* French Beach is named for James George French, who settled in this area around 1890, and was a pioneer conservationist.

ACCESS to *Sandcut Creek Trail* (Km 28.7) The trailhead is not signed along the West Coast Road but this trail is worth exploring. The Sandcut Beach parking area is about 4 km east of the Jordan River town site and has an accessible toilet. The 22-site campground is 3.6 km west of Sandcut Beach. From Victoria, allow 1 hour driving time.

HIKE DESCRIPTION

Sandcut Creek Trail Easy to moderate/250 m, one-way: A pretty rain forest trail (15 minutes down; 20 minutes up) with a moderately steep descent leads from the West Coast Road to the beach, primarily a day-use area. In wet weather, the trail can be very muddy and the boardwalks slippery. Salal thickets, huckleberries, Oregon grape and a variety of ferns line the route. Look for large stumps with notches in them, dating back to the hand-logging era. These cuts are where early loggers inserted springboards to assist in tree falling.

Near the sea the trail levels off, negotiates some boardwalks and crosses McManus Creek. After a small hill the path emerges on a long sand and pebble beach. A shoreline highlight is where Sandcut Creek splits into two waterfalls near tidewater. To the east you will spot Point No Point. A low tide beach walk from Sandcut Creek to Jordan River is about 3 km, one-way. Desolation Creek, at the halfway point, must be forded and may be impassable when in flood. The beach trail ends just east of the Jordan River bridge.

Near the mouth of the Jordan River, at the north end of Jordan River Regional Park, you can find ample parking, a picnic site, toilets, fire pits and picnic tables. The campground has drive-in and walk-in self-contained sites, and provides pit toilets, drinking water, picnic areas, and fire rings, not to mention waterfront views. This location is often lined with campers and RVs. The Jordan River bridge is at Km 32.5.

WORTH NOTING

- The Sandcut Creek campground (Jordan River Regional Park) is open year-round on a first-come, first served basis. Costs are less November 1–March 31.
- The area near Jordan River is known as a prime surfing "hotspot".

ACCESS to *China Beach* (Km 35.3/Km 36.7)   The entrance to the 78-site China Beach campground is on the left at Km 35.3. A trail from the campground descends to Second Beach. Continue just over a kilometre west to reach the China Beach day-use area, the first (southern) of four access points for the Juan de Fuca Trail. Turn left at Km 36.7 to the lower parking area. A trail begins here and goes down to China Beach. (The upper parking lot is for Juan de Fuca Trail users.) From Victoria to China Beach, allow 1.5 hours driving time.

HIKE DESCRIPTIONS

China Beach Trails   Moderate/1 km, one-way: From the China Beach campground, a steep 1 km trail, with a series of seemingly never-ending stairs, leads to the cobble shoreline at Second Beach. There are benches en route to the beach. From the China Beach day-use area trailhead (in the lower parking area) a 1 km gravel trail plunges through the forest to sandy China Beach. A viewing platform offers vistas of Juan de Fuca Strait and the beach. Hike west to a waterfall or east along the shoreline between Second and China beaches. There are very large Sitka spruce (some hundreds of years old and 60 m tall) in this area. Each trail takes about 15–20 minutes to hike, one-way. Allow extra time for the climb back up.

China Beach to Mystic Beach (moderate to strenuous/2.5 km, one-way)
From the upper parking lot at the China Beach day-use area, follow the
signed trail west to Mystic Beach. This is the first (or last) campsite on
the Juan de Fuca Trail and the beach is very busy on weekends. The
trail rises and falls a fair bit and some hills are steep. This "rooty"
trail winds through a sun-dappled second-growth forest, with several
sections of boardwalk, plank bridges, and the Pete Wolfe Creek
suspension bridge—a highlight of the hike. Watch for muddy patches
and large roots. In the final stretch to the beach, the trail narrows and
turns steep. Be extremely careful here. The final portion of the trail
is a scramble down to a gently curving crescent of cobble and fine
sand (perfect for children). Once at tidewater, turn east to a waterfall
that pours down a high sandstone bluff, behind the cobble and sand
beach. The shallow cave-like hollows under the bluffs offer lots of
exploring for children. Remember to dress warmly; Mystic Beach can
be windy.

WORTH NOTING

- Common birds to watch for here and in other coastal regions
  are Steller's Jay, grouse, Varied Thrush, woodpeckers, warblers,
  Common Raven, Belted Kingfisher, Rufous Hummingbird,
  sparrows, Pacific Wren and many more.
- Vancouver Island's wilderness beaches and trails offer excellent
  opportunities to observe marine life. Spring and fall brings the
  migrating Grey Whale. Scan the waves for Orca, sea lions, seals and
  otters. Osprey, Bald Eagle, gulls, cormorants and a variety of
  seabirds are plentiful.
- Wear good footwear. Please keep to designated trails.
- Tide tables are posted at some trailheads.
- Water is available at the China Beach campground.
- Beach fires are not permitted.
- Cycling is not permitted on park trails but is allowed on the
  campground road network.
- Contact BC Parks for information on day-use fees, campground
  fees and camping reservations for French Beach and China Beach.

ACCESS to *Sombrio Beach* (Km 56.8) A few kilometres west of the
Loss Creek bridge watch for the Sombrio Beach trailhead turnoff, on
the left at Km 56.8. It's about 2.2 km down a rough, steep access road

Confused about kilometres?
1 metre is 3.3 feet
1 kilometre is .63 miles

to the parking area and trailhead. Note that the access road to Sombrio Beach is very rough and it is recommended only vehicles with four-wheel drive and good clearance attempt the road. This second access point to the Juan de Fuca Trail is a popular destination for day hikers, and in the winter months, provides great wilderness surfing. From Victoria, allow 2 hours driving time.

HIKE DESCRIPTION

Sombrio Beach Trail   Easy/250 km, one-way: From the parking lot, a gravel trail, with a few steep parts, (about a 50 m drop) meanders through a second-growth forest. A little before the beach there is a signed junction. The right fork (marked Kuitshe Creek) leads west along the Juan de Fuca Trail to a suspension bridge over Sombrio River and the West Sombrio Beach campsite. The beach on this side of the river is strewn with cobblestones and boulders that make walking difficult.

Keep left at the junction and continue through a small stand of old-growth trees to the beach and the East Sombrio campsites. You can explore the shoreline southeast for about 1 km. The beach is sandy and rocky and has some tidal shelves. At its south end an orange marker ball hanging in the trees indicates the beach access to the Juan de Fuca Trail. From here you can extend your hike to Sombrio Point or Loss Creek, but start early in the day. Expect to do lots of tiring up-and-down climbing beyond East Sombrio Beach, on a rough route with muddy and overgrown sections.

WORTH NOTING   There are two designated wilderness camping areas at Sombrio Beach—one at the east of the beach and one at the west end.

ACCESS to *Parkinson Creek* trailhead (Km 66.4)   From the Sombrio cutoff, continue west on the West Coast Road towards Port Renfrew. The Parkinson Creek access road is on the left at Km 66.4. This rough, narrow secondary road twists and turns for 3.8 km to the parking area. The Parkinson Creek trailhead is the third access point for the Juan de Fuca Trail. From here you can hike east to Sombrio or west to Botanical Beach. On the way in, there are numerous spur roads; generally keep right when in doubt. From Victoria, allow 2 hours, 20 minutes driving time.

HIKE DESCRIPTION

Parkinson Creek Trail   From the parking area, a moderately difficult trail follows an old logging road and snakes through slash and clearcuts near Parkinson Creek to the beach access, a little over 1 km away. Low tide reveals exposed tide pools on the beach's rocky shelf.

At the bottom of a long grade the West Coast Road curves left to meet Deering Road (Km 72.4) near the Port Renfrew Recreation Centre. Stop in for trail and tourist information.

ACCESS to *Botanical Beach* (Km 74.3)   From the West Coast Road/ Deering Road junction in Port Renfrew continue straight ahead on West Coast Road to Cerantes Road, near the government wharf. Turn left onto Cerantes Road and head west for 3 km to the parking lot and trailhead. Botanical Beach is the fourth (northern) access to the Juan de Fuca Trail. The parking lot, the western terminus of the Juan de Fuca Marine Trail is located at Km 47 of the trail, and provides access to nearby Botany Bay and Botanical Beach itself. The Botanical Beach day-use area offers parking, pit toilets, visitor information and picnic areas. While hiking on the trail, cars can be left overnight in the

---

OF INTEREST

Botanical Beach's uniqueness, with tidal pools filled with a variety of marine life, is of particular interest to marine biologists and other naturalists. Dr. Josephine Tilden chose it as the site of the University of Minnesota's marine station in 1900. Access at that time was by steamship from Victoria to Port Renfrew, then on foot along a muddy track. This difficult access was a contributing factor in the station's closure in 1907.

Botanical Beach parking lot. Please do not leave anything of value in your vehicle. From Victoria, allow about 2.5 hours driving time.

HIKE DESCRIPTIONS

Mill Bay Trail   Moderate/1 km, one-way: Part way in to the Botanical Beach parking lot, you will pass the signpost (on the right) for the Mill Bay Trail. The somewhat steep trail drops quickly at first and then gradually levels out as it nears sea level at Mill Bay. This partially protected cove on Port San Juan features a shell and pebble shoreline. Low tide is the best time to investigate the cave at one end of the beach.

Botanical Beach Loop   Moderate/3 km loop: From the parking area it is possible to loop around the Botanical Beach area in either direction. The trail to the right leads 0.5 km to Botany Bay and the one on the left follows an old logging road 1 km to Botanical Beach. Seaward, a high, sandstone headland separates these shorelines, but a 1.5 km inland trail links them. When tides are low enough you can follow the shelf right around the headland. At higher tides, use the headland bypass route. Orange balls hanging in trees mark beach access points. Boardwalks cross muddier sections of the trail. At Botanical Beach's east end, the Juan de Fuca Trail continues east along the coast. Orca and Grey Whale have often been seen swimming past the beach or feeding just off the points. Harbour Seal are often seen offshore, and both California and Northern sea lions can be found here from late August through May.

The main highlight of Botanical Beach is the relative ease with which you can see a profusion of intertidal marine life exposed on the sandstone shelf. Within the sea-carved tidal pools (one called the Devil's Billiard Table) you may encounter sea star, sea anemones, barnacles, mussels, sea cucumber, plant life and small fish. Some deeper pools may even hold a small octopus. Never touch, disturb or remove any tidepool life.

WORTH NOTING

• Very low (1.2 m and less) or minus tides are most desirable for tide-pool viewing. Be sure to have precise tidal information prior to your hike. Remember to add one hour for Daylight Saving Time.

• Periodically and unpredictably an unusually large wave (rogue wave) or a series of larger waves will hit the beach. These dangerous waves can sweep unsuspecting visitors into the water. Never allow children to play near the surf. Be extra careful when crossing surge channels.

- The shoreline and sandstone shelf is rocky and slippery. Wear proper footwear.
- No camping or fires are permitted at Botanical Beach. The nearest walk-in campsites are located 6 km to the east, along the Juan de Fuca Trail.

NEARBY Nearby Botanical Beach is the *Avatar Grove Recreation Site*, about a 15 minutes drive from Port Renfrew. A phenomenal yet threatened stand of giant old-growth western redcedar and Douglas-fir stand alongside the Gordon River in this wilderness area. A boardwalk has been constructed but good balance and basic hiking experience is necessary in some areas. Enjoy amazing views of massive trees and waterfalls—well worth a visit.

ACCESS From Port Renfrew turn onto Deering Road and cross the big bridge over the San Juan River and continue down Deering Rd. staying to the right at the next Y. Cross a small single lane bridge and turn left at the T-junction onto Gordon River Road. Stay on the main paved road and after approx. 5 km go left at the "Y" and cross a tall, beautiful bridge over the Gordon River. After crossing the bridge stay on the Gordon River Road. You will soon cross a small bridge at Baird Creek. Park on the right immediately after the bridge and look for the signs at the entrances on both the left and right side of the road to reach the Upper and Lower Groves respectively. The entrance to the forest on the right will take you to the Lower Grove, which is flatter and has some giant burly cedars and large Douglas-fir trees. Heading up on the left side of the road, you can visit the Upper Grove and see "Canada's Gnarliest Tree" at the end of the trail! This side is a bit steeper and has many large cedar trees along side the path. Note that there are no facilities at this site.

Port Renfrew area

In the San Juan River Valley, east of Port Renfrew, are two easy-to-get-to hiking destinations.

ACCESS to *Fairy Lake* From the Port Renfrew Recreation Centre, take Deering Road, cross the bridge over the San Juan River's south arm and continue north to a second bridge (over the river's north arm) and T-junction. (Gordon Main is to the left.) Turn right onto Pacific Marine

Road and follow the signs for Cowichan Lake. Approximately 2 km east of the T-junction, opposite a small rock quarry, watch for the trailhead, on the right.

HIKE DESCRIPTION

Fairy Lake Nature Trail   Moderate/1 km, one-way: The trail runs from the mainline through second-growth timber to the BC Forest Service Fairy Lake campsite. About 100 m before the campsite is Stoney Creek, which flows into Fairy Lake. In the summer months it is easy to cross; in the wet season the stream may be impassable, forcing hikers to backtrack. Turn right onto the old logging road you crossed on the way in for an alternate route out.

ACCESS to *Lizard Lake*   From Port Renfrew, take Deering Road to the Gordon Main/Pacific Marine Road T-junction. Turn right onto Pacific Marine Road and continue 12.5 km to the Lens Creek Main junction. Keep left on Pacific Marine Road (following the Cowichan Lake signs) and travel another 1.5 km to the entrance for the BC Forest Service Lizard Lake campsite. Just beyond the recreation site look for an old logging road (blocked) on the right. Park well off the road. The trail begins to your left and heads east.

HIKE DESCRIPTION

Lizard Lake Nature Trail   Moderate/1.5 km loop: The Lizard Lake Trail is rough and zigzags around Lizard Lake, but at some distance from it, so the trail can be quite dark. There are plenty of blowdowns in the surrounding forest. The trail skirts the lake's west end campsite to emerge onto Pacific Marine Road once again. Allow 35 minutes to complete the loop.

NEARBY

San Juan River Valley Trails   There are other rugged San Juan River Valley trails to explore near Port Renfrew. Varying in length from 0.5 to 6 km, they lead to river sandbars, a waterfall, a plank road, and the site of a former railway logging camp, along an old railway grade and to large trees. Note that some of the area's trails are difficult to locate, receive scant maintenance and are often seasonally flooded. The amazing San Juan Spruce is off Lens Creek Main/Bear Main roads, one of the ways to get to the Red Creek Fir, Port Renfrew's most famous tree. The other route to get to the Red Creek Fir trailhead is rough and often not drivable. The deteriorating 12+ km access road is a 4WD road, rough but worth the journey. Contact: portrenfrew.com for directions, maps, updates and further information.

See also the Ancient Forest Alliance map at https://www. ancientforestalliance.org/docs/8.5x11-Avatar-Grove-Map-Port-Renfrew-Front.pdf for details for the above listed hikes.

OF INTEREST

It is now possible to drive the *Pacific Marine Circle Route* on the southern tip of the island. There are two loops—downtown Victoria north on Hwy #17 to Swartz Bay and back to Victoria via West Saanich Road and Hwy #17, or Victoria—Port Renfrew—Lake Cowichan—Duncan—Victoria, via Hwy #1, Hwy #18, the paved Pacific Rim Circle Route Road, and the West Coast Road (Hwy #14). Both routes treat you to scenic views and stretches of beautiful forested areas.

5

Regional Trails

5a1. Lochside Regional Trail   MAP 5a

DIFFICULTY/DISTANCE   Easy, level, some paved/29 km one-way

HIGHLIGHTS   The Lochside Regional Trail is a 29 km multi-use corridor stretching from Victoria to Swartz Bay. The trail is popular with hikers, cyclists, runners and horse riders. Portions are wheelchair accessible. The route follows old rail lines, crosses three trestles, and traverses wetlands, rural working agricultural land and urban areas. It is a mix of pavement through residential areas and gravel or dirt surface through farmlands, horse paddocks and fields. The CRD's website has good information and maps covering in detail the entire 29 km. The trail intersects with the Galloping Goose Regional Trail, the first section of the Trans-Canada Trail.

Best time to go   Any time of year, but best in spring and summer.

CAUTIONS
- The trestles can be very slippery on cold days. In hot weather, carry enough water.
- Parts of the trail share or cross public roads. Be alert and watch for traffic. Farm equipment has the right-of-way.
- Rural sections of the trail may be muddy and slippery following heavy rains.

ACCESS   From downtown Victoria, follow the Galloping Goose Regional Trail to the official starting point for the Lochside Regional Trail at the Switch Bridge, a 100 m pedestrian overpass over Highway #1 (Trans-Canada) near a large shopping centre. This start is located at the 4 km mark of the Galloping Goose Regional Trail. Nearby parking

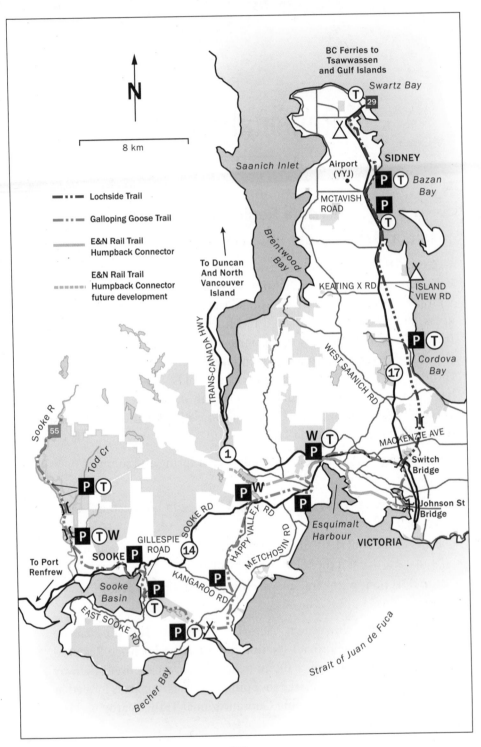

is available at the Saanich Municipal Hall and along Saanich Road, north of Lodge Avenue. There are several access points along the trail, including Lochside Park off Cordova Bay Road, Cy Hampson Park off Lochside Drive in Central Saanich, and Tulista Park off Lochside Drive in Sidney.

HIKE DESCRIPTION From the Switch Bridge, the Lochside Trail runs northeast under Blanshard Street and Vernon Avenue and passes the southern fringe of the Swan Lake Christmas Hill Nature Sanctuary. The trail crosses the 30 m Brett and the 140 m Swan Lake Trestle to emerge at Quadra Street. Use caution when crossing here and at the traffic lights at McKenzie Avenue. Continue north on Borden Street and follow the signs to Lochside Drive. At its end there is a parking area close to where the trail turns to gravel. Nearby is the signed junction with the Blenkinsop Greenway, a trail corridor that links the Lochside Trail with Mount Douglas Park and the Gordon Head area.

Next are the farmlands of the Blenkinsop Valley and a section of trail very familiar to horse riders. Pass with care. A highlight in this area is the 288 m Blenkinsop Trestle spanning Blenkinsop Lake. Stop on the bridge and have your picture taken with "Roy" (a bronze statue dedicated to the farmers of the Blenkinsop Valley). Bird blinds at Blenkinsop Lake Park assist visitors in spotting furtive lakeside wildlife. Just north of the lake you can detour along Lohbrunner Road to Blenkinsop Road and follow the Mercer Trail into Mount Douglas Park, or you can cut west at Donwood Park, a gateway to numerous urban trails in the Broadmead area. (see p.69).

Around the 6 km mark the trail crosses Royal Oak Drive. Opposite McMinn Park, Grant Park features a challenging trail that climbs to the top of Cordova Bay Ridge. Take a break at the Doris Page rest area, where there is a picnic shelter and a great ocean viewpoint looking out on James Island and the San Juan Islands. Doris Page Park provides a link to the Cordova Bay beach. Further north, detour west along Doumac Place to a lushly wooded ravine at Doumac Park.

The trail parallels Cordova Bay Road then picks up Lochside again at Lochside Park, near the 10 km mark. There are seasonal toilets and ample parking here. Expect to encounter horse riders from Lochside Park north to the Island View Road area. A side trip to Elk/Beaver Lake Park is possible via Cordova Bay and Sayward roads.

The Lochside Trail crosses the Saanich/Central Saanich border close to Dooley Road and enters Martindale Valley. This open stretch extends for several kilometres so, in hot weather, carry enough water. At Island View Road you can side trip to Island View Beach, 3 km to the east (see Nearby). The trail continues north to pass Heritage Acres, the agricultural and industrial museum operated by the Saanich Historical Artifacts Society. The route then runs through Tsawout First Nations land and parallels Pat Bay Highway (#17).

Just over the 16 km mark you will reach Mount Newton Cross Road. Zigzag right then left onto Lochside Drive. The seascapes of Cordova Channel dominate the backdrop. At North Saanich's Cy Hampton Park, near Bazan Bay, there are toilets and parking. Sidney's Tulista Park, near Washington State's Anacortes ferry terminal, also has parking and toilets, and features a promenade with beach access that is wheelchair accessible. From Sidney, the trail continues north alongside Pat Bay Highway and swings inland to Tsehum (Shoal) Harbour. Consider a side trip to Horth Hill (see p.19). The 29 km mark is the northern end of the Lochside Trail, at the Swartz Bay ferry terminal. From here you can travel to Tsawwassen or the Gulf Islands.

WORTH NOTING

- Interpretive signposts are located at numerous points along the route.

- Dogs must be leashed and kept on the right-hand side of Lochside Trail.

- Rare and uncommon breeding species of birds to look for near Blenkinsop Lake include Pied-billed Grebe, Green Heron and Wood Duck. Wintering waterfowl species include Eurasian Widgeon and Ring-necked Duck. Watch for eagles, Cooper's Hawk, Peregrine Falcon, swallows and Purple Martin.

- The Martindale Flats are an excellent destination to observe wintering freshwater ducks, raptors and Eurasian Skylark (an introduced species once common on the Saanich Peninsula, but now increasingly rare).

- BC Transit buses (low floor buses with bike racks and wheelchair lifts) stop at various points along the Lochside Trail.

- Contact CRD Parks for trail updates, regional regulations and information on the use of electric bicycles.

Island View Beach Regional Park (42 ha)   From Victoria, take Highway #17 (Pat Bay) and turn right at the traffic lights onto Island View Road. Turn left on Homathko Drive to the parking lot and beach. From Victoria, allow 30 minutes driving time. The park is open sunrise to sunset. This CRD regional park, on the Saanich Peninsula's east side, features one of Victoria's closest sandy beaches. The park offers easy hiking and the great seascapes of Haro Strait, the San Juan Islands and Sidney Spit. Spring and fall are excellent times to observe migrating shorebirds.

Do not trespass on the Tsawout Indian Reserve. On a minus low tide (an unusually low tide—when the lowest point of the tide is lower than the mean sea level), a 10 km one-way beach hike is possible from Island View Beach south to Mount Douglas Park with minimal rock scrambling. En route note the erosion of the Cowichan Head cliffs.

Check for signs and on the CRD Parks website regarding off leash areas and times. Many dogs like to chase waterfowl and this can be a problem when migrating waterfowl are feeding or resting on the beach. The birds feed between the high and low tide-lines and are essentially defenseless against dogs. Be sure to stay on the trails, clean up after your dog and do not allow your dog to chase wildlife.

The Lochside Trail accesses numerous hiking destinations, parks and beaches. For more information contact CRD Parks.

OF INTEREST

The first 2.3 km of the Lochside Trail follows what was known as the Saanich Spur, part of a Canadian National Railway (CNR) line abandoned in 1990. Borden Mercantile was the last freight customer. Canadian Northern Pacific Railway built the original rail line in 1917, offering passenger and freight service from Victoria to Pat Bay. The CNR took over operations in the 1920s. When the line was in active use, rail traffic was "switched" between tracks, hence the name "Switch Bridge" at the trailhead. The northern tip of the Lochside Trail follows the old Victoria and Sidney Railway bed.

5a2. Galloping Goose Regional Trail   MAP 5a

DIFFICULTY/DISTANCE   Easy to moderate/55 km in length

HIGHLIGHTS   The CRD's multi-use Galloping Goose Regional Trail (part of the Trans-Canada Trail) stretches 55 km, from downtown Victoria to Sooke and into the mountains of the Sooke River Valley. Hikers, bikers, joggers, horse riders and commuters use the route, which follows an old CNR rail line right-of-way. There are countless opportunities for urban walks and wildlife viewing. The trail runs close to parks, scenic lookouts and beaches. The trail intersects with both the Lochside Regional Trail and the E & N Rail Trail—Humpback Connector. There are three trestles along the trail, which intersects with the Lochside Regional Trail. The Galloping Goose Trail accesses numerous hiking destinations, parks and beaches. For more information, the CRD website has detailed maps and descriptions, or contact CRD Parks .(See p.226.)

Best time to go   any time of year, but best in spring and summer.

CAUTIONS
- The Selkirk Trestle can be slippery following rains.
- Proceed with caution at the many street crossings.
- Only about 14 km of the trail is paved, but the remainder is a wide flat gravel trail with slow elevation changes.

ACCESS   Designated free parking lots are located at Atkins Road, near the Highway #1 (Trans-Canada) overpass; off Sooke Road at Aldeane Avenue and at Glen Lake Road; off Happy Valley Road at Bilston Creek; off Rocky Point Road at Kangaroo Road and closer to Matheson Lake; at Roche Cove Regional Park (wheelchair accessible toilets). Parking fees apply at the two parking lots along Sooke River Road, one south of Sooke Potholes Provincial Park, the other to the north, at Sooke Potholes Regional Park. You can get on and off the Galloping Goose at many points along its length.

HIKE DESCRIPTION
The *Galloping Goose Regional Trail* begins east of the Johnson Street bridge, where the kilometre markers begin, and then follows the Selkirk Waterway. One of the trail's highlights is the 300-m-long Selkirk Trestle over the Gorge's Selkirk Waters. The trestle, built from hemlock and fir, is five metres wide. The route goes through Cecelia Ravine and

- The Galloping Goose Trail follows the right-of-way of an old Canadian National Railway line. Originally part of the Canadian Northern Pacific Railway, construction of the Victoria to Leechtown section began in 1911. The CNR transported mainly logs and freight. In 1922, the company operated passenger cars between Victoria and Sooke; the service was extended to Youbou, three years later.

- The type of coach used for the old Canadian National Railway was a clamorous gasoline-powered railbus (Number 15813) known as the "Galloping Goose". These were common throughout Canada. One person handled all the duties of conductor, engineer and baggage handler. In 1931, the CNR abandoned its passenger service. Freight service along a spur line continued sporadically until the late 1970s, then ended. The tracks were removed a few years later.

- The Leech River and Leechtown were named after Peter John Leech, who arrived with the Royal Engineers in 1858. Leech stayed on, to be part of the Vancouver Island Exploration Expedition in 1864, the time gold was discovered in the Leechtown area. By 1865, the mining boom was pretty much over, with Victoria merchants and outfitters profiting more than most of the miners, and Leechtown soon evaporated into a ghost town.

alongside a restored part of Cecelia Creek to a light industrial area near Douglas Street.

At the 4 km mark is the Switch Bridge, a 100 m pedestrian overpass over Highway #1 (Trans-Canada Hwy) near Uptown Shopping Centre. This is the junction with the Lochside Trail, a 29 km multi-use corridor stretching north up the Saanich Peninsula to Swartz Bay (see p.193).

The Galloping Goose swings west from the Switch Bridge to parallel Highway #1. There are some up and down sections as you pass through View Royal. There are toilets at the 10.5 km mark at the Atkins Road parking lot. Nearby Six Mile Road accesses Thetis Lake Regional Park (see p.95). The route crosses Millstream Creek on a sturdy bridge near the falls, which are especially striking on cold, bright days in winter.

Near Goldstream Avenue, the trail changes from paved to gravel. Pay attention at the many street crossings as you wind through Colwood and Langford. Though generally flat, the trail does have hilly sections.

Possible side trips include Fort Rodd Hill/Fisgard Lighthouse National Historic Site (see p.137), just over a kilometre down Ocean Boulevard, or the many walking trails near Hatley Castle at Royal Roads University (see p.135). The parking lot at Sooke and Glen Lake roads, close to the Luxton Fairgrounds, is at the 18 km mark.

The Galloping Goose enters Metchosin to pass through pastures, farmlands, rocky outcrops and hills. The trail roughly parallels Happy Valley Road for 7 km to the junction of Kangaroo and Rocky Point roads. A 1.5 km side trip east along Rocky Point Road, then Happy Valley Road to William Head Road will bring you to the historic Metchosin School. It opened in 1871 and is one of western Canada's first public schools. The Metchosin School (and the Metchosin Agricultural Museum and adjacent farm market across the street by the firehall) is open to the public on weekends in the spring, summer and fall. Check hours by calling the Metchosin Municipal Hall. Popular places to stop are My-chosen Cafe and the general store at the corner of Happy Valley, Metchosin and William Head roads. Washrooms are available on the school/museum grounds or in the cafe. Lombard Road (near the 26 km mark) leads to Devonian Regional Park, along William Head Road (see p.144).

From the second Rocky Point Road parking lot, south of Malloch Road near the 30-km mark, the trail narrows and heads west for 4.5 km through Matheson Lake, then Roche Cove regional parks. Here the route's semi-wilderness nature emerges (see pp.152 and 154). The parking lot at Roche Cove's west end has wheelchair-accessible toilets. Use extreme caution at the nearby Gillespie Road crossing due to a blind curve in the road.

The Galloping Goose runs north to a particularly scenic stretch that skirts numerous rocky headlands and pocket coves along Sooke Basin. You can access this area via Manzer Road, just past Glinz Lake Road. Near Hutchison Cove, the route plunges down to Veitch Creek, where the old railway right-of-way seems almost to hang out over the water. Take the time to stop near the bridge and savour the view of Veitch Creek. NOTE: From Veitch Creek to Sooke Potholes Regional Park is around 10 km, one-way, about a 3 hour hike.

At Cooper Cove, the trail crosses the busy Sooke Road. Next is the CRD's Ayum Creek Reserve (6.2 ha) (see p.156) that protects important salmon habitat near Goodrich Peninsula. No dogs are allowed here. Swans frequent these waters. The shoreline at the estuary is a good birdwatching spot. Look for Great Blue Heron, Bald Eagle, Osprey, shorebirds and other waterfowl. Boxes atop tall poles provide nesting areas for a variety of birds, including the Purple Martin. You can also reach the reserve by parking off Sooke Road, on the east side of the Ayum Creek bridge, near the 5600 block of Sooke Road. A creek-side trail, steep near the bridge, drops to tidewater. The path can be marshy and muddy at the tidal flats. Tread lightly in this environmentally fragile region. Ayum Creek is also known as Stoney Creek.

Eventually the route leaves the lowlands behind, swings north up the Sooke River Valley. The highlights here are the impressive river canyon and potholes. There is a designated parking lot off Sooke River Road (near the 45 km marker, approximately 500 m past Meota Drive) and another at the 48 km marker. The latter provides access to the CRD's Sooke Potholes Regional Park (see p.171). Please stay on the Galloping Goose Trail between the two parking lots to avoid trespassing on private property.

From the potholes area, the trail leads up to the refurbished trestles on Charters and Todd creeks. This is where most trail travelers turn around. You can continue north from Todd Creek on a steady 8 km climb up the Sooke River Valley. This is the most remote part of the Galloping Goose Trail and somewhat narrow and overgrown by trailside trees and bushes. The trail ends a little south of Leechtown, a mid-19th century gold mining town, long since deserted. Nothing of the town remains today.

WORTH NOTING

- Consideration between user groups is encouraged, with cyclists giving the right-of-way to hikers and hikers giving way to equestrians. Remember that horses are easily spooked. Safety dictates that all users should keep right, except to pass; courtesy dictates users should alert others when approaching from behind. Contact the CRD for trail updates, information on expected trail etiquette, regional regulations and rules pertaining to the use of electric bicycles.
- Most of the urban sections of the Galloping Goose are paved and many of the unpaved parts, including the section near the Luxton Fairgrounds, are suitable for wheelchair use.
- BC Transit buses (low floor buses with bicycle racks and wheelchair lifts) stop at various points along the trail. Check BC Transit website.
- The Galloping Goose is part of the Trans-Canada Trail, a coast-to-coast multi-use corridor that links Canada's regional trails.

Kapoor Regional Park (12.59 ha)   With habitat for Golden and Bald eagles, as well as Black-tailed Deer, Northern Alligator Lizards, Red Squirrels, and Pileated Woodpeckers, and easy trails for hikers, the park is at the north end of the Galloping Goose past Sooke Potholes Regional Park (see p.171) and the southern boundary of the Greater Victoria water supply area. Adjacent to historic Leechtown, there are numerous old trails and roads winding through the property, which includes almost two kilometres of riverfront. The park offers a bike rack, information kiosk and toilets at the rest area.

ACCESS   Follow the Trans-Canada Highway from Victoria, and take the Millstream Road exit (Exit 14) to Sooke. Follow Veterans Memorial Parkway, then turn right on Sooke Road. Turn right on Sooke River Road and follow the signs to Sooke Potholes Regional Park. There is no direct vehicle access. Visitors can access the park directly on bicycle via the Galloping Goose Regional Trail or on foot by walking from the Sooke Potholes Regional Park. It is a 7.3 km walk (one-way).

E&N Rail Trail - Humpback Connector

The E&N Rail Trail Connector forms part of the CRD's regional trail network, along with the Galloping Goose and Lochside Regional Trails. Construction of the E&N Rail Trail, a paved cycling and pedestrian trail, began in 2009 and will be developed in five sections over the decade.

When complete, it will be 17 km in length, the only rail-with-trail in the region. The E&N Rail Trail-Humpback Connector is, as the name implies, being constructed largely within the E&N Rail corridor, running along the south side of the E&N tracks beside the railway for much of the route. Hills on the new trails are where there were trestles on the railway itself. From the Johnson Street Bridge to Humpback Road, it will link Victoria to the western communities (see map p. 194). The railway is still officially active, so the CRD must comply with federal safety requirements. Along the trail this includes a safety fence, located between the active rail line and the trail and specific inter-section safety upgrades (barriers, signals and pedestrian crossings) that must be put in as part of the trail construction process. For more information and updates on progress, visit the CRD website (see p.226).

5b. Juan de Fuca Marine Trail   MAP 5b

DIFFICULTY/DISTANCE   Moderate to strenuous/47 km, one-way

HIGHLIGHTS   The Juan de Fuca Marine Trail, within Juan de Fuca Provincial Park (1528 ha), stretches 47 km along Vancouver Island's wild west coast. Designed as a wilderness hiking trail, extending from China Beach to Botanical Beach, near Port Renfrew, the trail features wilderness hiking and camping, breathtaking seascapes and excellent opportunities for wildlife viewing, nature appreciation and birdwatching. The trail leads to waterfalls, old growth rainforests of western redcedar, hemlock and Sitka spruce, ravines, estuaries, surf-lashed beaches, tide pools, sea stacks and rocky headlands. Conditions are always changing and hikers should get up-to-date information before hiking. From any of the four designated trailheads, take a day hike to a nearby beach or head off on a more challenging overnight or multi-day trek. (See the West Coast Road section on p.180 for information on day hikes.)

Best time to go   For maximum sunshine and spectacular views, spring, summer, or early fall is great. Summer months are generally the driest, but also potentially hottest, and wasps can be a problem. Wildlife viewing can be good year-round. Remember that rain, wind and fog can occur any time of the year, and can make many sections of the trail treacherous.

CAUTIONS

- The more remote parts of the Juan de Fuca Trail are best suited for experienced hikers, familiar with multi-day treks in a wilderness setting. Allow at least 4 to 5 days for the complete hike.
- Be prepared. The trail is designated as a wilderness hiking trail, and conditions can change quickly. It is not unusual to have washouts and mudslides along portions of the Juan de Fuca Marine Trail.
- Before starting your hike, check for a map and the latest trail information at BC Parks website (see p.226).
- Leave a detailed trip itinerary with someone reliable at home. Never hike alone and allow ample time for a return journey. BC Parks recommends you leave your pets at home.
- Be self-sufficient and carry emergency supplies. Pack out everything you bring in.

Map 5b   Juan de Fuca Marine Trail

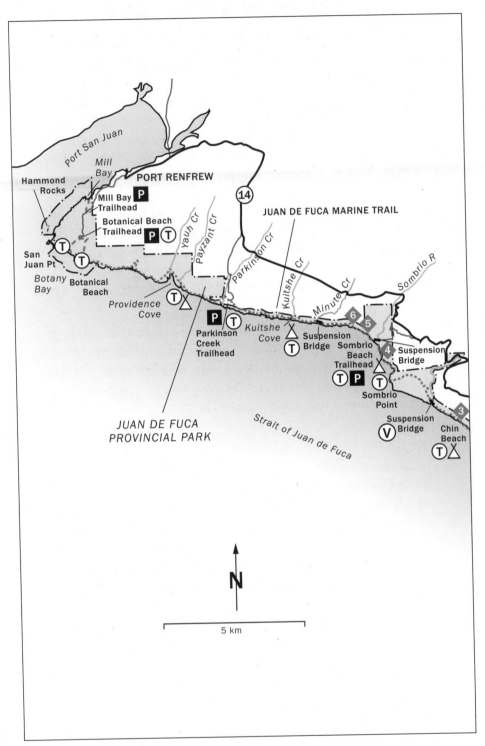

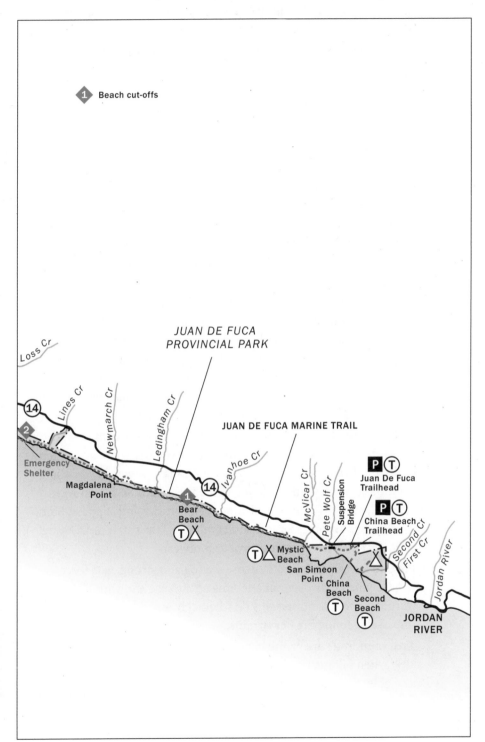

1 Beach cut-offs

Loss Cr

JUAN DE FUCA
PROVINCIAL PARK

Lines Cr

Newmarch Cr

Ledingham Cr

JUAN DE FUCA MARINE TRAIL

14

2

Ivanhoe Cr

Emergency
Shelter

Magdalena
Point

14

McVicar Cr

Pete Wolf Cr

Suspension
Bridge

P T
Juan De Fuca
Trailhead

P T
China Beach
Trailhead

Bear
Beach

T

T Mystic
Beach
San Simeon
Point China
Beach

Second Cr

First Cr

Jordan River

T

T

Second
Beach

T

JORDAN
RIVER

- Carry your own water on day hikes. Water is available at streams. Always boil, treat or filter water before drinking.
- Keep to designated trails and campsites to protect sensitive vegetation. Do not disturb or remove any plants, animals or marine life.
- To safely hike many of the trail's beach and sandstone shelf sections requires timing and the proper low tides. Be sure to have precise tidal information prior to your trip. Tide tables are usually posted at each trailhead. Remember to add one hour for Daylight Saving Time. Storms and steady winds may increase the heights of predicted high water.
- Tides may be problematic near Bear Beach's east end; at two spots at China Beach and at three separate headlands near Sombrio Point. Recurring slope failure at West Sombrio Bluff has blocked the headland bypass trail there. Hikers must follow the 0.6 km beach route and time their passage carefully with favourable lower tides.
- Some headlands (not all) may be skirted via bypass trails. Orange balls hanging in shoreline trees mark beach access points. When hiking on beaches, around headlands, on the tidal shelf and near surge channels beware of unexpected, unusually large rogue waves or a series of larger waves. Hikers have been swept off the rocks. Keep children safely away from the surf. Be aware that some beaches may be cut off from the trail during high tides and storms.
- Trails are usually muddy, root-prone and regularly climb up and down steep terrain in the numerous creek valleys. There are switchbacks and dense brush. Boardwalks and log crossings may be slippery. Use extreme caution along cliff edges, bluffs and open rock faces. The shoreline and sandstone shelf is rocky and slippery. Some beaches consist of rocks and large boulders. Use a staff or trekking pole. Travel slowly and wear proper footwear.
- Prepare for torrential rains, dense sea fog and strong, gale force winds, which may occur at any time of the year and with little warning. Creeks and streams flood quickly and some may be impassable following heavy rains.
- Area rainforests are prime habitat for Black Bear and Cougar. Be alert when hiking, particularly when travelling with children. If available, use the bear caches at designated campsites or hang your food securely in trees. Cook food away from camp.

- Nesting wasps are prevalent along parts of the trail, particularly in late summer.

- Driftwood campfires are permitted but only on beaches and below the high tide line. No fires are allowed at the China Beach day-use area, Botanical Beach or the designated forest campsites at Kuitshe or Payzant Creeks. Use a camp stove and set up your tent at the provided camping pads.

- You may meet logging trucks and other industrial traffic along the winding West Coast Road. Always yield the right-of-way and drive defensively. Use your headlights. Slow down and yield to oncoming traffic at the one-lane bridges.

ACCESS Four designated trailheads for the Juan de Fuca Marine Trail are located along the West Coast Road (Highway #14). Driving/cycling distances measured from the junction of the West Coast Road and Otter Point Road in Sooke (0) are: China Beach 36.7 km; Sombrio Beach 56.8 km; Parkinson Creek 66.4 km and Botanical Beach via Cerantes Road 77.5 km. China Beach is the east-most trailhead of the Juan de Fuca Marine Trail and is considered Km 0 for the kilometre signposts situated along the length of the trail. Note that the access road to Sombrio Beach is very rough and it is recommended only vehicles with four-wheel drive and good clearance attempt the road.

The Juan de Fuca Trail is open all year. Hikers must self-register at the trailheads. Except in the off-season, fees apply for overnight and multi-day hikes, with trailhead parking included. Consult the BC Parks website and map prior to your hike for current information, cautions and closures. Check also on fees for reservations and overnight stays at the China Beach campground (see Information Sources p.226).

At the trailheads, study the signed maps carefully to familiarize yourself with the trail and expected conditions. Carry good maps (ideally a topographic map) and be sure to have accurate tide information. Note that GPS units and cell phones may not work in all parts of the park.

There are six beach cut-offs along the trail—these indicate portions of the trail that can be alternate routes, subject to the tides.

Marker No.	Location	At km marker (approx.)	Passable below tide height of
1	Bear Beach	8.7 km*	3.00 m
2	Chin Beach (East)	20.6	2.75
3	Chin Beach (West)	21.3	2.75
4	Sombrio Beach (East)	28.0	3.00
5	Sombrio Beach (West)	29.6	2.60
6	Sombrio Beach (west west)	30.2	3.00

* from China Beach as Km 0

HIKE DESCRIPTIONS

China Beach to Sombrio Beach   Strenuous/29 km, one-way: This stretch of the Juan de Fuca Trail traverses rough terrain and is best hiked over two or even three days, with overnight stops at Bear Beach (Km 9—measured from China Beach as Km 0; trail marker 1) and Chin Beach (Km 21; trail markers 2 and 3).

From the China Beach trailhead, the trail leads 2.5 km west to Mystic Beach, the trail's first (or last) campsite. This is a popular day hiking destination. From Mystic Beach to Bear Beach, the trail keeps to the forest, but there are viewpoints along the cliffs west of Mystic Beach. Expect muddy sections at any time of the year. August is often the driest month. West of Ivanhoe Creek, the trail slowly drops to Bear Beach. The shoreline here is covered with slick stones and hard to traverse. Camp at the designated campsites.

The 12 km section from Bear Beach to Chin Beach is considered the toughest part of this hike and it can be very muddy. Elevation changes are endless since the trail rises and falls in every creek valley. The trail stays mainly in the forest until the slow descent to Chin Beach. An emergency cabin is located at the trail's 20.5 km mark if tides cut off the approach to Chin Beach's east side. There are several spots to pitch a tent at Chin Beach, and numerous beach access trails.

About 3 km west of Chin Beach is the Loss Creek suspension bridge, a hike highlight. Take some time to savour the view. The trail then curves inland, follows an old logging road and turns back toward the coast to hug the cliffs on the approach to Sombrio Beach. Beach camping is permitted at East Sombrio Beach (Km 27; trail marker 4) and on the tent platforms at West Sombrio Beach campsite (Km 29; trail marker 6). In between is the cutoff to the Sombrio Beach parking lot and trailhead (trail marker 5).

Sombrio Beach to Parkinson Creek   Strenuous/8 km, one-way: From Sombrio Beach, the Juan de Fuca Trail heads west to cross the Sombrio River suspension bridge to the Sombrio Beach campsite (with tent platforms). Due to slope failure near West Sombrio bluff, the bypass trail is severed. The beach route is the only option. Time your passage carefully for low tide. The up and down hiking in the creek valleys continues west of Sombrio Beach, but the hills are less steep. Fording the mouth of Minute Creek is hazardous on a high tide. Hike inland to the suspension bridge to cross this stream. Consider a stopover at the inland campsite at Little Kuitshe Creek (Km 33). The trail continues west, through logged forest to the Parkinson Creek trailhead (Km 37).

Parkinson Creek to Botanical Beach   Moderate/10 km, one-way: This final stretch of the Juan de Fuca Trail is a lot easier to hike than the eastern sections but there are still some elevation changes, muddy sections, uneven terrain and roots to contend with. Forest camping is available at Payzant Creek (Km 40) on the provided tent platforms. From here, the trail continues inland to a well-built bridge over Yauh Creek. A side trail leads to picturesque Providence Cove.

If the tides are low enough, hike the last 4 or 5 km via the beach. The inland trail has boardwalks over wet and muddy areas. There are many beach access points. Try to time your arrival at Botanical Beach with low tide. Tides of 1.2 m or lower are ideal for exploring diverse marine life in exposed tide pools on the sandstone shelf. From the east end of Botanical Beach (Km 46), follow an old logging road 1 km to the parking lot and trailhead. Extend your hike by heading west, past a headland, to Botany Bay and then take a second access trail to the trailhead.

For descriptions of more West Coast Road and Port Renfrew shoreline hikes, e.g., the Mill Bay Trail (1 km one-way, steep at first as it drops down and levels off as it nears sea level) and the Botanical Beach Loop Trail (3 km loop), see pp.188–189.

WORTH NOTING

- Suspension bridges have been installed at Sombrio River and also at Pete Wolf, Loss and Minute creeks. The views from these spans are outstanding.
- Watch for sea lions, seals, Orca, other large marine mammals and marine birds off the points of land. Grey Whale migrate north along the coast in March and April and return south in the fall.

- The Juan de Fuca Trail does not connect to the West Coast Trail. For information on trailhead bus service, contact www.trailbus.com. The company provides shuttle bus service (May 1 to September 30) from Victoria and Nanaimo to the trailheads and between the trailheads of the West Coast Trail and the Juan de Fuca Trail.

NEARBY

West Coast Trail   The Gordon River trailhead, near Port Renfrew, is the southern terminus of the West Coast Trail. This arduous 75 km trail extends north from Port Renfrew to Pachena Bay, close to Bamfield. The West Coast Trail is recommended for experienced backpackers only, those familiar with multi-day jaunts. You must be fit and well equipped. A daily quota system limiting hiking starts applies. The West Coast Trail is closed during the hazardous off-season. Contact Parks Canada (see p.227) for current details on reservation fees, ferry services and overnight use permits. Information is also available at Port Renfrew's West Coast Trail Information website—check for updates and advisories before you go (http://www.portrenfrew.com/wctlinks. htm)

Hikes by Level of Difficulty

(See p.11 for definitions of Easy—Moderate—Strenuous)

Please note that the difficulty rating is intended as a guide only. Depending on your experience, fitness level, and the trail conditions at the time you undertake the hike, you may find some hikes more or less difficult than rated in the list below. Consideration of these same factors is why we have refrained from indicating length of time for each hike—some description in the book will have times listed, but remember that those times are average, and you may take more or less time than described.

Easy

Albert Head Lagoon Trail	0.3 km	one-way
Beaver and Elk Lake – 10K Trail	10 km	loop
Colquitz River Trail	5 km	one-way
Colquitz to Knockan Hill Park	2.5 km	one-way
Colquitz to Panama Flats to Knockan Hill	5 km	loop
Cuthbert Holmes Park	2 km	loop
Cuthbert Holmes Park / Hyacinth Park loop	5+ km	loop
East Sooke Park – Aylard Farm to Becher Bay	0.4 km	one-way
East Sooke Park – Pike Road Trail	1.5 km	one-way
Esquimalt – Westsong Way	5 km	one-way
Esquimalt parks and waterfront	up to 5 km	loop
Francis/King Park – Elsie King Interpretive Trail	0.8 km	loop
Galloping Goose Regional Trail	55 km	one-way
Goldstream – Arbutus Trail	appr. 0.3 km	one-way
John Dean Park – Valley Mist Trail	0.5 km	one-way
Lochside Regional Trail	29 km	one-way
Mt. Douglas – Beach Trail	0.86 km	one-way
Mt. Work – Munn Road	0.63 km	loop
Oak Bay/Uplands – Bay to Bay Trail	6 km	loop

Oak Bay/Uplands – Bowker Creek Waterway	3.2 km	loop
Oak Bay/Uplands – Cattle Point to UVic	10.2 km	loop
Oak Bay/Uplands – Centennial Trail	6.8 km	one-way
Oak Bay/Uplands – Coast to Coast Trail	4.6 km	one-way
Rithet's Bog	3 km	loop
Roche Cove to Ayum Creek	10 km	loop
Roche Cove to Matheson Lake – Galloping Goose Trail	4.5 km	one-way
Sea Bluff Trail	1.2 km	loop
Sidney Island – East Beach and the Bluff	2.2 km	loop
Sidney Island – Lagoon and Hook Spit	4.5 km	loop
Sidney Island – Sidney Spit	2 km	one-way
Swan Lake – Lake Trail	2.5 km	one-way
The Flight Path (Airport Trail)	9.3 km	loop
Thetis Lake Park – Trillium Trail	2 km	one-way
Uplands Park, Willows Beach	5 km	one-way
UVic and vicinity – Mystic Vale/ Mystic Pond	2.9 km	loop
Victoria Waterfront – Ogden Point to Oak Bay	3+ km	one-way
Victoria Waterfront – Ogden Point to West Bay	3+ km	one-way
Whiffin Spit	1.2 km	one-way
Witty's Lagoon Regional Park – Tower Point	1.2 km	loop

Easy to Moderate

Broadmead	1.5-5+ km	one-way
Goldstream – Prospector's Trail	2 km	one-way
Goldstream – upper and lower trails	1-3 km	one-way
Horth Hill – Lookout Trail, Sunset Bridle Trail	5+ km	loop
John Dean Park – Merrill Harrop Trail	1.5 km	one-way
Lands End Area loop	7+ km	loop
Pearson College to Devonian Regional Park	7.4 km / 10+ km	one-way/ loop

Royal Roads, Esquimalt Lagoon, Fort Rodd Hill	2-8 km	one-way
Sooke Potholes	Up to 5 km	one-way
Swan Lake – Grand Loop	appr. 10k	loop
Thetis Lake Park – McKenzie Creek Trail	2.9 km	one-way
Thetis Lake Park – Two Lake Loop	4.5 km	loop
UVic and vicinity – Alumni Trail	4.5 km	loop
UVic and vicinity – Ten Mile Point loop	appr. 6 km	loop
West Coast Road – See 4g, p.180	Varies	one-way

Moderate

Bear Hill – Summit Trail	1.5 km	one-way
Cedar Hill Golf Course Trail	3.6 km	loop
Devonian Regional Park Beach Trail	0.9 km	one-way
East Sooke Park – Aylard Farm to Beechey Head	3 km	one-way
Francis/King Park – High Ridge Trail	2.8 km	one-way
Goldstream – Arbutus Ridge	2 km	one-way
Goldstream – Gold Mine Trail	3.5 km	one-way
Gowlland Tod – Rowntree Loop	1.9 km	loop
Gowlland Tod – Tod Inlet	1.5 km	one-way
Horth Hill – Ridge Trail	5 km	one-way
John Dean Park – Merrill Harrop Trail	1.5 km	one-way
John Dean Park – Pickles Bluff	0.5 km	one-way
John Dean Park –West Viewpoint	1 km	one-way
Lone Tree Hill	1.6 km	one-way
Matheson Lake Trail	3.4 km	loop
Mill Hill – Auburn Trail	0.8 km	one-way
Mill Hill – Calypso Trail	1.2 km	one-way
Mt. Douglas – Irvine Trail	1.6 km	one-way
Mt. Douglas – Merriman Trail	1.3 km	one-way
Mt. Douglas – Norn Trail	1.7 km	one-way
Mt. Douglas – Whittaker Trail	3.8 km	loop
Mt. Work – Durrance Lake Trail	1.7 km	one-way
Mt. Work – McKenzie Bight Trail	1.5 km	one-way

Portland Island – Kanaka Bluffs Trail	0.8 km	one-way
Portland Island – Pellow Islets Trail	0.8 km	one-way
Portland Island – Princess Margaret Perimeter Trail	6.5 km	loop
Portland Island – Royal Cove Trail	3 km	one-way
Roche Cove – Cedar Grove Trail	1.9 km	one-way
Swan Lake – Christmas Hill	1.25 km	one-way
Thetis Lake Park – Craigflower Creek Trail	2 km	one-way
Thetis Lake Park – Lewis J. Clarke Trail	1.4 km	one-way
Thetis Lake Park – Seymour Hill Trail	1.3 km	one-way
UVic and vicinity – Mount Tolmie Trails	0.5-2 km	loop
Witty's Lagoon Regional Park – Beach Trail	1.5 km	one-way
Witty's Lagoon Regional Park – Lagoon Trail	1.7 km	one-way

Moderate to Strenuous

East Sooke Park – Anderson Cove to Mt. Maguire	3.5 km	one-way
Gowlland Tod – Emma Dickson Trail to Jocelyn Hill via Ridge Trail	2 km	one-way
Gowlland Tod – Partridge Trail	5 km	loop
Gowlland Tod – Ridge Trail to Jocelyn Hill	1.2-2 km	one-way
John Dean to Centennial Park	4 km	one-way
Juan de Fuca Marine Trail	47 km	one-way
Mt. Douglas – South Ridge Trail	300m	loop
Sooke Hills – Harbour View Road to Sooke and Empress mountains, Sheilds, Crabapple, and Grass lakes	Up to 14 km	one-way
Sooke Hills – Sooke Potholes to Grass Lake	3 km	one-way
Thetis Lake Park to Stewart Mountain	8 km	one-way
Thetis Lake to Scafe Hill	7 km	one-way

Strenuous

Bear Mountain Resort to Mount Finlayson	2+ km	one-way

East Sooke Park – Coast Trail	10 km	one-way
East Sooke Park – Endurance Ridge Trail	2.9 km	one-way
Goldstream – Mt. Finlayson	4 km	return
Gowlland Tod – Timberman to Jocelyn Hill	5 km	one-way
Mt. Douglas – Blenkinsop Trail	0.6 km	one-way
Mt. Wells – Summit Trail	1.3 km	one-way
Mt. Work – Summit Trail	1.8-2.5 km	one-way

Accessible Areas

Accessibility allows a person with limited mobility or a disability to use an area and facilities with minimum assistance. Many of the trails mentioned here are also good for families with young children. In addition, other trails described in this book (or portions thereof) may be suitable depending on abilities. See also Information Sources, p.226.

- **Colquitz River (2i)**
  - Most of the trail from Tillicum Mall north to Hyacinth Park is accessible.
- **East Sooke Regional Park (4d)**
  - Aylard Farm Picnic Area – The accessible trail connects the parking lot with the picnic shelter and toilet facilities. A steeper trail to the beach could be accessed with assistance.
  - Pike Road to Iron Mine Bay – Accessible toilets are at both ends of the trail.
- **Elk/Beaver Lake Regional Park (2e)**
  - Beaver Beach – This beach has an accessible parking area, paved trails and accessible toilets.
  - Hamsterly Beach – The children's playground has accessible equipment. A drinking fountain, toilets and picnic tables are also accessible.
  - 10K Trail – The trail loops around the two lakes and is mostly flat and level. There are some narrow and uneven parts on the east side of Elk Lake, along the Pat Bay Highway.
  - Brookleigh Boat Launch – The boat launch provides easy and safe access to boats. The toilet facility is also accessible.

- Elk Lake Fishing Float – The parking area is reserved for disabled only and the toilet facility is accessible.
- **Esquimalt Lagoon (3c)**
  - An accessible picnic table and washrooms are available at the bottom of Lagoon Road.
- **Francis/King Regional Park (2j)**
  - The Elsie King Interpretive Trail is quite wide – most of the trail surface is hard-packed gravel or boardwalk. Note that the boardwalk can be slippery when wet. The Nature Centre and toilets are accessible.
- **Galloping Goose and Lochside Regional Trails (5a)**
  These connected regional trails are mainly wide and level, with pavement or hard-packed gravel.
  - Three sections of the Galloping Goose are favourites: Sooke Potholes to Todd Creek Trestle; Sooke River Rd. to Charters River Trestle; and Roche Cove to Rocky Point.
  - Near the Lochside Regional Trail, Island View Beach has a hard-packed gravel trail that follows the beach edge for some distance, and a group picnic shelter and toilet facilities are accessible.
- **Goldstream Provincial Park (2c)**
  - The Visitor Centre and several short trails from the day-use parking area are accessible.
  - Metchosin Shoreline (4b)
  - The Witty's Lagoon Nature Centre, picnic area and toilets are accessible.
  - Tower Point Trail in Witty's is also accessible but can be muddy and slippery in the rainy season.
  - Devonian Park parking lot, picnic area and toilets are accessible.
- **Mill Hill Regional Park (2l)**
  - The trails are not accessible but the picnic area and toilets are.
- **Mount Douglas Regional Park (2h)**
  - The main parking lot has a children's playground and picnic area and accessible toilets.
- **Mount Work Regional Park (2b)**
  - The north side of Durrance Lake is accessible.
  - The loop trail through the forest and toilets at the parking lot on Munn Road are accessible.

- **Swan Lake Nature Sanctuary (2g)**
  - The trail to the dock overlooking the lake is accessible.
  - Rithet's Bog – Some assistance will be required on uneven ground. No toilet facilities.
  - Near Swan Lake Nature Sanctuary, at Beckwith Park, the trail around the park and the toilet facilities are accessible.

- **University of Victoria (2n)**
  - The alumni chip trail is mostly accessible, with some parts requiring assistance.
  - Parking Lot 6, near the Interfaith Chapel and the gardens are accessible.

- **Victoria Waterfront (3b)**
  - The trail is level and wide enough for wheelchairs or scooters and accessible toilets are available.

- **West Coast Road (4g)**
  - The picnic/day-use area and toilets at French Beach are accessible.

- **Western Metchosin (3c)**
  - The Roche Cove toilets are accessible.

Nature Walks (includes Top Birding Spots)

In the mild climate that the Victoria area enjoys, natural areas provide habitat and food for all kinds of creatures, including amphibians, reptiles, insects, mammals, and birds (many of which nest on the ground). Almost anywhere and anytime you walk or hike, you will discover plants and various animals—help protect them by keeping on the trails (and do not pick the flowers), watching where you walk, and keeping your dogs under control to protect the fragile ecosystems. Some of the more spectacular sites in the Victoria area (as recommended by the Victoria Natural History Society) are listed below.

This is not an exhaustive list, and results will vary depending on weather and time of year. Don't forget to check the hike descriptions —wildflowers and birdwatching are highlights for many of them, e.g., wildflowers at Horth Hill and birdwatching at many spots such as Mount Work and along the Metchosin shoreline.

NOTE: an excellent resource when contemplating where and when to walk/hike is the Victoria Natural History Society's Nature Guide to the Victoria Region. This provides an introduction to the area's natural wonders—what to find and where—with sections for birds, butterflies, fungi, intertidal life, land and marine mammals, and more. The beautiful photographs and species lists are very helpful. VNHS organizes many walks/hikes to many locations—why not join and take your walks with them? Check the calendar at www.vicnhs.bc.ca.

Spring and Summer Flower Walks

- **Bear Hill (2e)**
  - There are many wildflowers to see including the delicate Sierra sanicle.
- **Beacon Hill Park (3b)**
  - Enjoy the fields of camas and occasionally yellow paintbrush.
- **Finnerty Gardens (2n)**
  - This University of Victoria landmark is known for its spectacular rhododendron and flower garden.
- **Francis/King Park (2j)**
  - This 100-year-old forest has some rare plants.
- **Gore and Oak Haven Parks (2a)**
  - These parks explode with carpets of colourful spring flowers in a Garry oak meadow.

- Gowlland Tod (2a)
  - Among this area's rare plants are the phantom orchid and some rare mosses.
- Horth Hill (1a)
  - The rare phantom orchid is sometimes found here along with many other wildflowers.
- Island View Beach (5a1)
  - The beach's fragile sand dune area is habitat to some rare and beautiful plant species.
- Lone Tree Hill (2a)
  - Among the countless wildflowers here you might spot the albino shooting star.
- Mill Hill (2l)
  - Look for the pink fairy slipper and as many as 40 species of wild-flowers.
- Mount Wells (2d)
  - This region features many, many varieties of wildflowers. Bring your wildflower field guide.
- Witty's Lagoon (4b)
  - Look for Fool's onion, harvest brodiaea and Howell's triteleia.

Fall and Winter Walks

- East Sooke Park (4d)
  - The headland at Beechey Head is the prime spot to see the annual Turkey Vulture migration or "Hawk Watch" in the fall.
- Goldstream Provincial Park (2c)
  - This park is a popular destination to observe the November salmon runs and for December eagle watching.
- Royal Roads (4a)
  - Look for mushrooms and fungi in the damp, shady forests.
- Sooke Potholes (4e)
  - Salmon spawn in the Sooke River in the fall.
- Thetis Lake, Six Mile Road/Millstream Creek (2k)
  - Enjoy the impressive waterfall and watch for mosses and lichens.
- Witty's Lagoon (4b)
  - Sitting Lady Falls are especially striking after heavy rains.

- **Blenkinsop Lake (5a1)**
  - Look for Marsh Wren, Song Sparrow and Trumpeter Swan (in winter); swallows and Black-headed Grosbeak (in spring), Bewick's Wren, Cooper's Hawk and Bushtit.

- **East Sooke Park (4d)**
  - This is the best place to be in September/October as hundreds of Turkey Vulture kettle here before crossing Juan de Fuca Strait. Many other raptor species, warblers, sparrows, gulls and shorebirds also stop here before departing south. Year-round there are Pacific Wren, Chestnut-backed Chickadee and other forest birds.

- **Esquimalt Lagoon (3c)**
  - This area has a large assortment of gull species, Black Turnstone, Black-bellied Plover, Mute Swan, Bald Eagle, ducks and grebes. On both sides of the peninsula watch for Kingfisher, Great Blue Heron, Osprey and many more. The lagoon is one of the better shorebird stopover points during migration and a great spot for winter birdwatching.

- **Goldstream Provincial Park (2c)**
  - Observe Red-breasted Sapsucker, American Dipper, Pileated Woodpeckers and Steller's Jay. Expect to see hundreds of Bald Eagle and thousands of mixed gull species during the fall salmon run.

- **Gowlland Tod Provincial Park (2a)**
  - You may spot Townsend's Solitaire, Hutton's Vireo, Purple Finch, Solitary Vireo and possibly Golden Eagle, among other upland and forest species.

- **Martindale Flats/Island View Beach (5a1)**
  - Watch for Peregrine Falcon, Bald Eagle, Cooper's Hawk, Red-tailed Hawk and other raptors. You may see Sky Lark, American Pipit and Horned Lark (in migration) and always a mixture of sparrows. In winter, the area is home to hundreds of wintering waterfowl, including Trumpeter Swan. If you are lucky, you might also see flocks of Snow Goose.

- **Mount Tolmie (2n)**
  - Spring brings Anna's Hummingbird, warblers and flycatchers. During migration, many rare species have appeared here.

- **Rithet's Bog (2g)**
  - You might see Virginia Rail, Cooper's Hawk, Song Sparrow, Bushtit and a mixture of duck species.
- **Viaduct Flats/Quick's Bottom/Panama Flats (2i)**
  - Here you will find an assortment of ducks and shorebirds in migration. Watch for Great Blue Heron, California Quail, many sparrow and warbler species, and owls in winter.
- **Victoria Waterfront: Ogden Point to Clover Point (3b)**
  - Observe Black Oystercatcher, Surfbird, Black Turnstone, Glaucous-winged Gull, and other seabirds. This is a great place for discovering rare migrants on top of the shoreline bluff.
- **Whiffin Spit (4f)**
  - The spit is an excellent winter birdwatching destination.
- **Witty's Lagoon/Tower Point (4b)**
  - This area features a nice mix of habitats for one location. Look for a variety of sparrows, ducks and seabirds, and watch for shorebirds and warblers in the spring and fall.

Family-friendly Hikes

Hiking as a family is a real gift you can give to children—one that can instill in them a sense of wonder and curiosity about nature. That said, it can be a challenge, especially with younger children. The trails listed in the Accessible Areas section are perhaps a good place to start, but for those ready for more, some of the hikes suggested here may be just what you want. Note that even some of the shorter hikes can be moderate to strenuous, with a number of steep and potentially slippery sections, so toddlers may need to be carried for portions of the trails. It is important that you be realistic about your family's needs and be prepared for all sorts of eventualities.

- **East Sooke Park – Coast loop (4d)**
  - Starting at Aylard Farm, this trail has lots of ups and downs.
- **Francis/King Park – Centennial/High Ridge Loop (2j)**
  - Goes through a variety of habitats, including a swampy area, and has several side trails that can be added.
- **Goldstream Provincial Park – Prospector's Trail (2c)**
  - Some footbridges and viewpoints add to the enjoyment of this trail. The trail is narrow in many areas and toddlers will likely need help.

- Gowlland Tod Provincial Park – Tod Inlet trail (2a)
  - Although not wheelchair accessible, the trail is mostly wide and gently sloping as it winds through the forest to the inlet.
- John Dean Park – Mt. Newton loop (1c)
  - Made up of five interconnecting trails, this route follows the Valley Mist, West Viewpoint, Woodward, ȽÁU,WELṈEW̱, and Lookout trails for a loop of approx. 3 km.
- Mystic Beach (4g)
  - One of the more strenuous hikes to attempt with children, as the trail rises and falls a fair bit and some hills are steep. It can be a magical route as long as you are careful.
- Sandcut Beach (4g)
  - A short but moderately steep trail to the beach, so take care.
- Sidney Spit Provincial Park (1d)
  - Trails are mostly flat and wide, and there are lots of things to look at along any of the trails. Great for all ages – especially the ferry ride over to the island!
- Sombrio Beach (4g)
  - A short gravel trail winds through the forest down to the sandy, rocky beach.
- Witty's Lagoon Beach Trail and Tower Point Trail (4b)
  - The Beach Trail is fairly steep, taking you past a waterfall and skirting the lagoon and estuary on the way to the beach. Tower Point Trail, accessed from the parking lot on Olympic Drive rather than the main Witty's parking lot, is an easy loop – great for learning about the geology of the area.

Dog-friendly Hikes

Most dog owners look for opportunities to get outside together with their dogs, and the Greater Victoria area and vicinity offer some great places, including a number of leash-optional areas. Dogs are welcome in most parks and trails, but must be under control at all times. Specific information on leash requirements and when/if dogs are allowed is generally posted and easy to see. Nearly all parks require dogs to be leashed. Remember that unleashed dogs can chase wildlife and damage fragile ecosystems—don't let your dogs chase birds! Please be responsible for their behavior (stay on the trails) and always clean up after your pet. Some hikes described in this edition include notes about dogs, but rules are changing, so please look for signs where you wish to hike.

The City of Victoria has a *Paws in Parks* program (see City of Victoria website for detailed information). BC Parks, the Capital Regional District (CRD), and area municipalities have **seasonal restrictions, particularly in beach areas**, i.e., between May 1 and the end of October. Dogs on leash are allowed to pass through but not allowed to stay in beach and picnic areas. Note also that there are places where dogs are **prohibited year-round**, such as Swan Lake Nature Sanctuary, Quick's Bottom Park, Rithet's Bog (except the perimeter trail), Ayum Creek Regional Park Reserve, Coles Bay Regional Park and Sherwood Creek in Devonian Regional Park. Please obey the signs.

The list below is not an exhaustive list, and there may well be additional areas where dogs are welcome. Some areas are great for playing but not really a walk or hike—pick the spot that offers the most fun for you and your friend. Some listed here (at the time of writing) are leash-optional* and a few allow swimming **at certain times and in specific areas**—check signage for current restrictions.

- **Saanich Peninsula, including near islands:**
  - Island View Beach (5a1) – excellent swimming; some areas leash-optional
  - John Dean (1c)
  - Portland Island (1e) – swimming
  - Sidney Spit (1d) – swimming

- **Saanich, Highlands and adjacent municipalities**
  - Bear Hill (2e)
  - Elk/Beaver Lake (2e)
  - Francis/King (2j)
  - Goldstream/Mount Finlayson (2c)
  - Gowlland Tod (2a) – swimming in Tod Inlet
  - Lone Tree Hill (2a)
  - Mill Hill Regional Park (2l)
  - Mount Douglas (2h) – good swimming at low tide
  - Mount Tolmie (2n)
  - Mount Work (2b)
  - Mystic Vale (2n) – dogs must be leashed at all times
  - Thetis Lake (2k) – some swimming areas

- **Victoria, Oak Bay and Esquimalt**
  - Alexander Park* (3b)
  - Arbutus Park* (3b)
  - Banfield Park* (3b)
  - Bayview-Hilltop Songhees Park* (3b)
  - Beacon Hill Park (3b)
  - Cattle Point, Uplands Park (3a) – swimming
  - Coles Bay (1a) – swimming
  - Cordova Spit – excellent swimming (area restricted during May through August)
  - Dallas Road, Clover to Ogden Point (3b) – swimming
  - Gonzales Park* (3b)
  - McCaulay Point Park (3c) – limited to the area from the parking lot to the top of the hill
  - Oswald Park* (3b)
  - Pemberton Park* (3b)
  - Redfern Park* (3b)
  - Topaz Park* (3b)
- **Western Communities to Port Renfrew**
  - Devonian Regional Park (4b) – ocean swimming, NOT in the pond
  - East Sooke Park (4d) – dogs not permitted in Aylard Pond; good swimming at Anderson Cove
  - Juan de Fuca Trail (5b) – dogs are allowed but must be leashed at all times. Backcountry sections of this trail are not suitable for dogs due to bear and Cougar problems. BC Parks recommends that dogs be left at home.
  - Matheson Lake (4c) – swimming
  - Roche Cove (4c) – swimming
  - Whiffin Spit (4f) – good swimming except at the end of the spit
  - Willows Beach (3a) – swimming
  - Witty's Lagoon (4b) – ocean swimming outside the lagoon area
- **Regional Trails**
  - E&N Regional Trail – dogs must be leashed at all times
  - Lochside Regional Trail (5a1) – dogs must be leashed at all times
  - Galloping Goose Regional Trail (5a2) – dogs must be under control

Vancouver Island Trails Information Society

The Vancouver Island Trails Information Society (VITIS) is a non-profit society dedicated to providing accurate information to the public about parks and trails on Vancouver Island. The object of the society is to increase the interest of the general public in the outdoors and in hiking, by publishing information relating to these activities.

The first edition of *Hiking Trails, Victoria & Vicinity* was published in 1972, followed by *Hiking Trails 2, Southeastern Vancouver Island* in 1973 and *Hiking Trails 3, North Vancouver Island*, including Strathcona Park in 1975. Originally the society was formed as the Outdoor Club of Victoria Trails Information Society under the direction and leadership of Editor, Jane Waddell Renaud. In 1993, to eliminate confusion, the society changed its name to the Vancouver Island Trails Information Society. The names of the three books have changed slightly over the editions; the three books in the series are now titled:

Hiking Trails 1, Southern Vancouver Island,
 Greater Victoria and Vicinity. 14th edition (2017)
Hiking Trails 2, South-Central Vancouver Island and the
 Gulf Islands. 9th edition (2010)
Hiking Trails 3, Northern Vancouver Island. 10th edition (2008)

The society has an unbroken 44-year history of producing hiking trails books covering all of Vancouver Island. We also maintain a website with additional support and resource information. Our volunteer members maintain the operation of the society and guide the production of the Hiking Trails books.

Information is gathered with the assistance of dedicated hikers and climbers who have contributed accurate descriptions of trail conditions, suggested corrections and pointed the way to new hiking destinations. We would also like to thank the many individuals, agencies and organizations that have also provided helpful information (see Acknowledgements).

For more information about VITIS
e-mail: trails@hikingtrailsbooks.com
website: www.hikingtrailsbooks.com
telephone: 250-474-5043 or
toll free 1-866-598-0003

Information Sources

Information sources change rapidly with increased availability on the Internet. A relative few of the multitude on offer that provide information and maps are listed below. Check with local municipalities and regional districts, area hiking clubs and outdoor organizations, and see the Vancouver Island Trails Information Society (VITIS) www.hikingtrailsbooks.com for links and contact information. NOTE: VITIS does not endorse these sites and is not responsible for any misinformation therein.

AllTrails
www.alltrails.com

Ancient Forest Alliance
www.ancientforestalliance.org

BC Ferries (schedules and fares)
www.bcferries.com

BC Parks
www.env.gov.bc.ca/bcparks

BC Species and Ecosystems Explorer
http://a100.gov.bc.ca/pub/eswp/

BC Transit (bus information)
www.bctransit.com

Birding in BC
www.birding.bc.ca

Capital Bike + Walk
www.capitalbikeandwalk.org

Capital Regional District Parks (CRD)
www.crd.bc.ca/parks

City of Langford
www.cityoflangford.ca

City of Victoria leash-optional areas
www.vacs.ca/leash-optional-areas

Clubtread
www.Clubtread.blogspot.com

Cordova Bay Hikers
www.Cordovabayhikers.wordpress.com

CycloTouringBC
www.Cyclotouringbc.com

Discover BC
www.ourBC.com

District of Central Saanich
www.centralsaanich.ca

District of Metchosin – parks/trails
www.district.metchosin.bc.ca/content/parks-and-trails

District of North Saanich
www.northsaanich.ca

District of Saanich
www.saanich.ca

District of Sooke
www.sooke.ca

ExploreVancouverIsland.com
www.explorevancouverisland.com

Federation of BC Naturalists
www.bcnature.ca

Fisheries and Oceans Canada (regional tide and current information)
www.dfo-mpo.gc.ca

Freak Maps – GIS cartography
www.freakmaps.com

Galloping Goose Trail
www.gallopinggoosetrail.com

Gulf Islands National Park Reserve
http://www.pc.gc.ca/eng/pn-np/bc/gulfvisit.aspx

Meteorological Service of Canada (regional weather information)
www.weatheroffice.ec.gc.ca

Opencyclemap.org
www.opencyclemap.org

OpenStreetMap
www.openstreetmap.org

Outdoor Club of Victoria
www.ocv.ca

Parks Canada
www.pc.gc.ca

Port Renfrew
www.portrenfrew.com

Royal Roads
www.royalroads.ca

Secret Lakes of Southern Vancouver Island
www.secretlakes.ca/maps

T'Sou-ke First Nation
www.tsoukenation.com

Township of Esquimalt – parks and recreation
www.esquimalt.ca/parksRecreation/parks

TrailPeak.com
www.trailpeak.com

User-friendly Trails in CRD
https://www.crd.bc.ca/docs/default-source/parks-pdf/userfriendly-trails.pdf?sfvrsn=2

Vancouver Island Health Authority (health information)
www.viha.ca/mho

Vancouver Island Vacation Guide
www.vancouverisland.travel/regions/south-island/greater-victoria-and-downtown/

Victoria Harbour Ferry
https://www.victoriaharbourferry.com/

Victoria Natural History Society
www.vicnhs.bc.ca

Victoriahiatus.com
www.victoriahiatus.com

Walking in Victoria
www.walkinginvictoria.com

Water taxi Sidney Spit/Portland Island
www.alpinegroup.ca/businesses/sidney-spit-ferry/
www.ecocruising.com/taxi.html

West Coast Rail Express – shuttle service for the West Coast Trail and Juan de Fuca Trail
www.trailbus.com

West Shore Parks & Recreation
www.westshorerecreation.ca

Suggested Reading

The publications listed below are just a few of the many titles available to enhance your walking and hiking experience. Some titles may be out of print but can still be found online or in second-hand bookstores.

50 Best Dog Walks/Hikes Around Victoria by Leo Buijs

A Guide to User-friendly Trails by CRD Parks, IACDI, and West Shore Parks and Recreation

Amphibians & Reptiles of British Columbia by Matsuda, Green & Gregory

Backroad Map Book, Vol. 2 – Vancouver Island by Wesley & Russell Mussio

Birder's Guide Vancouver Island: A Walking Guide to Bird Watching Sites by Keith Taylor

Birds of Coastal British Columbia by Nancy Baron & John Acorn

Birds of Victoria by Bovey, Campbell & Gates

British Columbia: A Natural History by Richard Cannings and Sydney Cannings

Butterflies of British Columbia by John Acorn

Coastal Wildflowers of the Pacific Northwest by Elizabeth L. Horn

Common Seashore Creatures of the Pacific Northwest by J. Duane Sept

Essential Wilderness Navigator: How to Find Your Way in the Great Outdoors by David Seidman

Geology of Southern Vancouver Island by Chris Yorath

Hike Victoria by John Crouch

Hiking Adventures With Children: Southern Vancouver Island and the Olympic Peninsula by Kari Jones & Sachiko Kiyooka

Hiking On The Edge: West Coast Trail – Juan de Fuca Trail by Ian Gill

Hiking the West Coast of Vancouver Island by Tim Leadem

Hiking Trails 2: South-Central Vancouver Island by Richard K. Blier

Hiking Trails 3: Northern Vancouver Island including Strathcona Park by Gil Parker

Hiking Vancouver Island by Shannon & Lisa Cowan

Juan de Fuca Marine Trail by Matthew Payne and Adam Vaselevich

Leave No Trace: A Guide to the New Wilderness Etiquette by Annette McGivney

Mosses, Lichens & Ferns of Northwest North America by Vitt, Marsh & Bovey

Mushrooms of Northwest North America by Helene Schalkwijk-Barensen

Native Trees of British Columbia by Halter & Turner

Nature Guide to the Victoria Region by Ann Nightingale and Claudia Copley, Victoria Natural History Society

Nature Walks Around Victoria by Helen Lansdowne

Pacific Coast Bird Finder: A Manual for Identifying 61 Common Birds of the Pacific Coast by Roger Ledere

Pacific Coast Fern Finder by Glenn Keaton

Plants of Coastal British Columbia by Jim Pojar & Andy Mackinnon

Some Common Mosses of British Columbia by W.B. Schofield

Trans Canada Trail: The British Columbia Route by Mussio

Victoria-Nanaimo Nature Walks, The Easy Guide by John Henigman

Walk Victoria by John Crouch

West Coast Trail: One Step at a Time by Robert J. Bannon

Where To See Wildlife on Vancouver Island by Kim Goldberg

Acknowledgements

I am indebted to the editors and contributors of previous editions of this book, without whose work mine would have been so much more difficult. Throughout the years and various editions, every effort was made to compile accurate and interesting descriptions of the trails in the area, and these formed a wonderful starting point for this edition.

Special thanks are due to Patrice Snopkowski and Annie Weeks, of Beacon Hill Communications Group, not only for their work on the maps—starting completely fresh and achieving consistency of style and format was a huge job—but also for coaching me through some stages in the publication process. They also acted as a check on me—the maps and descriptions had to match, and they caught some things I might have missed, making me look good.

Thanks, too, to Frances Hunter, for her creativity and perhaps most of all, her patience, as she guided me through the process from layout to printing. Her calm advice was much appreciated.

Also deserving of thanks, for assisting me with everything from advice regarding which websites to check to providing personalized accounts of specific hikes, are: Gemma Norton-Wilks, for her attention to detail on the hikes involving Pearson College and other hikes in the Metchosin area; staff of CRD Parks, B.C. Parks, and Parks Canada, and municipal staff in Sidney, North Saanich, Central Saanich, Highlands, Saanich, Oak Bay, Victoria, Esquimalt, View Royal, Langford, Colwood, Metchosin, and Sooke; and members of various hiking clubs and outdoor organizations and others who have provided updates and verified information.

And finally, special thanks to the VITIS Editorial Committee members, John W.E. Harris, Joyce Folbigg, Graham Ruxton, Betty Burroughs, Irm Houle, Bernadette Harris, and Neil Burroughs. Sadly, both Graham and Betty passed away before they could see their efforts for this edition come to fruition. Their assistance was most valuable.

A Postscript from VITIS (excerpt from the 13th edition):

To all those both past and present, who had the foresight to recognize the need to preserve the green spaces and unique features of beautiful Vancouver Island, how do we thank you—Parks Canada, BC Parks, Capital Regional District, Saanich Parks, and the many other agencies who have been involved in the purchase, protection and maintenance of the special natural areas that we enjoy so much? As well, there are the hundreds of individuals who volunteer their time, energy and talent to maintain these areas. What a gift you have given us!

Index

About the Editor

Gail F. Harcombe

A long-time resident of the Victoria area with a strong interest in the natural world, Gail Harcombe has explored many of the areas described in this book.

Gail is a biologist who worked for the B.C. Ministry of Environment for many years. The fall, winter and spring in the first few years were spent illustrating and co-authoring an identification guide to the conifers of B.C., and two such guides to the vascular plant families of B.C. The summers of those first years were spent doing fieldwork, giving Gail the opportunity to explore various parts of the province—including some very exciting helicopter trips doing vegetation inventory!

For the majority of her career, Gail worked as a technical editor of scientific publications and web content. This led to an awareness of the incredible diversity and fragility of the environment in which we live. A concern for and a desire to see more of the different habitats, flora, and fauna was a direct result of this.

In recent years, her interest in nature, and especially in birding, has grown even stronger, and has been the "excuse" to go to places like Colombia, Ecuador, Mexico, South Vietnam, Hawaii, Costa Rica, and southern Africa, not to mention a good number of states and provinces in North America. The more of the world Gail sees, the more appreciative she has become of the amazing biodiversity southern Vancouver Island has to offer. Gail takes great delight in introducing children and grandchildren to such wonders, be it standing on a rocky hilltop where you can see hawks and Turkey Vultures, walking a beach "hopping" with sandpipers, or examining the intricate textures and colours of mosses, lichens and fungi found in our forests.

Gail has been the editor of The Victoria Naturalist, a bi-monthly newsletter published for members of the Victoria Natural History Society, since 2012, and has collaborated on a number of articles and technical papers for municipal and provincial clients.

Also in this series:

Hiking Trails 2
South-Central Vancouver
Island and the Gulf Islands

Hiking Trails 3
Northern Vancouver Island

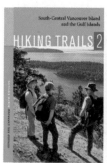

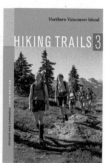